MW01077956

The Fighting
FLYING BOAT

The Fighting
FLYING BOAT

A HISTORY OF THE MARTIN PBM MARINER

RICHARD ALDEN HOFFMAN

Naval Institute Press
Annapolis, Maryland

Naval Institute Press
291 Wood Road
Annapolis, MD 21402

Library of Congress Cataloging-in-Publication Data
Hoffman, Richard Alden, 1926–
   The fighting flying boat : a history of the Martin PBM Mariner /
Richard Alden Hoffman.
     p. cm.
     Includes bibliographical references and index.
     ISBN 1-59114-375-6 (alk. paper)
     1. Mariner bombers—History. I. Title.
     UG1242.B6H4725 2004
     359.9'4834—dc22

                          2004000011

To all the brave and dedicated men who flew and supported the Mariner.
And to my wife Dorothy for her patience and support.

Contents

Preface and Acknowledgments

Although I flew the Mariner during the Korean War, I had little appreciation for its rich history. After leaving my Mariner squadron in 1954, memories of the lumbering flying boat faded as I moved on in my naval aviation career.

In 1993 I joined the Mariner/Marlin Association (MMA), a veterans group of pilots and crewmen who had flown and supported the Mariner and its successor, the Marlin. Becoming part of MMA awakened my interest in Mariner history. Under the auspices of the MMA, Capt. Albert L. Raithel Jr., USN (Ret.), Lt. Comdr. David Rinehart, USCGR (Ret.), and Robert M. Smith wrote *Mariner/Marlin: "Anywhere, Any Time."* It gave a broad overview of the Mariner story and included many personal accounts of Mariner operations. The MMA also publishes a quarterly newsletter that contains fascinating, mostly firsthand, bits of Mariner history. But pieces of the story were missing. I began hunting for a book that traced Mariner employment through World War II and its subsequent postwar exploration activities, service with the U.S. Coast Guard, and involvement in the Korean War and cold war. No book was found. Very little foreign military and commercial activities had been documented in any depth. This book, therefore, attempts to fill in the blanks by presenting the complete history of the Mariner.

The book's completeness is due to the contributions of many people: former Mariner crewmen, historians, and aviation enthusiasts throughout the world. Stan Piet, director of the Glenn L. Martin Museum, freely contributed his knowledge of the company's archives, records, and photographs. Capt. Dick Knott, author of *The American Flying Boat,* was of great help in understanding the competition leading to the development and procurement of the Mariner. Capt. Al Raithel sent me a copy of the official U.S. Navy history of fleet air wings during World War II. This history clearly showed the deployments of Mariner squadrons, base assignments, and supporting seaplane tenders in both oceans. Don Sweet provided squadron histories and wonderful photographs. Historian Bruce Barth provided a copy of a U.S. Navy document, titled "Aircraft Expended or Lost Outside the Continental U.S. December 1941 to August 1945."

Capt. Andy Sinclair shared his recollections of the involvement of USS *Norton* in Operation Nanook. Dave Rinehart, Dick Erb, and Virgil Hoffman expanded on the stories of the Red Chinese MiG attacks on the VP-50 aircraft.

Mike O'Rourke of the Ancient Order of Pterodactyls provided U.S. Coast Guard Mariner employment statistics. Comdr. Dan Abel, USCG, led me to the coast guard fatality records. Capt. Mitch Perry, USCG (Ret.), provided recollections of a 1953 open-sea rescue attempt.

Paul Warrener, RAF (Ret.), was an essential member of the research team. He contacted Graham Day of the Royal Air Force (RAF) Historical Records Branch, Ministry of Defence, London, for Mariner records and uncovered Ken Meekcoms's *British Air Commission and Lend-Lease,* which correlated RAF with U.S. Navy serial numbers. Jack Durbin, a neighbor, provided a firsthand account of the 1943 sinking of RAP Mariner JX 101 in Bermuda. Colin Pomeroy, author of *The Flying Boats of Bermuda,* provided source information for RAF delivery photos.

David Wilson, of the Royal Australian Air Force (RAAF) Archives and History Branch in Canberra, Australia, provided copies of the RAAF Mariner's aircraft record cards, the monthly reports of the commanding officer of No. 41 Squadron, and other valuable historical papers. Wilson also put me in contact with Paula Wilkins, assistant to the curator of the RAAF Aviation Heritage Museum of Western Australia in Bull Creek, for the information on the Mariner "carvans." Wynnum Graham, an Australian historian, provided the correlation of RAAF to U.S. Navy serials.

Marco Borst and Gerben Tornjii of the Netherlands put me in contact with Dr. P. C. van Royen, director of the Netherlands Institute for Maritime History in The Hague. Van Royen arranged for Ing. Nico Geldhof, an aviation historian, and Dr. C. A. C. W. van der Feltz, of the institute, to provide information and data on the procurement, sparing, training, and deployment of the Dutch Mariners. Theo Dingemans, a former Dutch PBM flight engineer, provided valuable background and crash details of the Dutch Mariners.

Dan Hagedorn, of the National Air and Space Museum (NASM), is perhaps the most knowledgeable person in the United States on the history of South American aviation. He graciously shared his files on the South American PBMs and put me in contact with historians in Argentina and Uruguay. Jorge Nunez Padin of Argentina provided complete and accurate information on the procurement, operation, and losses of the Argentine Mariners. Saul Alvarez, a former pilot of the Argentine Mariners and a member of MMA, provided firsthand data on Argentine Mariner procurement, delivery, and operations. MMA member George T. Damoff provided an eyewitness account of the Argentine 2-P-22 fire in Trinidad. Hagedorn arranged my contact with Eduardo Luzardo, an Uruguayan aviation historian, who provided many wonderful illustrations and articles describing the Uruguayan delivery flights and the A-811 rescue mission. Luzardo also forwarded the beautiful artwork of Pedro Otto Cerovaz and a copy of the Mariner section of a comprehensive history of Uruguayan Naval Aviation being written by Nelson P. Acosta and Alberto Del Pino. Comdr. David K. Tibbetts, USN, Office of Defense Cooperation Montevideo, acted as liaison with Capitan de Navio Federico Strasser, commandant of Uruguayan Naval Aviation, in obtaining usage data on the Uruguayan aircraft.

Over many years Rich Frangella collected documents, photographs, articles, and reminiscences pertaining to The Flying Lobster of Air Lanes, Inc. (TFLALI). He graciously contributed his entire collection to the Mariner/Marlin Association archives. In 2002 I was fortunate enough to meet with Harry O. Lee, the proprietor of TFLALI. He provided the complete story of the Lobster and its predecessor.

Most of the Naviera Colombiana story is due to the research of Rich Frangella and the memorabilia of Emil "Chick" Tkachick. Chick filled in some missing details on the delivery and final fate of the Colombian aircraft. The correlation of the Colombian registration numbers of the aircraft to their original U.S. Navy bureau numbers was provided by aircraft historian John M. Davis of Wichita, Kansas.

The story of the two Portuguese commercial Mariners was an elusive one. I first became aware that the operation had even existed from a footnote in David Oliver's *Flying Boats and Amphibians since 1945*. I had no idea how to proceed until I noticed the name of a Portuguese historian, Carlos Guerreiro, on the Internet. I contacted Guerreiro and he referred me to Lt. Duarte Monterio of the Portuguese Air Force magazine *Mais Alto* and Portuguese historian Mario Canongia Lopes. Lopes graciously sent me copies of his files on the Portuguese Mariners and Monteiro pointed out that official records might be available from the Portuguese Instituto Nacional de Aviacao Civil (INAC). INAC's director, Commandant Lopes, referred me to Luis Lima da Silva, of the accident investigation bureau. Da Silva provided me a copy of the accident report on the lost aircraft and registration documentation on both Aero Topografica SA (ARTOP) Mariners. After my ARTOP article was published in *Propliner* magazine, I was contacted by Jose Mergulhao, the son of ARTOP's founder. He sent me previously unavailable information, personal reminisces, and marvelous photographs. Dave Wilton added notes extracted from the official history of the U.S. Air Force's 56th Air Rescue Squadron that provided a wonderful overview of the massive search-and-rescue effort for the ARTOP Mariner.

Jennifer Till, of the U.S. Naval Institute's photographic archives, located photos of the various seaplane tender classes that serviced Mariners. Al Raithel provided a newsletter clipping about the "Three Domed Mariner." Stan Piet provided photos and background on the XP5M-l and the Martin M-270 as well as information about the Naval Air Test Center (NATC) hydroski experiments. Capt. Ralph Frame added details about the sinking of the Lake Washington Mariner. Gary Larkin contributed a fascinating video of the Kwajalein Mariner. Dan Cain was the source of information on the restoration of the Pima PBM-5A.

My sincere thanks to all for their contributions to the Mariner story.

Introduction

Although the Martin PBM Mariner served the U.S. Navy for nearly twenty years, it is relatively unknown and unappreciated. The only well remembered World War II–era navy flying boat is the PBY Catalina. However, there were more Mariner than Catalina squadrons during World War II.

The history of the Mariner is a significant part of U.S. Navy history from the beginning of World War II through the Korean War. First deployed in the Atlantic in 1941, Mariners sank ten German U-boats, some in pitched battles in which Mariners were shot down and casualties were suffered. *The Fighting Flying Boat: A History of the Martin PBM Mariner* details each Mariner versus U-boat engagement.

In 1942 transport versions of the Mariner became a mainstay of the Naval Air Transport Service. They provided the vital air link from Hawaii to the South Pacific and Australia. Combat Mariners were deployed to the Pacific at the end of 1943, and Mariners participated in all the major offensive campaigns, including the Marianas and the liberation of the Philippines, Iwo Jima, and Okinawa. Operating from seaplane tenders under primitive conditions, Mariners made the sighting that led to the "Marianas turkey shoot," sank Japanese submarines, attacked and sank hundreds of thousands of tons of Japanese shipping, and shot down sixteen Japanese aircraft. Mariners attacked Japanese naval forces and participated in the sinking of the superbattleship *Yamato*. Mariners also were the main air sea rescue platform during these campaigns, saving hundreds of airmen and seamen in spectacular open-sea rescue operations. Mariners bombed mainland Japan and were the first aircraft into Tokyo Bay after the Japanese surrender.

In the postwar years, Mariners supported the occupation forces, participated in Arctic (Operation Nanook) and Antarctic (Operation Highjump) explorations, and performed a vital role in support of the Operation Crossroads atomic testing. On station in the Far East when the Korean War began, Mariners exploded mines in North Korean harbors and patrolled the Formosa Straits and the Yellow Sea. They flew shipping reconnaissance, weather, and electronic intelligence-gathering missions for United Nations task forces. Mariners survived five attacks from Red Chinese MiG-15 jet fighters. Firsthand accounts describe these attacks.

More than eighty Mariners served with the U.S. Coast Guard beginning in 1943. Many Mariner crews performed spectacular open-ocean rescue missions. Fourteen Mariners were lost during these hazardous missions.

Mariners also served with the armed forces of Great Britain, Australia, Argentina, Uruguay, and the Netherlands. Research for this book covered each foreign service and never-before-published photographs were unearthed. War-surplus Mariners were also used commercially in the United States, Portugal, and Columbia.

This book details many Mariner assignments and missions. It also describes the organization of Mariner units. Most important, it attempts to provide a comprehensive history of this aircraft and its aviators, crews, and leaders. Whenever possible full names as well as rank or enlisted rating are given. The appendix pays tribute to Mariner casualties during the 1941–59 period.

Despite its historical importance, not a single Mariner flying boat was preserved by the U.S. Navy. One Mariner amphibian, sold by the navy as surplus in 1958, survived. It was restored by the Mariner/Marlin Association in 2001 and is currently on display at Pima Air and Space Museum in Tucson, Arizona. The story of its survival and restoration is also presented in this book.

The PBM Mariner is usually referred to as the "fighting flying boat." The deeds of Mariner crews have contributed a proud chapter to naval aviation history.

The Fighting
FLYING BOAT

CHAPTER ONE

DESIGN, DEVELOPMENT, AND PRODUCTION

Genesis, 1935–1939

Development of the Glenn L. Martin Company's Mariner flying boat began in the 1930s. In 1935 the U.S. Navy designated its new Catalina patrol plane a "patrol bomber" and promulgated a requirement for follow-on heavily armed flying boats that would be capable of bombing naval shore bases as well as performing the traditional naval missions of locating and attacking warships. Consolidated, Sikorsky, and the Martin Company submitted four-engine designs to meet this requirement. These aircraft became known in the popular press as the "flying battleships" and the "flying dreadnoughts."

In 1936 contracts were awarded to Consolidated and Sikorsky to build

prototypes: the XPB2Y-1 and the XPBS-1, respectively. Both the XPB2Y-1 and the XPBS-1 were flown in late 1937. The XPB2Y-1 was the one selected for production and became known in service as the PB2Y Coronado. After the competition, the XPBS-1 was used by the navy as a transport and made several high-priority trips to the South Pacific in the early days of World War II. It was wrecked in a landing accident at Alameda, California, on 30 June 1942 with Adm. Chester W. Nimitz, commander in chief of the Pacific Fleet, on board.

Even though the Glenn L. Martin Company's design model 160 was not awarded a development contract in the four-engine battleplane competition,

Martin continued to explore the design with company funds. As part of its research, Martin constructed a one-quarter scale, man-carrying flying model of the model 160. Even though the model 160 project was eventually canceled, this man-carrying model is an important element of Martin's PBM story.

Four-engine patrol bombers were expensive. A single PB2Y cost as much as three PBY Catalinas. In the austere economy of 1937, cost was of great significance to navy procurement officials. Therefore the navy invited proposals for a two-engine version of the battleplane.

The Glenn L. Martin Company proposed its design model 162, a new flying

boat that used two Wright R-2600 Cyclone engines. The model 162 offered speed, load, and armament advantages over the PBY, and it cost much less than a four-engine aircraft.

On 30 June 1937 Martin received a development contract for a single prototype, designated XPBM-1. To speed development and improve its position for a production contract, Martin converted the one-quarter scale model of the model 160 into a three-eighths scale model of the model 162. Framed in wood and covered with aluminum sheeting, the model 162A "Tadpole Clipper" was powered by a Martin-modified Louis Chevrolet light-plane engine driving two propellers by means of belts. Ready in mid-November 1937, extensive testing of the model 162A confirmed Martin's performance projections for the XPBM-1.

A possible competitor was Consolidated's model 31, developed with company funds. It was an innovative and promising design, using the powerful Wright R-3350 engines, a low-drag Davis wing, and self-contained tricycle beaching gear. Designed as a commercial transport to carry up to fifty-two passengers, Consolidated's model 31 had the potential to be a fine navy patrol bomber. The model 31 flew on 5 May 1939 but demonstrated poor hydrodynamics characteristics at high gross weight. After much modification, it

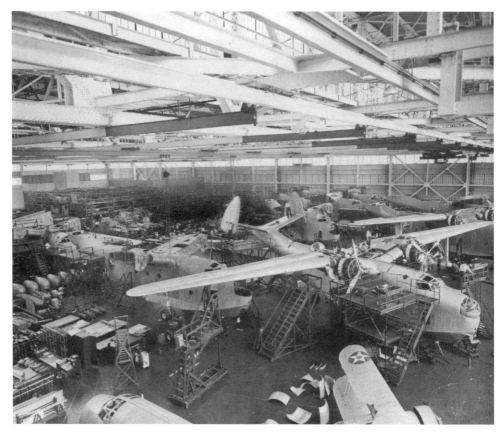

PBM-1 production at the Martin Company factory, Baltimore, 1939. *Glenn L. Martin Museum*

was acquired by the navy in April 1942 as the XP4Y-1 "Corregidor."

Martin's Tadpole Clipper testing was very timely. In spring 1937 Maj. Reuben Fleet, the colorful president of Consolidated, went to Washington, D.C. He stormed into the U.S. Navy's procurement offices, disputing Martin's performance claims for the model 162 and threatening political action if Consolidated lost the next navy contract.

Supported by the Tadpole Clipper test data, the navy awarded Martin a production contract on 30 December 1937. The navy covered its bets by the politically astute move of splitting the 1937 procurement: twenty-one PBM-1s were ordered from Martin for $5.1 million and thirty-three PBYs were ordered from Consolidated for $4.5 million.

The XPBM-1

The XPBM-1, Bureau Number (BuNo) 0796, first flew on 13 February 1939. The

XPBM-1 had a 118 foot gull wing and twin tails. It was powered by two 1600 horsepower Wright R-2600-6 engines. It was double-decked forward. Aft of the cockpit, the flight deck had standup room for a navigator, a radio operator (and later a radar operator), and a flight engineer. A complete galley was located beneath the flight deck. It had powered bow and dorsal turrets with single 50-caliber guns and 50-caliber waist guns in unpowered gimbal mounts. Enclosed bomb bays were located in extended engine nacelles, each with a capacity for six 500-pound bombs. The wing floats were located well inboard from the wingtips and retracted inboard for flight. The XPBM-1 was a sturdy and businesslike design that served the navy well for many years.

Flight tests of the XPBM-1 went well. Major faults uncovered were poor directional stability and the tendency to "porpoise" (develop hydrodynamically induced oscillations) at high water speeds. The porpoising tendency was reduced by moving the main step of the hull slightly aft and directional stability was improved by giving the horizontal stabilizer dihedral. The vertical stabilizers remained fixed at 90 degrees to the horizontal stabilizers, giving the PBM a unique cranked tail appearance.

The XPBM-1 had a remarkably long career for an X-model aircraft. It served in a training role with patrol squadrons VP-55 and VP-56, received a major overhaul in Norfolk in 1941, and was assigned to the aircraft armament units at Norfolk, Virginia, and Patuxent River, Maryland, until stricken in May 1944.

The PBM-1

Even as the XPBM-1 prototype flight test continued during 1939, the Martin

Post-test flight modification to horizontal stabilizer of the XPBM-1, 1939. *Used with permission and under copyright of Squadron/Signal Publications, Inc.*

Company began series production of the service model PBM-1. Thanks to the performance data verification by the Tadpole Clipper, which had allowed the early production decision, deliveries of the production PBM-1s (Bureau Numbers 1246 through 1266) to fleet squadrons began in October 1940, only nineteen months after the first flight of the prototype. Deliveries were complete by May 1941. The PBM-1s were almost immediately deployed to the North Atlantic for neutrality patrol missions.

The PBM-2

The second production PBM-1, BuNo 1247, was redesignated XPBM-2 and modified to test the concept of achieving extra-long range by catapult launching of an overloaded flying boat. Fuel capacity was increased from 2,700 to 4,815 gallons. The structure was reinforced and fittings were added for catapult launching. The Baldwin Locomotive Works built the XH Mark 3 catapult that was installed on a catapult lighter (AVC-1) intended as a mobile base. Specifications for AVC-1 have not yet been located, but extrapolation of its size from two photographs indicate that it was approximately three hundred feet long with a seventy foot beam. Successful tests of the catapult with dead loads of up to sixty thousand pounds were completed in 1942. However, the requirement for the extra

long-range flying boat was canceled and the XPBM-2 remained at the Naval Air Material Center in Philadelphia as a static test article until it was stricken from the navy inventory in June 1944.

The PBM-3

As part of President Franklin D. Roosevelt's massive rearmament program, an order for 379 PBM-3s was placed in November 1940. The PBM-3 displayed significant differences from the PBM-1. The retractable wing floats were replaced with fixed, strut-mounted floats, the nacelles were lengthened to increase the bomb-bay capacity, and the size of the aft hatches was increased. The gimbaled waist guns were replaced with 50-caliber guns that were arranged to fire from the aft hatches. Armor was added for crew protection and Wright R-2600-12 engines of seventeen hundred horsepower were installed. The basic airframe configuration of the PBM-3 remained unchanged for the rest of PBM production.

The pilot's handbook for the PBM-3D provided an excellent description of that aircraft (and the later PBM-5):

Maximum speed was about 215 miles per hour, with a service ceiling of approximately 20,000 feet; fuel capacity with droppable bomb bay tanks was 3,496 gallons, and range was 2,300 to 2,400 miles. Maximum weight was about 58,000 pounds.

Armament consisted of eight 50-caliber type M-2 machine guns: two each in the bow, deck, and tail turrets, and one mounted at each of the two waist hatches. The turrets were all electro-hydraulic, controlled with Mark VIII electric gun sights. The waist guns, also 50-caliber M-2s, had hydraulic controls or could be used manually. A bomb load of 4,000 pounds (bombs, depth charges, or mines) was carried in bomb bays located at the aft end of the engine nacelles. Also, two Mark XIII torpedoes could be carried, one under each wing, between the hull and engine nacelle.

The fuselage of the plane was divided into five watertight compartments by bulkheads provided with watertight doors. (1) The bow compartment contained the bow turret and the bombardier's station. Aft of the bow compartment to about three feet forward of the leading edge of the wing, the fuselage divided into two floor levels. The upper floor was the flight deck, which contained the raised pilot's control station at the forward end, with a seat for the pilot on the left and for the copilot on the right; a navigator's station on the left behind the pilot; a seat between the pilot and navigator for the radar operator; a radio operator's station on the right behind the copilot and the flight engineer's station at the aft end of

the flight deck. The lower level was (2) the galley compartment, with refrigerator and electric range. Directly aft was (3) the fuel compartment and the lavatory. Beneath the center wing structure were two small compartments. The forward one was the bunk room and the aft held a fuel tank (the saddle tank). Above that was the auxiliary power unit, on what was called the putt-putt deck. This unit supplied power for the plane when the engines weren't running. The navigator's hatch was also on that deck. Aft of that was (4) the after hull compartment, containing the waist gunner's stations and the deck turret. A tunnel from the aft hull compartment provided access to (5) the tail compartment, which contained the tail turret.

A passageway extended from the bulkhead under the front spar, down through the center of the plane, and back to the tail turret. Forward of the front spar, the passageway extended down the left side of the plane to the galley compartment. A flight of stairs led to a door on the right, which opened on the flight deck just forward of the flight engineer's station. Two manholes in the bottom wing skin, in the fuel compartment, allowed access to the center wing section and the bomb bays.

Personnel protection against gunfire consisted of two pieces of armor plate behind the pilot's and copilot's seats, six pieces of armor plate for protection of crew

members on the flight deck, one piece of armor plate on the aft section of each waist hatch door for protection of the waist gunners, and face and body armor plate for the projection of each turret gunner.

One unique feature of the PBM-3 design was the addition of four "vortex airfoils" to the horizontal stabilizers. The PBM-1 had suffered an undesirable tail flutter or "buzz" caused by the airflow pattern at the intersection of the vertical and horizontal stabilizers. To cure this problem on the PBM-3, Ellis (Sam) Shannon, a Martin test pilot, conceived the idea to install small airfoils on the horizontal stabilizer to smooth the flow. This installation solved the problem and the "Shannon vortex airfoils" became another unique PBM feature.

The PBM-3 was produced in a numbers of variants: PBM-3C patrol bombers, PBM-3S antisubmarine versions for the South Atlantic campaign, PBM-3R transports, one PBM-3E radar testbed, and the PBM-3D patrol bomber that had self-sealing tanks, increased armor, and nineteen hundred horsepower R-2600-22 engines. A total of 677 PBM-3s were built.

The PBM-4

By 1941 the U.S. Navy recognized that the PBM needed more power and ordered 230 PBM-4s to be powered by the twenty-two horsepower Wright R-3350 engine. Correspondence detailed concern as to whether or not the existing Mariner empennage design was a satisfactory match for these power plants, but the question became moot when national priorities directed all R-3350 engine production to the B-29 Superfortress. The PBM-4 project was canceled before a prototype could be built.

The PBM-5

With the cancellation of the PBM-4, another approach to increasing Mariner power was necessary. Two PBM-3s, Bureau Numbers 45275 and 45276, were designated XPBM-5 and used as testbeds for the installation of Pratt and Whitney R-2800-22 engines of twenty-one hundred horsepower. The design was satisfactory and delivery of the PBM-5 began in mid-1944. In addition to more powerful engines, the PBM-5 had provisions for four of the newly developed rocket assisted takeoff (RATO)/jet assisted takeoff

(JATO) bottles of one thousand pound thrust each. These rockets would prove invaluable in rough water operations in the Pacific. A total of 628 PBM-5s were delivered. Delivery continued after the end of World War II although many of the postwar aircraft went directly from the factory to storage. This postwar production was justified because of the way contract termination costs were structured. It was cheaper for the navy to take delivery than it was to cancel the contracts. The postwar production decision was a sound one. Most of the stored aircraft were later activated to serve in the Korean War and during the cold war era.

The PBM-5A

The versatility and military usefulness of an amphibious aircraft was well demonstrated

Shannon Vortex Airfoils

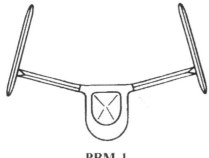

PBM-1

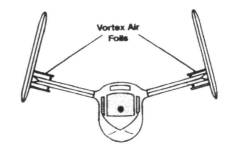

PBM-3 and Subsequent PBMs

Shannon vortex airfoils added to the empennage of the PBM-3 in 1940 to improve airflow. *Used with permission and under copyright of Squadron/Signal Publications, Inc.*

PBM-5 in markings of Patrol Squadron 34, Korean War era. *Capt. Al Raithel*

during World War II by the PBY-5A amphibian version of the Catalina. The navy decided to expand the operational utility of the Mariner by building an amphibious version. A standard Mariner flying boat, PBM-5 BuNo 59349, was converted into the prototype XPBM-5A amphibian and delivered in April 1946 to the Naval Air Test Center in Patuxent River, Maryland. Tests of the prototype were successful and thirty-six production PBM-5A amphibians were ordered. The final Mariner delivery was a PBM-5A on 9 March 1949.

The XPBM-6?

Martin Company archives refer to "a proposed PBM-6 design proposed in 1945," but apparently the navy took no action on this proposal; no navy record of a PBM-6 designation was found.

Bob Smith, the founder of the Mariner/Marlin Association in 1986, erroneously stated in his 1986 *PBM Mariner in Action* that "[a] single PBM-3D (45274) was modified and delivered under the designation XPBM-6. Further details are unavailable." The U.S. Navy Bureau of

Aeronautics aircraft history card for PBM BuNo 45274 shows no reference whatsoever to this aircraft being delivered as an XPBM-6.

Aircraft history cards for PBMs Bureau Numbers 45275 and 45276, however, provide a possible explanation for the XPBM-6 story. These seaplanes were PBM-3Ds that had been converted into the prototypes for the PBM-5. On their cards, in the space for "Model" was typed "PBM-5." This was crossed out and

"XPBM-6" was handwritten. Subsequently, the "6" was crossed out and a "5" written in, thus providing the proper "XPBM-5" designation.

Total Production

From February 1939 to March 1949, total Mariner production was 1,367 aircraft: 1 XPBM-1, 21 PBM-1s (including the XPBM-2 conversion), 677 PBM-3s, 632 PBM-5s, and 36 PBM-5As.

CHAPTER TWO

THE MARINER IN THE ATLANTIC THEATER DURING WORLD WAR II

Prelude to War, 1940–1941

At the outbreak of World War II in Europe in September 1939, President Franklin D. Roosevelt declared American neutrality and directed the U.S. Navy to establish a neutrality patrol extending from the high latitudes of the North Atlantic to the northeast coast of South America and out to three hundred miles from the coastline. The Atlantic Squadron was tasked to execute the patrol. It was directed to observe and report the movement of foreign warships. The scope and intensity of the patrol gradually expanded to ensure the delivery of supplies to Great Britain. It grew from a purely defensive maneuver to a condition slightly short of war.

Patrol Squadron 55 (VP-55) was estab-

PBM-1 in VP-55 markings, early 1941. *U.S. Naval Institute Photo Archive*

lished on 1 August 1940 specifically to operate the PBM-1. Deliveries of the new aircraft began in October 1940. Patrol Squadron 56 (VP-56), also designated a Mariner squadron, was established on 1 October 1940 and started to receive Mariners in December 1940. Delivery of the PBM-1 to both squadrons was completed by early 1941.

On 1 February 1941 the U.S. Atlantic Fleet was established under the command of Adm. Ernest J. King. On 1 March 1941 the Support Force U.S. Atlantic Fleet was created. The Support Force included a patrol wing comprised of five squadrons and the tenders *Albemarle* (AV-5) and

George E. Badger (AVD-3). The Patrol Wing, Support Force was charged to establish naval aviation in the strategically placed islands to the north and east of the United States and to ensure the safe passage of war materials to Great Britain.

In late April 1941 Mariners from VP-55 and VP-56 began fleet operations and flew night missions from *Albemarle* in the Rhode Island area. Crews learned to live and work with the seaplane at anchor and practiced fueling and rearming from both the ship and the ship's boats. On 9 May 1941, the chief of naval operations directed that at least six patrol planes with suitable tender support be established at

Argentia, Newfoundland. The directive also ordered that four patrol planes and a tender, which would be based for this mission in Iceland near Reykjavík, carry out a reconnaissance to determine the presence or absence of any Axis detachments in the Scoresby Sound area of Greenland.

To perform the Greenland reconnaissance, *Belknap* (AVD-8) was dispatched to Iceland, arriving on 21 May. A detachment of four PBM-1s of VP-56 was designated the Greenland East Coast Reconnaissance Flight with Lt. William C. Asserson, the squadron's executive officer, as senior naval aviator in charge.

The specific orders of the reconnaissance flight detachment were to conduct aerial reconnaissance of the region between Mackenzie Bay and Cape Browser with a primary purpose of determining possible German activities. A secondary purpose was to obtain as much data as possible to assist in a complete survey of the Angmagssalik area at a later date. The detachment was also charged to obtain aerial photographs of all settlements and stations and to photograph possible landing fields and anchorages in the Angmagssalik area.

Although the complete records of this mission have not been found, surviving parts of Asserson's report indicate the four Mariners departed Argentia on 24 May 1941 and flew missions from Iceland on 31 May and 3, 5, 6, and 7 June. Although

no German activities were observed, Danish and Norwegian settlements and radio stations were photographed. Also, a possible landing field and a seaplane anchorage were identified. The flight returned to *Albemarle* at Argentia. Asserton's report was dated 12 June 1941.

In a fleetwide redesignation on 1 July 1941, the Patrol Wing, Support Force became Patrol Wing 7, VP-55 became VP-74, and VP-56 became Operational Training Squadron (OTS). OTS was redesignated Transitional Training Squadron Atlantic (TTSA) on 1 August 1941.

On 19 July VP-74 sent a three-plane detachment of its PBM-1s to Argentia. The base was still under construction and the men of the detachment lived aboard the planes and *Albemarle*. While at Argentia the aircraft were moored at buoys where preventative and minor maintenance work was done, supported by *Albemarle* and *Pocomoke* (AV-9). Plane crew performance set the tone for flying boat crews throughout World War II. The aircraft were flown to Norfolk for major maintenance.

During the previous maintenance at Norfolk the PBMs had been fitted with an early British radar that had the antennae installed along the side of the hull. Constant trouble was experienced because servicing boats frequently broke off the antenna splines.

No training flights were conducted at Argentia. Each neutrality patrol mission in itself was a training flight under the most difficult weather conditions.

On 27 June small seaplane tender *Goldsborough* (AVD-5) arrived at Reykjavík, Iceland, to establish a base for twelve flying boats. Five PBM-1s of VP-74 and six PBYs of VP-73 arrived on 8 August. Using moorings borrowed from the Royal Air Force (RAF), the Mariners began operations immediately from Skerja Fjord. They provided convoy coverage as far as five hundred miles from base and maintained patrols in the Denmark Strait between Iceland and Greenland. At first the aircraft carried no bombs, but merely reported submarine contacts. Orders were changed to "sink on sight" after the destroyer USS *Kearney* (DD-432) was torpedoed by a U-boat near Iceland on 15 October 1941.

Conditions in Iceland were extremely primitive. Shore facilities were almost nonexistent. Even after the tender *George E. Badger* joined *Goldsborough* as many personnel as possible berthed aboard the tenders. Others slept in the planes and others slept in tents provided by the U.S. Army and in huts borrowed from the RAF. *Goldsborough* was relieved by *Belknap* in October.

On 13 September six more PBM-1s arrived to relieve the first detachment. It was deployed back to Argentia in bad weather, which was the norm for the Reykjavík PBMs. Frequently fog closed in on the base before planes on patrol could be recalled. Returning aircraft would have to circle the base until the weather cleared. Instrument landing equipment had not yet been developed. That flying boat operations were conducted at all in Iceland from October through January is a tribute to the courage and skill of the crews. As early as October 1941 it was recognized that the use of flying boats in the Icelandic winter was not practical. The navy recommended that they should be replaced with land planes and amphibians as soon as possible. PBY-5A amphibians were scheduled to replace the PBMs and PBY flying boats by December. On 2 November 1941 VP-74's plane 8 (BuNo 1248) became the first Mariner operational loss. After circling the base until fuel was almost gone, the pilot was forced to attempt a landing and flew into the surrounding hills. All hands were lost.

The Mariner Goes to War, 1942

Albemarle arrived in Iceland on 9 January 1942. The end of all flying boat operations in Iceland was signaled when a wind of hurricane force struck on 15 January. Three PBYs and two of VP-74's PBM-1s (Bureau Numbers 1255 and 1256) were sunk at their moorings.

In January 1942 six of VP-74's PBM-1s

were deployed to the more suitable climate of Bermuda. They would be tended by *Gannet* (AVP-8). Now under the operational control of Patrol Wing 5, the Mariners were initially based at the RAF flying boat base at Darrell's Island. The Mariners used the night landing facilities of Pan-American Airways. Beaching facilities were not available for Mariners and the planes were kept at the buoy. Major checks and engine changes were made at Norfolk. When the new U.S. Naval Air Station (NAS) Kings Point was ready in May, the unit shifted to that base. It was during operations from Bermuda that the Mariner began to show its mettle.

The first open-sea rescue by a Mariner occurred on 11 February 1942. Nine survivors of a torpedoed merchant vessel were picked up and returned to Bermuda. Three more rescues were made in April.

June 1942 brought both tragedy and triumph for the Mariner. Ens. John Cushman (BuNo 1250) and his crew were lost at sea on 3 June while on a search mission. On 7 June two PBMs of VP-74 landed in very rough sea conditions to rescue twenty-two survivors of the seaplane tender *Gannet,* which had been torpedoed by German submarine U-653. The PBMs directed the destroyer minesweeper *Hamilton* (DMS-18) to the rescue of forty others.

On 30 June Lt. Richard E. Schreder and his crew sank U-158 off Bermuda. In Capt.

Albert Raithel et al.'s *Mariner/Marlin: "Anywhere, Any Time,"* Schreder recalled:

I was flying a day patrol from Bermuda in a PBM-1 on June 30, 1942. This Mariner had an early ladder-type radar that could detect targets for about fifteen miles. Targets (suspected submarines) often disappeared as they could dive before being reached. We had been alerted by the base that a bearing had been obtained of a submarine sending a message to Germany. This bearing was near my search sector, but there was no fix. We intercepted the bearing course and were flying just above scattered cumulus clouds at 3500 feet, located the target on our radar and then sighted the submarine speeding on the surface at high speed leaving a long wake. Men were running for the conning tower where the captain stood with folded arms looking directly at us. I made a low level conning tower–high run directly from the stem at our maximum speed to drop depth charges with a pickle switch, at my command. We had four 500 pound depth charges and a single .50 caliber machine gun in the bow turret. After dropping the depth charges, I climbed sharply to the right to observe the drop and saw only one depth charge explosion about 100 feet astern of the submarine. Ensign Jack K. Gierisch, handling the pickle, informed me that only two of the four depth charges had released and that the second one that dropped struck the unusually broad deck.

I immediately began a second attack hoping that the two remaining charges would release. The submarine crash-dived before we could reach it a second time, but an underwater explosion clearly outlined the submerged submarine. It was now evident that the second depth charge had lodged in the deck super-structure and detonated at its fused depth of 50 feet.

We observed, during the initial bomb run, that there was an unusual length of broad flat deck. We circled the scene for an hour and photographed much floating deck lumber and debris, indicating that we had sunk a supply submarine. There were no survivors seen. Incidentally, we took the two depth charges back to base, as they failed to drop a second time.

Schreder added an interesting aspect of the attack:

The submarine commander failed to see the second depth bomb hit his deck and lodge there. He ordered a crash-dive after seeing only one explosion, which did not damage the submarine. He thought that it was safe to dive when all crewman had cleared the deck.

The bomb racks were defective. If the third and fourth depth charges had dropped, the submarine would surely have been damaged enough to force it to stay on the surface where the crew could have abandoned ship.

Additional rescues were performed in late June and July. In September, Lieutenant (junior grade [j.g.]) Lafferty was the patrol plane commander (PPC) of 74-P-5 (BuNo 1251). Engine failure occurred and the seaplane crash-landed and sank. After forty hours in life rafts, the crew was rescued by 74-P-2 flown by Lieutenant Hickman.

In September 1942 VP-74 was relocated to NAS Norfolk with a two-aircraft detachment in San Juan, Puerto Rico. In Norfolk, the squadron traded its PBM-1s for newer PBM-3s. On 22 September the squadron was transferred to Trinidad, British West Indies, to perform antisubmarine patrols and rescue missions under the control of Patrol Wing 11.

On 1 November 1942 the patrol wings were redesignated fleet air wings (FAWs). During the Atlantic campaigns, PBM squadrons were under the operational control of its assigned FAW. The six Atlantic Fleet air wings were FAW-3, Albrook Field, Panama Canal Zone; FAW-5, NAS Norfolk, Virginia; FAW-9, NAS Quonset Point, Rhode Island; FAW-11, Naval Station, San Juan, Puerto Rico; FAW-12, at NAS Key West, Florida; and FAW-16,

PBM-1 of
VP-74 at
anchor in
Bermuda,
early 1942.
U.S. Navy

established 16 February 1943 at Naval Air Facility, Recife, Brazil.

The U.S. Navy's aircraft history cards show that a total of 111 PBM-3 Mariners were delivered in 1942. As the new Mariners began to flow from the Martin production lines, crews were rapidly trained at TTSA. Between September and December 1942, eight Mariner squadrons were commissioned: VP-201 through VP-208. The squadrons were established and underwent training at NAS Norfolk under FAW-5 before being deployed to operating bases.

The PBM-3 aircraft history cards docu-ment that as many as fifty of the first 1942 deliveries were configured as desperately needed PBM-3R transports. Ten of these PBM-3Rs were assigned to Pan American Airways and two to American Overseas Airways to support the newly formed Naval Air Transport Service (NATS). In 1942 there were no suitable cargo/transport aircraft, either military or civilian, to support the far-flung military operations in the South Pacific or in the South Atlantic and Caribbean. The PBM-3R could carry an eight thousand pound payload, a respectable load for the time, and could be

Early PBM-3 of VP-74 on patrol, late 1942. *U.S. Naval Institute Photo Archive*

fitted for up to thirty-three passengers. In the Atlantic, the cargo Mariners based in Miami were the only air logistic support to the antisubmarine forces in Brazil, Panama, and the Caribbean islands.

Because the Mariner would be employed in areas where there was no enemy air threat, its configuration was optimized for the antisubmarine mission. Self-defense gun turrets and armor were removed and an extra four hundred gallons of fuel and improved radar were added. This configuration was designated PBM-3S; ninety-four were delivered by Martin.

Although this configuration may have initially been done solely to reduce weight to ease the strain on the engines, a loaded PBM-3S was of similar all-up gross weight to an unstripped PBM-3C. At the same gross weight, the PBM-3S gave a 25 percent increase in combat radius over the PBM-3C. Delivery of the PBM-3S antisubmarine configuration began in November 1942.

On 1 December 1942 PBY squadron VP-32 received five new PBM-3Cs and began transition training at NAS Coco Solo, Panama Canal Zone. On 10 December

1942 VP-203 began deploying to San Juan, Puerto Rico, and to Guantánamo Bay, Cuba, for training. On 18 December 1942 VP-74 was transferred to the Naval Air Facility (NAF), Natal, Brazil, to be tended by *Humboldt* (AVP-21).

The Mariner Comes into Its Own, 1943

The 1943 year did not open well for the Mariner. According to Clay Blair, in his monumental *Hitler's U-Boat War: The Hunted 1942–1945,* "[T]he PBM-3 was plagued by innumerable faults: severe engine weaknesses, poor aerodynamic characteristics, erratic performance of the bombing system, and inadequate spare parts, to name only the most important." There is no question that the Mariner suffered serious engine problems that were not completely resolved until the production of the Pratt and Whitney R-2800–fitted PBM-5 in 1944.

Despite its shortcomings, Fate had the Mariner at the right place at the right time. The Mariner's scope of operations vastly expanded in 1943. Eight more squadrons were commissioned: VP-209 through VP-216. VP-209 through VP-212 were established at NAS Norfolk between January and March 1943. VP-213 through VP-216 were established at NAS Harvey Point, North Carolina, in October and

November 1943. VP-216 never became operational in the Atlantic. After training at Harvey Point and Key West, it was transferred to the Pacific Fleet in March 1944.

On 22 January 1943 VP-207 was assigned to San Juan, Puerto Rico, under the operational control of Commander Fleet Air Wing 11 (CFAW-11). After three weeks the squadron was transferred to Naval Auxiliary Air Facility (NAAF) Salinas, Ecuador, and a detachment was sent to NAAF Galápagos, Seymour Island, arriving on 11 February. The squadron flew patrol between Salinas into the Galápagos, and to Corinto, Nicaragua. During the first month at Salinas, three aircraft were on detached duty to Jamaica for the prosecution of antisubmarine warfare (ASW) hot spots. Although it may seem odd that Atlantic squadrons operated in the Pacific, the Atlantic Fleet supported the Panama Sea Frontier and the Panama Sea Frontier was responsible for the defense of both the Atlantic and the Pacific approaches to the Panama Canal. At the time there was a real fear that the Japanese might attack the canal from the Pacific side. The patrols between Ecuador, Nicaragua, and the Galápagos were intended to detect any approaching Japanese warships approximately six to seven hundred miles from the canal in order to provide timely warning to canal defenses.

On 8 February 1943 VP-202 was relocated to Key West, Florida, with a three-plane detachment at Grand Cayman Island. The squadron's principal duties until November were patrol and convoy coverage. On 24 February VP-74, operating from Natal, Brazil, experienced its first encounter with the German tactic of remaining on the surface to fight with quad-mount 20-mm antiaircraft guns. Ens. W. J. Barnard spotted a U-boat in the act of torpedoing a ship. During his subsequent attack, the submarine surfaced and commenced heavy and accurate 20-mm cannon fire. There were no injuries to the PBM crew, but the U-boat escaped.

In March 1943 VP-204 completed training in San Juan, Puerto Rico, with support from *Pelican* (AVP-6). The squadron then began antisubmarine patrols and convoy escort from San Juan and Trinidad. Trinidad was one of the few sources of critically needed bauxite, essential in aluminum production. Squadron advanced base detachments were maintained at various times at Antigua; Coco Solo; Essequibo, British Guiana; Cayenne, French Guiana; Paramaribo; Suriname; and Guantánamo Bay, Cuba. From March through August VP-204 aircraft attacked U-boats on eight different occasions and on three of these attacks antiaircraft fire from the submarine damaged the attacking aircraft. An attack on 30 July by BuNo 6718 at 07°58' N, 54°58' W resulted in the death of Lt. (j.g.) R. K. Hersey from submarine gun fire. The U-boat involved was possibly U-572, which was sunk on 3 August by VP-205.

VP-203 returned to Norfolk in March and began convoy escort and ASW patrols under the operational control of FAW-5. On 12 March VP-208 was assigned a home port of Key West and began operational patrols from an advanced base at Pelican Harbour, British West Indies. The squadron was supported by *Christiana* (YAG-32).

On 1 April 1943 VP-206 was transferred to NAS Coco Solo, Canal Zone, with support from *Rockaway* (AVP-29). VP-206 began flying antishipping, convoy coverage, and shipping barrier patrols. Detachments were established at Salinas, Ecuador, and Seymour Island in the Galápagos. Additional detachments flew from Jamaica and Corinto, Nicaragua.

FAW-16 established headquarters at Recife, Brazil, on 14 April 1943. The fleet air wing's control included Mariner squadrons VP-74, VP-203, and VP-211. Mariners operated from bases at NAF Aratu, NAF Bahia, and NAF Galeo at Rio de Janeiro. They were serviced by six small seaplane tenders: *Barnegat, Humboldt, Lapwing, Rehoboth, Rockaway,* and *Sandpiper.* On 28 April, ten VP-74 aircraft established a detachment at NAF Aratu near Bahia, Brazil.

The U-boat fleet in the North Atlantic

had received crippling blows from the Allies in 1942 and early 1943. In May 1943 alone, forty-one U-boats were destroyed. The North Atlantic was now an Allied lake. Grand Adm. Carl Doenitz, commander of the German submarine forces, gradually began withdrawing U-boats from the North Atlantic. A complete withdrawal was ordered on 22 May 1943. Doenitz planned to continue the war of attrition against Allied shipping in the supposedly safer waters of the Caribbean and South Atlantic. Twenty U-boats were assigned this mission: thirteen to the Caribbean Panama Canal approaches and seven to Brazilian waters. The Mariner was positioned and ready to counter this new U-boat deployment.

While patrolling off Bahia in support of a convoy southbound from Trinidad to Bahia on 16 May 1943, a VP-74 Mariner attacked U-128, Kapitanleutnant Herman Steinert commanding. The Mariner's depth charges fell wide and U-128 escaped. During the night Steinart proceeded on the surface toward Recife. Near dawn he submerged and picked up the convoy on sonar. After he established the convoy's course and speed, Stienart surfaced in order to make a high-speed run to a better firing position. On 17 May VP-74's plane 5 piloted by Lt. Howland Davis and plane 6 piloted by Lt. Howard C. Carey detected the submarine on radar and attacked with a total of twelve depth charges, wrecking U-128. Two destroyers, *Moffett* (DD-362) and *Jouett* (DD-396), arrived on the scene and finished off U-128 with 5-inch gunfire at position 10°00' S, 35°35' W. *Moffett* rescued fifty-one U-boat crew members including Steinart.

On 21 May 1943 new squadron VP-211 was homeported at Naval Auxiliary Air Station (NAAS) Elizabeth City, North Carolina. On 27 May new squadron VP-201 was deployed to Bermuda. By 8 July a squadron Mariner piloted by John D. Hitchcock strafed and depth charged U-134, commanded by Kapitanleutnant Hans-Gunther Brosin. Although the submarine had been caught on the surface, its accurate defensive fire allowed it to escape. The PBM was heavily damaged during the attack and was forced to return to base. On 18 July U-134 shot down the attacking blimp K-74 with the loss of one crewman.

German records indicate that by this time seven U-boats patrolled "inside" the Caribbean. U-759, commanded by Kapitanleutnant Rudolf Friedrich, had entered via the Mona Passage on 29 June 1943. From a position south of the Windward Passage, Friedrich patrolled the Key West–Trinidad convoy route. He sank a sailing ship with gunfire on 30 June; the sinking vessel was unable to alert Allied forces. On 5 July Friedrich sank the thirty-five hundred ton American freighter *Maltran* from a small convoy. Two days later he found convoy Trinidad-Aruba-Guantánamo (TAG) 70, consisting of eight freighters and six escorts. He sank the ninety-three hundred ton Dutch cargo vessel *Peolau Roebiah*. An escort, the old four-stack destroyer *Tattnall* (DD-125), counterattacked, but Friedrich evaded and slipped away. A navy scout plane found the U-boat again on 8 July and dropped depth charges and summoned surface ships. In the ensuring seven-hour chase, Friedrich successfully eluded the warships.

Friedrich reported this long chase to U-boat control on 10 July, adding that there were no casualties. This was the last communication from U-759. According to a postwar German reassessment, a VP-32 Mariner piloted by Robert C. Mayo was escorting yet another convoy, TAG 74, in the early hours of July 15. Mayo found U-759 on the surface. His depth charges sent U-759 to the bottom at 18°06' N, 75°00' W with the loss of all hands. U-759 had been one of only two U-boats of the seven total to sink any ships inside Caribbean waters.

Seemingly oblivious to the Allied ASW measures in Brazilian waters, Kapitanleutnant Fritz Guggenberger (Knight's Cross with Oak Leaves) in U-513 continued to hunt on the surface. On 16 July 1943 he torpedoed and sank the seventy-two hundred ton American Liberty ship *Richard Caswell*, which had been sailing alone about four hundred miles south of Rio de Janeiro. The seaplane tender *Barnegat* (AVP-10), supporting the Mariners of VP-74 based at Florianpolis, rescued the survivors. The sinking of the *Caswell* intensified the use of Mariners on submarine search missions.

Three days later a VP-74 Mariner piloted by Roy S. Whitcomb found Guggenberger's U-513 on the surface not far from the scene of the *Caswell* sinking. Guggenberger saw the plane, but dismissed it as an "old crate" flown by Brazilians. He manned his 37-mm and 20-mm guns to give battle. After a few rounds, the 20-mm jammed, but Guggenberger remained on the surface as Whitcomb bore in and dropped four depth charges. Two of the charges hit very close, destroying U-513. The submarine sank instantly at 27°17' S, 47°42' W.

The blasts threw a number of Germans, including Guggenberger, into the sea. Seeing them, Whitcomb made a low pass and dropped two life rafts and life jackets. He then notified *Barnegat*. When the seaplane tender reached the scene about dusk, it could find only one life raft containing Guggenberger and six enlisted men. Forty-six Germans perished. After extensive interrogation, Guggenberger was incarcerated at a prisoner of war (POW) camp, Papago Park, on an Indian reservation in Arizona. Earlier, Guggenberger in U-81 had sunk the British aircraft carrier *Ark Royal*.

U-359, commanded by Oberleutnant Heinz Forster, patrolled inside the Caribbean south of Hispaniola. On 26 July 1943 a Mariner of VP-32's San Juan detachment, was being piloted by Ralph W. Rawson. He found U-359 at 15°57' N, 68°30' W and attacked through heavy flak. The Mariner dropped four depth charges. Rawson was credited with "probable damage" to a U-boat. But, in fact, U-359 did not survive this attack. It was the third U-boat to be sunk within two weeks by the PBM-3 Mariners of VP-32, a record not exceeded by any other land-based ASW squadron in the war.

Oberleutnant zur See Heinz Beckmann in U-159 was assigned to patrol the Panama Canal area. He entered the Caribbean via the Anegada Passage. While southeast of Haiti on 28 July 1943, a VP-32 Mariner piloted by Lt. (j.g.) D. C. Pinholster caught U-159 on the surface. The VP-32 after-action report described the incident:

Approach and Contact. Flying at altitude 1500 feet, a radar contact was obtained bearing 150 forward of the port beam, distance 5 miles. Visual contact was established immediately thereafter. Submarine fully surfaced, estimated speed 15 knots. Approach with maximum power was made with a wide turn to port in order to cross target from astern.

Attack. The plane's bow turret first opened fire at a range of 3 miles. It then ceased fire and re-opened at $^3/_4$ mile. Numerous hits were observed on the conning tower. The submarine held the plane under AA [antiaircraft] fire throughout the approach without effect. The submarine made a sharp evasive turn to port as the plane reached the release point. Four Mk [Mark] 44 depth bombs, with fuzes set to function at 25 feet were released in train by intervalometer with a 60 feet spacing. Altitude of release 25 feet, air speed 180 knots, target angle 250 deg.

Reported Evidence of Damage. It was reported that after the explosions at the time of the attack the submarine lost headway rapidly until almost dead in the water. One or two large oil slicks were sighted in approximately the same position on the following morning and afternoon.

Subsequent Action of Aircraft. After release of bombs, the plane was put in a sharp left turn to permit strafing from crown and tail turrets. After one complete circle of the submarine the plane was hit by anti-aircraft fire which produced injury to two crew members and materiel damage comprising 3 or 4 holes six to twelve inches across in the fuselage and about 170 small holes scattered over the side of the plane.

Although it was not positively confirmed at the time, U-159 sank with the loss of all hands. U-boat control had no clue to its loss. Originally, the U.S. Navy incorrectly credited the sinking of U-159 to a VP-32 Mariner piloted by Robert C. Mayo.

On 3 July 1943 U-199, commanded by Kapitanleutnant Hans-Werner Kraus (Knight's Cross), was located by two Brazilian aircraft. Later in the afternoon U-199 was attacked by a VP-74 Mariner (BuNo 6571) piloted by Lt. (j.g.) Harold C. Carey. Carey had participated in the sinking of U-128 in May. U-199's flak brought down Carey's aircraft with the loss of all hands.

On 24 July U-199 attacked the forty-two hundred ton British freighter *Henzada*. The first three torpedoes missed, but one of two stern shots struck and the ship broke in half and sank in twenty-nine minutes. A week later, sixty miles off Rio de Janeiro, Kraus chased a lone ship until dawn on 31 July. Responding to the ship's call for assistance, a VP-74 Mariner piloted by William F. Smith found U-199 on the surface. Flying into the heavy 20-mm and 37-mm flak, Smith attacked, dropping six depth charges in his first run and two more in a second run. The explosions of the depth charges badly damaged U-199, but Kraus kept up the flak and ran west toward shallow water, where he intended to bottom and make repairs.

Holding on to his target, Smith continued to rake U-199 with machine-gun fire and radioed for help. Two Brazilian planes

promptly responded, a Hudson and a Catalina. The Hudson dropped two depth charges that fell wide. Piloted by S. C. Schnoor, the Hudson strafed the U-boat. Piloted by Alberto M. Torres, the Catalina finally sank U-199 with four depth charges at 23°54' S, 42°54' W. Twelve of U-199's sixty-one-man crew, including Kraus, the first and second watch officers, a midshipman, and a warrant quartermaster, survived and were rescued by *Barnegat*. Kraus ended up with Guggenberger at the Papago Park POW camp. Kraus and Guggenberger escaped together on 23 December 1944 but were soon recaptured.

U-572, Oberleutnant Heinz Kummetat commanding, was assigned to patrol an area to the east of Barbados and Trinidad. On 14 and 15 July 1943 he sank by gunfire two British sailing vessels southeast of the latter place, the 114-ton *Harvard* and the 176-ton *Gilbert B. Walters*. He then returned to an area well to the east of Trinidad and searched in vain for Allied shipping. On 31 July he reported to U-boat control "heavy air" activity and that U-572 had repelled an aircraft attack. Possibly he was referring to the attack by a VP-204 Mariner in which Lt. (j.g.) R. K. Hersey died.

About that same time, two of the other U-boats that were also patrolling from Trinidad southward to French Guiana had tangled with Allied aircraft: U-406 commanded by Kapitanleutnant Horst

Dieterichs, and U-653 commanded by Korvettan Kapitan Gerhard Feiler. Feiler in U-653 is credited with the sinking of the seaplane tender USS *Gannet* on 7 June 1942. Because both U-boats had expended a great deal of flak ammunition in these engagements, Dieterichs requested a rendezvous with Kummetat to take on ammunition and gun grease.

The Allies learned of the proposed rendezvous from radio intelligence. On 3 August a VP-205 Mariner (BuNo 6722) piloted by Lt. (j.g.) Clifford C. Cox arrived at the rendezvous point. After reporting his position he said: "Sighted submarine, making attack." The submarine engaged was probably U-572 because twenty minutes earlier Kummetat had radioed Berlin from near the same position. Cox probably sank U-572 and Kummetat probably shot down the Mariner because neither was heard from again. Dieterichs in U-406 reported to U-boat control on 5 August that U-572 had failed to keep the rendezvous. When U-572 did not respond to repeated queries, U-boat control presumed that it was lost at 11°35' N, 54°05' W. Owing to the crash of the Mariner the exact details of U-572's loss will never be known. Lieutenant Cox was awarded a posthumous Distinguished Flying Cross (DFC).

Kapitanleutnant Ralph Kapitzky, in command of U-615, entered the Caribbean via the Anegada Passage. He cruised southwest to the islands of Curaçao and Aruba. On 12 July 1943 he found and chased a tanker without success. On 28 July he sank the Dutch tanker *Rosalia* en route from Lake Maracaibo. Kapitzky's subsequent radio report to U-boat control was picked up by the radio direction finding station in San Juan and set in motion what historian Adm. Samuel Eliot Morison has described as "perhaps the best example in the entire war of a fiercely aggressive, fearfully costly, but finally successful air antisubmarine hunt." In his *History of United States Naval Operations in World War Two, Volume X, The Atlantic Battle Won,* Morison's description of the engagements with U-615 is accurate and colorful:

First to attack was an Army B-18 out of Aruba on the night of 29 July 1943. The pilot, 2nd Lieutenant T. L. Merrill USA, made one good bombing attack but lost contact when his flares flickered out— again, no searchlight. On 1 August a B-24 out of Curaçao dropped one bomb on the submarine; next day PC-1196 made a depth-charge attack of no avail. U-615's crew were working hard to make repairs, and the boat had made only 200 miles easting by the night of 5 August when it was caught surfaced near Blanquilla by a Trinidad-based Mariner commanded by Lieutenant (jg) J. M. Erskine USNR. This plane made three runs but failed to inflict further damage. The following afternoon another Mariner of the same squadron (VP-205), piloted by Lieutenant A. R. Matuski USNR, attacked once, caused heavy flooding, radioed to Port of Spain, "Sub damaged with bow out of water making only two knots, no casualties to plane or personnel," banked for a second attack and then radioed, "Damaged—damaged—fire." Those were Matuski's last words; U-615 shot him down and all hands were lost.

In the meantime more aircraft were hastening to the spot or warming up at Trinidad. That very afternoon (6 August) a Mariner piloted by Lieutenant L. D. Crockett USNR located the crippled submarine a few miles from the latest contact, delivered a bombing attack against heavy antiaircraft fire, and received an incendiary bullet in the starboard wing, which immediately burst into flames. While the flight engineer smothered the blaze with CO2 [carbon dioxide] and his shirt, Lieutenant Crockett bore in and at 1631 dropped a string of bombs that detonated close on the submarine's port quarter. Nevertheless U-615 managed to withstand five subsequent strafing attacks. At 1635, a Ventura piloted by Lieutenant (jg) T. M. Holmes USNR appeared on the scene, slipped through the U-boat's flak without a scratch, and straddled it. U-615 submerged, surfaced within a minute, the submariners springing to their guns as Crockett, Holmes and, at 1815, a Mariner

piloted by Lieutenant (jg) J. W. Dresbach USNR, prepared to make a coordinated attack. The U-boat's gunfire killed Dresbach and caused a premature release of his bombs; but the co-pilot, Lieutenant (jg) O. R. Christian USNR, pulled out of the dive and banked for a high-level bombing attack. By this time, the U-boat's deck was littered with dead and wounded. At 1834 August 6 there arrived another PBM (fifth of that type to take part), making three aircraft on the spot; its pilot, Lieutenant Commander R. S. Null, made two attacks which resulted only in killing more Germans. Night was now falling and the planes were running out of gas; an Army B-18 from Zandery Field reached the scene and attacked at 2118, the boat lighted by flares from a sixth PBM. So ended this memorable 6th of August.

U-615 was still afloat at 0010 August 7 when a seventh PBM made radar contact and lighted flares but, uncertain whether the boat was friend or foe, dropped no bombs. Destroyer *Walker*, dispatched from Port of Spain the night before, sighted the submarine at 0552. Kapitzky, seeing the destroyer approaching, knew that his time was up, ordered all hands into life rafts, and grimly took his boat down for the last time. *Walker* rescued 43 submariners.

Kapitzky was mortally wounded during the attack. He died in a life raft and was buried

PBM-3Ss of VP-211 passing Sugarloaf Mountain, Rio de Janeiro, December 1943. *U.S. Naval Institute Photo Archive*

at sea by his crew. U.S. records show VP-130, VP-204, VP-205, and Army Squadron 10 sharing credit for the kill of U-615. Navy pilots Crockett, Christian, and Dresbach were awarded DFCs for the action.

On 3 August 1943 Lt. (j.g.) E. C. Scully of VP-211 attacked and damaged the surfaced U-566, Kapitanleutnant Hans Hornkohl commanding, off the coast of Elizabeth City, North Carolina. On the first and second bombing runs, the aircraft's electrical bomb release malfunctioned. By the third run the submarine had submerged, but the seaplane's manual bomb release was used. The U-boat was blown back to the surface. Although Scully made additional strafing runs, heavy antiaircraft fire damaged the hull of the Mariner. Scully was forced to break off the attack. He was able to land safely and beach his aircraft on a sandspit before it sank. U-566 survived. It sunk the gunboat *Plymouth* (PG-57), originally the German-built Vanderbilt yacht *Alva,* on 5 August.

The first section of VP-210 arrived at NAS Guantánamo, Cuba, on 11 August 1943. The squadron commenced flying convoy coverage, antisubmarine sweeps, and rescue missions. VP-210 remained at Guantánamo for the remainder of the war with detachments at Great Exuma Island. On 23 August VP-209 commenced convoy coverage patrols from NAS Norfolk, Virginia.

U-161, Kapitanleutnant Albrecht Achilles (Knights Cross) commanding, sailed from France to Brazilian waters on 8 August. After rendezvousing with the Japanese submarine I-8 near the Azores and later with U-198 in the South Atlantic, Achilles reached his patrol area and sank two freighters: the fifty-five hundred ton British *St. Usk* on 20 September and the five thousand ton Brazilian *Itapage* on 26 September. The day after he sank the second ship, U-161 was found by VP-74's plane 2, piloted by Lt. (j.g.) Harry B. Patterson. He attacked with machine guns and depth charges. U-161 sank with all hands at 12°30' S, 35°35' W. Two PBM crewmen were wounded by fire from the U-boat.

On 30 September 1943 VP-212 was transferred to San Juan, Puerto Rico, to fly convoy coverage and ASW sweeps. A detachment was maintained at Antigua. In October VP-203 was ordered to Aratu, Brazil, to relieve VP-74. VP-203 also operated a detachment from Natal, Brazil.

Lt. (j.g.) Daniel T. Felix Jr. and his VP-210 crew made a radar contact on a surfaced U-boat while covering a Guantánamo-Trinidad convoy on 12 October. The U-boat submerged after flares were dropped, but reappeared with heavy antiaircraft fire. The U-boat submerged again before a bombing attack could be made. It is probable that the U-boat was U-214, commanded by Kapitanleutnant Rupprecht Stock, because U-214 reportedly laid mines off of Panama on 10 October.

On 16 October 1943 VP-211 arrived at Aratu, Brazil, and established a detachment at Galeao, Rio de Janeiro. On 15 November VP-208 relocated to Grand Cayman Island to replace the VP-202 detachment. VP-202 was sent to Norfolk to transition to the PBM-3D. After its transition, VP-202 was transferred to the Pacific Fleet. The squadron began ferrying its aircraft west on 28 December.

Lt. H. M. Walling and his crew from VP-212, providing night convoy coverage for ships en route to Curaçao, came across a surfaced submarine on 17 December. It was U-516, commanded by Kapitanleutnant Hans-Rutger Tillessen. The Mariner was driven off by antiaircraft fire, but successfully interrupted the U-boat's attack on the Spanish tanker *Campestra*. At nightfall the next day, Admiral Robinson, commanding the Trinidad sector of the Caribbean Sea Frontier, organized a search by three Mariners equipped with radar and L-7 searchlights. U-516 was detected by radar and illuminated by searchlight by a Mariner flown by Lt. Robert E. Pearce. He attacked with machine guns and depth charges. Although Tillessen reported considerable damage from the attack, he was able to escape and returned safely to Germany.

A Safer Atlantic, 1944

In the beginning of 1944 three of the four Mariner squadrons established in October and November 1943 joined the Atlantic Fleet. Although U-boat activities did not end completely in Mariner operating areas, they sharply declined as Doenitz pulled back his forces for the defense of Europe. His foray into the South Atlantic had been a disaster; ten of his twenty U-boats had been sunk.

In January FAW-16, which had been experiencing great difficulty in getting spare parts, established a cargo detachment in Natal, Brazil, at the seaplane base next to the Pan Am docks. The detachment consisted of two PBM-3Ss (Bureau Numbers 6505 and 6580) and three crews. Lt. Richard Watson was transferred from VP-203 to head up the detachment.

FAW-16's home base was at Natal, but the spare crew generally laid over in Norfolk. A plane was scheduled to leave Norfolk each Thursday. The payload was weight limited to eight thousand pounds, although occasionally volume was the controlling factor. Routing southbound was Norfolk to Banana River, San Juan, Georgetown in British Guiana, Belem, and finally Natal. The facility in British Guiana on the Essequibo River was a

small satellite seaplane base for Trinidad. It had only one ramp and the most difficult current of any known Mariner seadrome. Southbound was into the wind. Loaded with cargo the trip took five days. The north-bound routing was sometimes the reverse, but more often the trip was from Natal to Paramaribo, Dutch Guiana (using the Pan Am dock), Trinidad, Guantánamo Bay, and then Norfolk. The northbound trip took four days, all downwind. Usually the seaplanes were lightly loaded, mostly with personnel being transferred or on leave.

On patrol from Natal, Brazil, on 5 January 1944 and near the end of its 640 mile search, a VP-203 Mariner flown by Lt. Stanley V. Brown spotted a suspicious-looking merchant vessel. Brown transmitted such an accurate description of the vessel that Fourth Fleet headquarters was able to identify it as the 7,320 ton German blockade runner *Burgenland*. *Burgenland* was intercepted and sunk by *Omaha* (CL-4) and *Jouett* (DD-396) on the same day.

Lt. Richard Boehme of VP-207, flying from San Juan on 15 March 1944, spotted a U-boat on the surface and began to circle in preparation for an attack. The U-boat was probably U-518, commanded by Oberleutnant zur See Hans-Werner Offermann. Offermann had sunk the Panamanian tanker *Valera* on 7 March. Antiaircraft fire from the U-boat damaged the aircraft before an attack could be made and wounded Ens. Douglas K.

Kelsey. The damaged Mariner landed at Coco Solo for repairs. On 17 March another VP-207 Mariner, flown by Lt. (j.g.) Bowen S. Larkins attacked what was probably the same submarine without results. Although Offermann escaped destruction, his sinking of the *Valera* was his only victory during his 106-day cruise.

On 1 April 1944 Lt. (j.g.) G. R. Gregory of VP-212 attacked a surfaced U-boat northwest of Puerto Rico. Although a "perfect straddle" of depth charges was dropped, damage was assessed as minimal. The U-boat may have been U-218, commanded by Kapitanleutnant Richard Becker. Becker's original mission was to lay mines off Trinidad, but due to intense ASW opposition, he was forced to cancel that operation. He did lay mines off Port Castries, St. Lucia, on 23 March and off San Juan, Puerto Rico, on 1 April. Neither minefield sank any ships.

A VP-203 Mariner, based at NAF Galeo, Brazil, made a strafing run on a surfaced U-boat at 08°42' S, 22°33' W on 4 April. The U-boat, possibly U-129, was forced to dive, but apparently was unharmed.

A direct Mariner attack on a U-boat was conducted on the night of 5 June off the coast of Puerto Rico. A VP-204 aircraft used its new wing-mounted searchlight and claimed damage to the submarine, but this claim was not substantiated by a postwar examination of German records. Possibly the U-boat was U-539, commanded by Kapitanleutnant Hans-Jürgen Lauterbach-

Emden. On 12 June U-539 was attacked by a Mariner despite intense flak from the submarine, but the U-boat got away.

On 28 September 1944 a VP-211 Mariner, east southeast of Recife, Brazil, located U-863, Kapitanleutnant Dietrich von der Esch commanding, but was driven off by heavy antiaircraft fire. The Mariner's sighting and accurate position report resulted in U-863 being located and sunk the following day by two PB4Y-1 Liberators of VB-107.

The designation of Mariner squadrons was changed from patrol squadron (VP) to patrol bombing squadron (VPB) on 1 October 1944 to more accurately describe the expected employment of these squadrons in the Pacific. In November, VPB-205 and VPB-208 were transferred to the Pacific Fleet.

For the remainder of 1944 U-boat activity in Mariner areas was light. Mariners continued providing convoy coverage, checking neutral shipping activity, and providing air-sea rescue services.

Atlantic Wrap-up, 1945

During the first part of 1945, Mariners continued their duties. As soon as the war in Europe ended in May, almost all the Atlantic Mariner squadrons were rapidly disestablished. Personnel were reassigned and the aircraft were "disposed of." A U.S. Navy document, titled "Aircraft Expended or Lost Outside the Continental U.S. December 1941 to August 1945," shows that approximately ninety-five of the Atlantic early PBM-3 series were "expended outside the continental United States" in May, June, and July 1945: Nine in Bermuda, fifty-two in San Juan, Puerto Rico, and thirty-four in the Panama Canal zone. Contemporary photographs show the Bermuda aircraft being scuttled at sea, and the San Juan and Panama aircraft were probably disposed of in the same manner.

Despite its recurring engine problems, the Mariner and its crews established an impressive record during World War II in the Atlantic. Mariners directly participated in the sinking of ten U-boats; this was more than any other land-based type of aircraft. Mariners located a German blockade runner so it could be sunk by surface ships and were responsible for the ocean rescue of hundreds of seamen and airmen. Three Mariners were shot down by U-boats with the loss of all hands and eight were damaged by U-boat antiaircraft fire. At least sixteen others were lost in operational accidents.

The opportunity to engage U-boats by Atlantic Fleet's Mariner squadrons was largely dependent on the squadron's geographic deployment. Obviously, squadrons operating from Ecuador, Nicaragua, and the Galápagos had no chance at all.

Although only two of the Mariner squadrons, VP-32 and VP-74 were awarded Navy Unit Commendations, the activities cited in VP-74's award was shared by all the squadrons:

For outstanding heroism during operations against enemy forces in the Atlantic from June 7, 1942 to July 31, 1943. Undaunted by perils of weather and sea conditions and the ever present danger of being forced down in the broad expanses of the Atlantic Ocean while fulfilling an extremely vital assignment in connection with anti-submarine warfare, Patrol Squadron 74 compiled an imposing record in the sighting of 29 hostile submarines, in attacking 16, in destroying five and in inflicting damage upon two others. Individually courageous and operating in a smoothly functioning team, its pilots and crewmen effected numerous hazardous open-sea landings to rescue 220 stranded airmen and Mariners, and in addition, dropped supplies to survivors of merchant disasters and directed surface craft to their rescue. The outstanding record of service and combat achievement attained by this gallant fighting unit contributed notably to the Allied success in crushing the U-boat menace and reflect the highest credit upon Patrol Bombing Squadron 74 and the United States Naval Service.

All personnel attached to Patrol Squadron 74 during the above period are hereby authorized to wear the Navy Unit Commendation Ribbon.

—JAMES FORRESTAL, SECRETARY OF THE NAVY

CHAPTER THREE

THE MARINER IN THE PACIFIC THEATER DURING WORLD WAR II

Mariners Begin Pacific Service, 1942

In early 1942 there were very few long-range cargo/transport aircraft. The only aircraft capable of carrying a payload from California to Hawaii were the six Pan American Boeing and three Martin Clippers, and the U.S. Navy's sole Sikorsky XPBS-1. Because warfare in the vast Pacific would require air logistic support, the Naval Air Transport Service (NATS) was formed in March 1942. On 1 April Air Transport Squadron 2 (VR-2) was commissioned at Alameda, California, with a mission to establish cargo and passenger service from the continental United States to Australia and the South Pacific. The navy converted Consolidated PB2Y Coronado patrol bombers to the PB2Y-R "GI Clipper" transport configuration for the long California-Hawaii leg. Because the need was so urgent, the first fifty PBM-3s were delivered as PBM-3R transports.

The transport Mariners pioneered NATS flights southbound from Hawaii in October 1942. Graham Kelly, a former VR-2 pilot, recalled that eventually there were twenty-seven Mariners operating from Honolulu. Their routes extended to Australia and New Zealand in island-hopping relays via Palmyra, Canton, Wallis, Suva, and Nouméa. A hub with eight planes was established at the Pan American Clipper base in Nouméa. Later the Mariners shuttled across the east-west routes with a service from Suva to Nouméa and through Tonga, Upola, Espiritu Santo, and Efate. NATS PBMs were part of the aerial supply line to Guadalcanal when American troops started the conquest of Japanese-held islands. As Mariners fed supplies into Espiritu Santo for trans-shipment to the Solomons, they often were attacked by Japanese planes based in the New Hebrides. Mariner crews recalled these early operations as days when flight crews did their own loading and unloading. There were few surveyed seadromes among the undeveloped islands.

Ten of the NATS Mariners were assigned to Pan American Airways' Pacific Division: Bureau Numbers 6459 through 6466, and 6503 and 6504. The Pan American Mariners received cargo configuration improvements at the airline's Treasure Island Base in San Francisco Bay. They operated under NATS direction from Pan American's Pearl City terminal on Oahu, with maintenance performed at NAS Ford Island.

Preparations for Pacific Combat, 1943

The first known Mariner air-sea rescue "Dumbo" mission in the Pacific was performed by a NATS Pan American PBM.

At 0530 on 12 November 1943 the troop transport SS *Cape San Juan* was on its second voyage from San Francisco to Townsville, Australia, with 1,429 passengers. It was hit by a torpedo from a Japanese submarine. The explosion killed many of the U.S. Army troops on board and released oil that spread onto the surrounding water. A false word to abandon ship quickly spread and all but about two hundred men went over the side into the sea. They were immediately were coated with a layer of oil. Survivors swam for jettisoned life rafts or clung to floating debris and kapok jackets. *Cape San Juan* listed on its starboard side as damage control tried shoring up the gaping hole and pumping out the incoming sea. The stricken ship remained afloat for another twenty-four hours.

The liberty ship SS *Edwin T. Merideth* rescued 443 people, including those remaining aboard *Cape San Juan. McCalla* (DD-488), *Dempsey* (DE-26), and minesweeper YMS-241 picked up 840 additional survivors. The sea then became rough as a storm system passed through the area, bringing swells that were up to fifteen feet high. These conditions exacerbated the situation for the men in the water.

A Pan American Mariner, just arriving in Suva, Fiji, on a cargo run, volunteered to assist in the rescue mission. Captain Moss gives his account in Lee Roy Way's "First PBM Rescue" article:

> We arrived at Suva at 1030 hours and were informed of the *Cape San Juan's* dilemma and the plight of the many survivors in the water. Our cargo was unloaded and we were airborne about noon. Our entire crew plus Navy Pharmacist Mate A. L. Burress volunteered for the mission and after three hours flying the *Cape San Juan* was sighted listing in 15 foot swells. We circled the ship 3 times without seeing anyone in the water. We were just about ready to give up when a New Zealand land plane was spotted circling some distance from the ship. Dropping lower and closer we sighted clusters of men in the water spread out for about 3 miles. Some were in life rafts, one life boat was drifting and others were in life jackets in the middle of the oil slick.

> A landing was made in a relatively smooth area of the oil slick with 15 foot swells all around us. Unable to taxi very close to the survivors, we trailed life rafts behind the Mariner and survivors clambered in as the rafts passed by. In all, 48 survivors were brought aboard.

All known survivors were rescued when the Pan American Dumbo began its takeoff. Not only was this the first Mariner open-sea rescue in the Pacific, no other aircraft ocean rescue before or since is known to have picked up so many people.

Preparations for the deployment of Mariner combat squadrons to the Pacific began in late 1943. In December VP-202 was re-equipped with new PBM-3Ds at Norfolk, Virginia. The PBM-3D was an upgraded model with three power turrets, increased armor, the Norden bombsight, and Wright R-2600-22 engines of nineteen hundred horsepower. VP-202 began moving its aircraft to the West Coast on 28 December. Another squadron programmed for immediate Pacific service was VP-216, which had been established in November 1943 at NAAS Harvey Point, North Carolina.

Pacific Deployment, 1944

VP-216 was re-equipped with the new PBM-3D in January 1944 but almost immediately valve seat insert failures began to occur in the new engines. VP-216's aircraft were grounded until the end of February 1944 when improved parts solved the problem.

Eleven new Mariner squadrons slated for Pacific service were established in 1944: VP-16 through VP-22, and VP-25 through VP-28. All were initially equipped with the PBM-3D. Most of the new squadrons were formed at Norfolk or Elizabeth City and received advanced tactical training in Key West. They then flew across the country to Alameda, California, on San Francisco Bay. A common routing included a refueling stop at NAS Corpus Christi, Texas, or at Eagle Mountain Lake near Dallas. After arriving at Alameda the Mariners were prepared for transpacific flight by Commander Fleet Air Wing 8 (CFAW-8). CFAW-8's official history notes that between April and September 1944 it was necessary to change all the cylinders of approximately fifty PBM-3Ds due to unsatisfactory valve seats.

From Alameda the PBMs made the eighteen-hour flight to Kaneohe, Hawaii, where final preparations for deployment to the combat areas were made under the direction of Commander Fleet Air Wing 2 (CFAW-2). As the war progressed, three more Atlantic squadrons joined the Pacific Fleet: VPB-205 and VPB-208 in November 1944, and VPB-32 in August 1945. Total Mariner Pacific employment in

World War II would reach a total of sixteen patrol bombing squadrons, three training squadrons, and four rescue squadrons.

The Pacific's strategic situation dictated a different employment of the Mariner than it was in the Atlantic. In the combat area, Mariners would operate under the command of five fleet air wings:

CFAW-1, South Pacific area
CFAW-2, Hawaiian/Gilberts area
CFAW-10, New Guinea/Philippine
   area
CFAW-17, Philippine area
CFAW-18, Guam/Tinian

The northward advance of U.S. forces had begun with the campaigns of Guadalcanal and New Guinea in 1942 and 1943. By November 1943 U.S. control had been extended to the Gilbert Islands with the conquest of Tarawa, and then to the Marshall Islands when Kwajalein and Eniwetok were taken in February 1944.

The first operational Pacific Mariner squadron was VP-202, the former Atlantic Fleet squadron commanded by Comdr. Robert W. Leeman. VP-202 arrived in Hawaii in early January 1944. After four days at Kaneohe, under the operational control of CFAW-2, the squadron began to deploy to Tarawa on 15 January with a mission to patrol the Japanese-held Marshall and Gilbert Islands.

On 29 January 1944 Lieutenant Hunt and his crew took off from Tarawa and made the first bombing raid on Japanese territory by a Mariner. Hunt made three separate runs over the airstrip on the Japanese-held Taroa Island in the Marshalls. All bombs hit the runway, barracks, and other installations.

On 31 January Leeman and his crew took off from Tarawa and attacked Taroa Island in another night raid. All bombs hit in the vicinity of the runway and the barracks area, where incendiary bombs started several fires. Although antiaircraft fire was encountered, the Mariner did not suffer any damage.

The squadron's base was moved to Majuro in February and later on to Kwajalein. On 14 February Hunt and his crew attacked a two thousand ton Japanese freighter off Ponape Island and scored several near misses on it with bombs and strafed it severely. They encountered heavy antiaircraft fire from ship and shore batteries, but sustained no damage.

While on a search mission on the night of 11 February Lieutenant Schwerdt and crew suffered an engine failure, but were able to fly their plane on a single engine from the vicinity of Ponape Island to Kwajalein, a distance of about 450 miles. On 13 February Lt. John Schreffer and his crew, flying off Ponape, sighted a seven thousand ton Japanese freighter and two escort ships. When they broke through the clouds to attack, the Mariner was met by a thick barrage of antiaircraft fire. Tail Gunner W. B. (Bill) Pierce was momentarily knocked unconscious, but recovered in time to give the ship a severe strafing. During this run Mariner gunners put eleven hundred rounds of 50-caliber ammunition into the enemy ship.

VP-202 was sent on to Eniwetok on 24 February 1944 after the invasion forces secured the seadrome area. One hundred and one missions were flown from Eniwetok before the squadron returned to Kaneohe for repairs and refitting. Although surviving records are not definitive, VP-202 was probably tended by *Casco* (AVP-12) and/or *Chincoteague* (AVP-24) during this operation. From this promising beginning, Mariners would go on to participate in the major Pacific campaigns: Marianas, Palau, Philippines, Iwo Jima, and Okinawa.

Marianas, June 1944

The strategic value of the Marianas Islands was nicely described by Michael G. Kammen in his *Operational History of the Flying Boat,* an extensive study of tender-based open-sea seaplane operations:

> The Marianas represented the next logical stepping stone. They lay directly across our path north to the Imperial homeland and

west to the Philippines. The Marianas enabled the Japanese to stage land-based aircraft to any island in the western Pacific. The larger islands of Saipan, Guam, Rota. Tinian, and Pagan were valued as bases for defense and communications. Tanapag Harbor, Saipan, had provided the Japanese with a fueling and supply station for ships en route to and from the Empire. The American objective was the establishment of air and surface bases from which future operations against Japan might be launched. The airfields on Saipan, Guam, and Tinian would provide bases for long-range bombers, while fleet facilities at Guam would be useful in the establishment of advanced fuel and supply bases nearer the home grounds of the Japanese fleet.

The Marianas campaign presented an operational scenario that made use of the flying boat essential. The closest U.S.–held support base, Eniwetok, was a thousand miles away. The Marshalls lay fifteen hundred miles to the east. These distances made the use of tender-based flying boats a necessity to perform protective searches. No land planes had sufficient range to patrol the approaches to the Marianas from Eniwetok.

The PBM-3 was now available to support the operation, and Garapan anchorage and Saipan Harbor were planned to be the initial seadromes. On 15 June 1944, after several

days of bombing Guam, Rota, Saipan, Tinian, and Pagan by carrier-based aircraft, landing forces went ashore on Saipan.

On 16 June small seaplane tender *Ballard* (AVD-10) arrived at the Garapan anchorage on Saipan and laid seaplane mooring buoys in the open sea about three miles from the reef off Tanapag Harbor while within range of enemy guns ashore. The next day, five VP-16 Mariners arrived from Eniwetok. Within two hours they and the tender *Ballard* were attacked by an enemy dive-bomber. In the melee one PBM taxied out to sea and was temporarily lost. The other four took off shortly before midnight on 17 June in very rough water with the help of illumination provided by the destroyer *Phelps* (DD-360).

On the second night of the operation, takeoff conditions were again poor, but one plane made an important contact with the Japanese fleet. The aircraft conducted searches to the west, and at 0115 on 19 June Lt. H. F. Arle's aircraft located an enemy fleet of about forty ships 470 miles west of Guam. Unable to contact the base because of radio problems, the pilot was forced to fly back to Saipan to deliver his contact report. The information did not reach Adm. Raymond A. Spruance, commander of Task Force 58, until nearly eight hours after the contact. This delay precluded Spruance from launching a direct attack on the Japanese fleet, but he was able to launch Task Force (TF) 58 aircraft in time to catch the enemy aircraft as they approached the invasion forces. The resulting air battle became known as the "Marianas Turkey Shoot," the opening day of the Battle of the Philippine Sea.

On 18 June tenders *Pocomoke* (AV-9) and *Onslow* (AVP-48) arrived at Saipan and the rest of VP-16 followed. The PBMs had to operate from the open roadstead off Garapan. The water was frequently rough. On dawn patrol 19 June, one PBM was severely damaged and one of its crew was killed after being attacked by four F6F Hellcats that evidently mistook it for a Japanese Kawanishi Mavis. Another PBM was sunk off Saipan by a fuel barge trying to come alongside in a heavy ground swell. A third PBM (BuNo 45216), whose identification friend or foe (IFF) apparently was not functioning, was shot down by destroyers of TF 58, and the entire crew of twelve was lost.

On 20 June 1944 a detachment of three PBMs of Rescue Squadron 1 (VH-1) arrived. Heavy weather made it necessary to move the seadrome closer inshore. Although this reduced the exposure to rough water, it exposed the aircraft to antiaircraft fire during takeoffs into the offshore wind. VP-16 was followed by VP-216 23 June with PBMs and a detachment of VP-72 PBYs. Weather conditions at Saipan continued to make seaplane operations difficult through 30 June. The Japanese still held the town of Garapan and Tanapag Harbor. Because of shore fire, it was impossible to move the seaplane anchorage into the harbor. From 22 June until 17 July VP-202, based at Ebeye Island in Kwajalein, provided daily mail flights between Saipan and Kwajalein via Eniwetok. This was the only air connection with the outside world during the early days of the invasion. VP-202 was then forward deployed to Saipan on 17 July, operating off *Pocomoke, Chandeleur* (AV-10), and *Mackinac* (AVP-13). *Onslow* also assisted VP-202, with *Yakutat* (AVP-32) supplying subsistence and quarters for a patrol aircraft service unit (PATSU). VP-202 flew a daily average of four daylight and one night patrol out to a six hundred mile range.

Before Saipan had been fully captured, seven seaplane tenders and four Mariner squadrons were operating in the rough waters in the sea off the island. The flying boat units provided the vital search, patrol, reconnaissance, and rescue services that were necessary for the success of the initial phase of the operation.

By 10 July 1944 Saipan was sufficiently secured to allow Mariners to use the Japanese-built seaplane base and the protected waters of Tanapag Harbor. However, Japanese stragglers presented a threat and armed shore patrols were necessary to protect the aircraft.

PBM-5 refueling from bowser boat, Saipan, 1944.
U.S. Naval Institute Photo Archive

Mop-up operations at Saipan continued into August. On 1 August VP-18 arrived in Saipan. The squadron was based afloat in Tanapag Harbor, with two detachments aboard *Yakutat* and *Shelikof* (AVP-52) under the operational control of CFAW-18. On 9 September 1944 the detachment aboard *Yakutat* relocated to *Coos Bay* (AVP-25). Both day and night patrols were conducted in the vicinity of Saipan to provide antisubmarine screening in addition to mail flights between Saipan and Ulithi, hunter-killer standby, and Dumbo standby.

In August CFAW-1 moved to Saipan from the Solomons and assumed overall responsibility for patrol aircraft operations in the central Pacific. Also in August the commander of naval air forces of the Pacific Fleet announced a new policy. Henceforth, squadrons in the forward areas would not be rotated as units, instead complete flight crews would be replaced. Consequently VP-100, a PBY training squadron at Kaneohe, was expanded to include PBM crew training, and VP-98 was established at San Diego to train replacement Mariner crews.

Palau, September 1944

After Saipan was secured, plans were made to secure bases in the Western Carolines in preparation for the invasion of the Philippines. The magnificent atoll of Ulithi, which was destined to become a major fleet base, was seized without a fight, but taking the Palau Islands group of Peleliu, Anguar, and Ngesebus required a major amphibious assault. Patrol planes were tasked to carry out the wide-ranging search, patrol, bombing, and photo reconnaissance missions necessary to support this assault.

In the Palau operation, it was again necessary to use seaplanes as the advanced patrol force until the arrival of land-based aircraft. The seadrome was established in the Kossol Passage, an open roadstead, on 16 September 1944. Mariner squadrons VP-16, VP-17, VP-21, VP-202, VP-216, and VH-1 participated in this operation, working in very rough water conditions. The seadrome was maintained by *Chandeleur* (CFAW-1's flagship), plus *Pocomoke, Mackinac, Yakutat,* and *Onslow.* In addition to covering the western Caroline operations, Mariner patrols were

flown in support of the capture of Morotai, Netherlands East Indies.

The first three aircraft of VP-216 arrived at the Kossol Passage on 10 September. They were joined by the rest of the squadron and by VP-202 and VP-16 on 17 September. The squadrons conducted night antishipping patrols and Dumbo missions in the area around the Palau Islands group.

All Mariner squadrons were designated patrol bombing squadrons (VPBs) on 1 October 1944. On the night of 1–2 October 1944, a VPB-16 Mariner, flown by Lt. Floyd H. Warlow Jr., attacked a suspected submarine target fifty miles northwest of Palau. The next day a hunter-killer group located a badly damaged submarine twelve miles from Warlow's attack, indicating that the attack had crippled the submarine. *Samuel B. Miles* (DE-183) sank the submarine, which was identified in postwar U.S. Navy records as I-177 commanded by Lt. Comdr. Masaki Watanabe.

VP-202 was moved to Ulithi on 27 September and was tended by *Onslow.* Antishipping patrols around Ulithi commenced immediately. By 13 October VPB-17 was also moved to Ulithi and was supported by *Onslow* and *Hamlin* (AV-15). VPB-21 was relocated to Kossol Passage from Eniwetok on 17 October. The squadron began daily patrols, supported by *Chandeleur* and *Mackinac.*

Carrier sweeps covering the southern Philippines had been conducted in support of the western Carolines operation. When Japanese air opposition was found to be minimal, the date for the invasion of the central Philippines was advanced to October 1944.

After the Carolines were secured, Ulithi became a major fleet base for the invasion of the Philippines. But Ulithi was not immune to Japanese attack. VPB-17 and VPB-202 flew continuous antishipping and antisubmarine patrols, and Ulithi became the target of suicide submarine assault. In Capt. Albert Raithel et al.'s *Mariner/Marlin: "Anywhere, Any Time,"* Lt. (j.g.) Frank Dunigan of VPB-17 relates:

In November 1944 the squadron was based on the tender USS *Hamlin,* anchored at Ulithi Atoll, along with hundreds of ships in Admiral Halsey's Task Force. One of the few successful attacks by Japan's new "Kaiten Weapon," suicide submarines, occurred here. Our Crew #1 flew five all-night patrols around Ulithi in November, encountering Kaiten submarines twice.

The "Kaiten" was developed as a desperate attempt, like the "Kamikazes," to inflict huge losses on American Naval Forces. The little submarine was about 54 feet long, and carried as much as 1,800 kilos of explosive in the head, about four times the weight of a normal torpedo. On November 8 three Japanese submarines

left Kure Harbor, each with four Kaiten submarines attached to their hulls for the first Kaiten Weapon strike against U.S. ships. I-36 and I-47 headed for Ulithi, and I-37 for Kossol Passage, Palau.

Our PBM was at the end of an all-night patrol around Ulithi on November 16 and about to return to base as daylight was beginning to break. As co-pilot to Lt. j.g. Jack Healy, PPC [patrol plane commander], I looked through field glasses to see if I could get a visual sighting on a radar target that had been reported by our radar operator. We turned toward the target. As we approached, the almost-fully-surfaced conning tower of an underway submarine appeared in my field-glasses! With "General Quarters" sounding in our plane, we began what we hoped would be a depth-charge run on the submarine. Apparently, the Japanese submarine had sighted us also and crash-dived. They were considerably below the surface when we reached the spot where we had seen it. The spot was bracketed with sono-buoys to start tracking the sub's movements. We requested an aircraft replacement since fuel was low. A TBM appeared and we returned to our base.

During the night of the 19th, Japanese sub I-47 launched four "Kaitens" and I-36 launched one, all headed for ship-packed Ulithi. My crew had been had been flying all night and about the time we were returning to the seadrome, a huge explosion erupted from the fleet oiler *Mississinewa,* which was loaded with 400,000 gallons of aviation gasoline. The ship sank at her mooring with a loss of fifty officers and men. Several aircraft carriers and battleships were anchored nearby.

Ulithi immediately became a "boiling pot" of activity, with destroyers and destroyer-escorts dropping depth charges and trying to ram the midget subs. No additional damage was done to U.S. Forces, and I-36 and I-47 returned safely to Kure, but I-37 was sunk at the western entrance to Kossol Passage by the USS *McCoy-Reynolds* and the USS *Conklin.*

On 21 January 1945 a Kaiten was sunk in Ulithi lagoon by a VPB-21 PBM Mariner flown by Lt. (j.g.) Richard L. Simms. The aircraft crew spotted the midget submarine in the lagoon and attacked with four depth charges. The Kaiten had been released earlier by the submarine I-36 for an attack on shipping in Ulithi lagoon. Four midgets had been launched, but only one scored a hit on the ammunition ship *Mazama* (AE-9). None of the Kaitens returned to I-36 after the attack.

Philippines, October 1944

The liberation of the Philippines, which began with landings at Leyte on 14 October, was eventually supported by fourteen patrol bombing squadrons including Mariner squadrons VPB-17, VPB-20, VPB-25, and VPB-28. These squadrons and Rescue Squadron 1 (VH-1) operated more or less independently of each other in all areas of the Philippine theater. The primary mission of the Mariner squadrons was the interdiction of Japanese supply routes and air-sea rescue. The activities of these squadrons paint a vivid picture of the Mariner's contributions to the war effort in the Pacific.

As operations expanded through the Philippines, missions were flown against the Japanese forces throughout the southwest Pacific area. In January 1945 major landings took place at Lingayen Gulf on the island of Luzon. This operation was supported by VPB-71 with PBYs; VPB-104, VPB-111, and VPB-119 with PB4Ys; and VPB-17, VPB-20, VPB-25, VPB-28, and VH-4 flying PBMs. From the bases secured by the liberation of the Philippines, the Japanese-occupied areas in Southeast Asia and along the coast of China and Formosa provided fruitful targets for patrol bombing operations.

VPB-20

VPB-20 was the first of the Mariner squadrons to support the Philippine liberation. It was ordered to proceed to the seaplane base at Los Negros, Manus, Admiralty Islands, in groups of three aircraft. The first group of VPB-20 arrived on

24 October 1944, coming under the operational control of CFAW-10. As each group of aircraft arrived, they were painted flat black in preparation for night operations. Operating with black painted aircraft, in operations similar to those of the famous PBY "Black Cats," the black PBMs were known as the "Nightmares," but the name never caught on with the public. A detachment of two aircraft was sent on 28 October to Mios Woendi Island, followed on 29 October by a detachment of two aircraft to Morotai. The latter group of aircraft was provided tender support by *Tangier* (AV-8). Nine aircraft remained at Manus, relieving VPB-29. Operations during this period were carried out in the vicinity of the Mindanao Sea, Celebes Sea, Sulu Sea, Makassar Straits, and along the borders of islands in those waters. On 14 November 1944 a VPB-20 aircraft on a night patrol attacked and claimed damage to a *Shokaku*-class carrier in Philippine waters.

At the end of November the squadron, except for the Morotai detachment, was ordered to report to Leyte for further assignment. The first three crews to arrive were assigned night search missions out of Leyte. While in this area, the squadron was berthed aboard *Currituck* (AV-7). On 25 November the Morotai detachment rejoined the squadron at Leyte. A routine of three daily daytime searches was begun on 26 November.

On 27 November a submarine was spotted on radar in Ormoc Bay by Lt. (j.g.) John B. Muoio and his crew. Muoio had been providing air coverage for DESDIV [Destroyer Division] 43 engaged in bombardment of enemy positions. The sighting was reported to the destroyer flotilla commander and the destroyers quickly located the submarine and sank it with gunfire. Postwar examination of U.S. Navy records indicate only one submarine sunk in that vicinity on that date, Yu-2, a Japanese army submarine of the *Yu-1* class. The *Yu-1* class was built by the Japanese army without any assistance from naval constructors. It was an inexpensive, short-range transport submarine with a sole mission to supply Japanese army garrisons cut off by U.S. forces. The sinking of the submarine was accomplished by *Waller* (DD-446), *Pringle* (DD-477), *Saufley* (DD-465), and *Renshaw* (DD-499). The commanding officer of Yu-2 was 1st Lt. Seikichi Ueki. Besides the crew of the submarine there was an army detachment of fifteen men aboard when it was sunk. Only a total of fifteen men from the submarine survived the sinking.

During the Mindoro invasion landings in December 1944 the squadron provided coverage for convoys and night combat patrols in the face of intense opposition. On 26–27 December a four-plane attack was made on a Japanese task force that was bombarding the beachhead in Mangarin Bay, Mindoro. Two aircraft were shot down, but both crews were rescued. Lt. Warren M. Cox's aircraft was hit by intense antiaircraft fire and ditched in the bay. Lt. James V. Fallon's Mariner was riddled by fire from a Japanese destroyer and ditched a half mile away from the scene of the battle. Fallon and his crew reached Canipo Island two days later. They were aided by guerrillas and were able to return to the squadron three weeks later.

In January 1945 VPB-20 departed Leyte Gulf for Lingayen Gulf in company with Task Group (TG) 73.1. Through the end of the month the squadron provided support for convoys and the invasion groups at Marinduque, Lingayen, San Antonio, and Nausbu with night patrols and search and attack missions.

Lt. (j.g.) Wesley O. Glaze attacked a twenty-four-ship Japanese task force on 19 January 1945, damaging a *Hayataka*-class (or *Hiyo*-class) carrier, most likely the much-abused *Junyo* that was damaged by VPB-20 on 14 November 1944. Glaze approached the carrier at an altitude of fifty feet, barely clearing the flight deck, and dropped his three bombs in train (two 250-pound and one 500-pound), scoring two direct hits. Glaze was lost on 29 March in a similar attack.

On 21 January 1944 a squadron aircraft was being flown by Lt. Frank A.

Yourek. He and his crew sighted a submarine west of Ulithi and attacked it with two depth charges and a Mark 24 mine. The submarine escaped but was damaged by the attack. Three destroyers—*Conklin* (DE-439), *Corbesier* (DE-438), and *Raby* (DE-698)—observed the aircraft attack. The next day they made a contact that resulted in the sinking of the submarine. Postwar U.S. Navy records indicate the Japanese submarine lost was I-48 with a crew of 122. Comdr. Zenshin Toyama and his crew had been on a Kaiten mission against shipping in Ulithi lagoon, but apparently none of the Kaiten midget submarines were launched before VPB-20's attack.

In February 1945 VPB-20 was re-equipped with PBM-5s and relocated to Jinimoc and then to Mangarin Bay, Mindoro, and Sangley Point, Luzon, to conduct antishipping patrols in the South China Sea and off the Indochina coastline.

In March four squadron aircraft were sent to join VPB-17 at Puerta Princessa, Palawan Islands, aboard *Pocomoke*. The crews participated in a formation attack on a Japanese convoy sixty miles south of Hainan Island on 29 March, in which Lt. (j.g.) Wesley O. Glaze's aircraft was shot down with the loss of all hands.

The Sangley Point aircraft of VPB-20 joined the detachment on *Pocomoke* when it moved to Tawi Tawi, Sulu Archipelago, on 1 May 1945. The squadron provided convoy coverage and reconnaissance flights in support of the invasion of Borneo. During the month numerous enemy small craft were sunk. During June squadron activities were concentrated on mine spotting for convoys and task groups involved in operations around Borneo at Brunei Bay and Balikpapan.

On 4 June 1945 Lt. Deland J. Croze and his crew were patrolling off the east coast of Borneo. They eventually ran across two Sugar Dogs (small Japanese transports) with a subchaser as escort. Croze immediately mounted an attack on the three ships. The subchaser gun crew was pumping out heavy antiaircraft fire, but Croze had bits on both Sugar Dogs, and one immediately sank. The antiaircraft fire was being delivered very accurately from the subchaser, and the Mariner was hit twice in its gas tanks, causing two men to be wounded and one to later lose his foot. Croze knew he could not make it back to base, so he landed at Lingayen Island, just off the Japanese-held Celebes. He went ashore but learned nothing, so he secured for the night.

In the morning one of the radiomen tried to make contact with the base, but the Japanese saw him and he was killed. That precipitated an every-man-for-himself movement, and the nine other crewmen scattered. Three men hid in the water for three days, but the sharks found them and attacked, mangling the left arm of one of

them, Dale Hunt. Fortunately, just after the shark attack a Mariner from VPB-21 picked up the three survivors from the water and one from the brush. Hunt lost his arm in short order. Four crew members were never seen again. After the war was over, however, it was discovered that all four of them were captured and beheaded. The Japanese officer responsible was tried for war crimes and hanged.

VPB-20 continued in July and August with detachments at the Lingayen Gulf, Tawi Tawi, and Sangley Point. In late August it was moved to Okinawa for courier and rescue service. After the Japanese surrender, VPB-20 moved to Shanghai, China. VP-20's outstanding service in the Philippine liberation was recognized by the award of the Navy Unit Commendation. The citation, signed by Secretary of the Navy James Forrestal, read:

The Secretary of the Navy takes pleasure in commending PATROL SQUADRON TWENTY for outstanding heroism in action against enemy Japanese forces in Indo-China, Borneo, the Netherlands East Indies from November 1, 1944, to June 1, 1945. Engaged in night and day offensive searches, night convoy coverage and barrier patrol missions throughout this period, Patrol Bombing Squadron 20 maintained its flights with persistent determination despite the hazards of heavy enemy antiaircraft fire and hostile fighter opposition to destroy over 42,000 tons of vital Japanese shipping and to inflict severe damage on more than 82,000 additional tons. Individually heroic and aggressive, the pilots and aircrewmen flew in support of the Tarakan Island, Brunei Bay and Balikpapan operations, not only providing effective protection for amphibious forces proceeding from the staging area, but also carrying out low-level coastal and river armed reconnaissance missions to thwart the enemy's attempts to evacuate his troops from the Sulu Archipelago to Northern Borneo. This valiant record of combat in missions excellently planned and executed was made possible only by the courage, skill and superb teamwork of the pilots, the flight crews and the men who serviced and maintained the planes. Their perseverance, high standards of achievement and unwavering devotion to duty reflect the highest credit upon Patrol Bombing Squadron 20 and the United States Naval Service.

VPB-17

A detachment of VPB-17 was deployed on 12 February 1945 from Ulithi to San Pedro Bay, Philippines, under the operational control of FAW-17 and based aboard the tender *Orca* (AVP 49). A second detachment was

deployed to Lingayen Gulf, berthed temporarily aboard the tender *Currituck* (AV-7). The remainder of the squadron arrived at San Pedro Bay on 20 February and the crews were relocated to *San Pablo* (AVP-30). In early March VPB-17 was relocated to Jinamoc Island, Philippines, and rejoined by the detachment previously operating from Lingayen Gulf. The seaplane base at Jinamoc Island was completed on 31 March 1945, providing berthing and repair facilities ashore for the squadron.

Bombing runs were made at Iloilo, San Carlos, Panay, Zamboanga, Davoa, Mindanao, Cebu, Negros, Legaspi, and Luzon. There were plenty of targets. A daring rescue was made on 20 February 1945 of a Corregidor prisoner while delivering supplies to guerrilla forces on Palawan. The squadron performed many such air-sea rescues. In Raithel et al.'s *Mariner/Marlin*, Lt. (j.g.) Frank Dunigan tells of a rescue that his crew made:

During March 1945 our crew flew a number of "Dumbo" air-sea rescue flights in the Philippines. Six of these were in support of Marine Air Operations aimed at softening up and participating in the invasion of Iloilo, the third largest city and capital of the Island of Panay. These flights were from March 8 through March 16 during the landings at Iloilo.

On March 4th, our crew was assigned to cover Marine air strikes at

Zamboanga in Southern Mindanao. A Corsair pilot making a run on an enemy airstrip was hit by enemy fire requiring him to bail out over water adjacent to the target. Our Mariner was contacted by the pilot's squadron, who said they would make dives over his position so we could locate him. The Marines also promised air-cover.

The pilot, Lt. Jack O'Bringer had parachuted, inflated his one-man raft and started paddling away from shore. We spotted him, landed, and taxied toward him. The water became more shallow and we had to parallel a reef to avoid grounding. In the meantime O'Bringer had been "bracketed" by native canoes. Not knowing their intent, the Marine pilot pointed his pistol at the head of one of the canoe-paddlers. Lieutenant O'Bringer was 19 or 20 years old. His combat attire included a neck scarf which seemed to fit his jaunty pose.

On 22 April 1945 the squadron regrouped and moved to the *Tangier* (AV-8) at Lingayen Gulf and flew Nightmare night reconnaissance flights until 29 June. It was assigned good hunting sectors off Western Formosa and along the China coast. Each flight began with 2,500 gallons of gas, four 250 pound and six 100 pound general purpose bombs, 3,500 rounds of .50-caliber ammunition, and six to eight fragmentation bombs. These flights were flown at 250 feet or lower on lean power settings. The Mariner's superb radar permitted entry into bays and rivers. Weather was often horrible and the crews were under continual strain. The enemy was also busy. One Mariner returned with three hundred bullet holes, but no injuries to the crew. However, the squadron did sustain casualties on other flights.

The squadron's most publicized attack was a mission flown by Lt. Warren Lasser and reported to the world on 23 May 1945 by famed war correspondent Merrill Mueller. Lasser sank five Japanese ships during one night's patrol as the ships were attempting to run the air-sea blockade that had been erected between Japan and their southern possessions. He made a run on the group of ships from dead ahead. A large vessel was damaged from near misses of bombs, and the fifty-five hundred ton ship began to lose way and settle in the water. Then the Mariner went after the second large vessel with machine guns. The tracers started large fires that provided light for the attack on other ships. With the first ship sinking and the other burning brightly, Lasser took sights on the remaining vessels. For more than an hour the Mariner strafed the three vessels until they sank and the survivors took to life rafts. The second ship became completely covered by fire and was obviously doomed, so the Mariner returned to the first ship it had attacked, but the vessel had sunk with the crew abandoning it before the aircraft could make its final run. Toward the end of the action, enemy aircraft appeared, but the Mariner departed without damage and continued its scheduled patrol over China waters.

On 25 May 1945 one of VPB-17's planes was shot down by a Japanese destroyer off the China coast. Lt. (j.g.) Fred Forman, the patrol plane commander, was knocked unconscious when the plane exploded and crashed. Ens. Bob Bunge, who also survived, found an inflated life raft and got Forman into it. For four long days and nights, with little water and no food, they drifted. Finally, on the fifth day, they saw land. Shortly afterward, a junk appeared with eight men aboard. They picked the two men up. After a long and arduous journey over land, using every means of transport—-rickshaw, horseback, walking—-they made it to safety.

Eventually, the squadron ended up at Tawi Tawi flying ASW patrols. Then an unusual opportunity arose: the chance to fly for the Allied Intelligence Bureau (AIB) personnel to guerrilla groups (Australian agents knowledgeable of the Philippines). These flights carried supplies and personnel from Morotai to the coast of North Borneo. Captain Chipper of the Australian army often flew with the crew and was an excellent source of information about Semporna, Labuan Island, and Maradu

Bay. As the war began to wind down, VPB-17 was instrumental in evacuating some POWs who had been captives of the Japanese in North Borneo.

VPB-25

VPB-25 began their Philippine deployment in San Pedro Bay, Leyte Gulf, in late November 1944, supported by *Half Moon* (AVP-26) and *San Pablo* (AVP-30). VPB-25 began its first daytime combat sector patrols on 1 December.

On Christmas Day 1944 VPB-25 received orders to transfer its operations to Mangarin Bay, Mindoro, Philippines. Aircrew personnel were transferred temporarily to *Barataria* (AVP-33) while the rest of the squadron, aboard *Half Moon* and *San Pablo,* proceeded to the new station. On 29 December the squadron aircrews flew from San Pedro Bay to rejoin the rest of the squadron and the two tenders at Mangarin Bay. The squadron began conducting sector searches from the new location the next day. Searches from this base covered the coastline of French Indochina and north toward Hainan Island.

Crew 8 of VPB-25 consisted of Lt. J. L. Stevenson, Ens. Dwaine Meridith Peterson, Ens. William (Bill) Arthur Quinn, Aviation Machinist's Mate 2nd Class Frederick C. Bames, Aviation Machinist's Mate 3rd Class Warren H. Daley, Aviation

Machinist's Mate 3rd Class Donald H. Douglas, Aviation Machinist's Mate 3rd Class Thomas J. McGowan, Seaman 1st Class Joseph N. Venditti, Aviation Ordnanceman 3rd Class Gordon H. Yates; Aviation Radioman 3rd Class Vincent M. Grady, and Aviation Radioman 2nd Class Charles L. Hamilton. The crew had participated in thirty-five missions before their luck ran out.

On 16 January 1945 the crew crashed in PBM BuNo 45277, three hundred miles west of Lingayen Gulf. For twelve hours the crew worked feverishly amidst fifty-foot waves to keep afloat. They were rescued by *Hopewell* (DD-681).

Ten days later, they again were forced to ditch because of a mechanical failure in BuNo 45309 off the coast of French Indochina near Tam Quan Point. The crew salvaged all possible gear from their sinking PBM, paddled ashore in a raft, and hurried into the jungle to begin a three-month saga of escape and evasion.

The rescue plan for crew 8 was to be evacuation by submarine from the vicinity of Sa Huyhn. Only Hamilton made it aboard an Australian sub. Enemy advances prevented further rescue attempts by submarine.

Crew 8, now with a French underground unit, moved regularly to various locations in the country. They were joined by Lt. (j.g.) Donald A. Henry who had

been shot down on 12 January, flying with *Essex*'s VT-4. Burned and wounded, Henry underwent six weeks of treatment at My Tho before transferring to Catecka plantation near Pleiku.

The plan now was to evacuate the crew and Henry by air, along with Michael Purcell, an escaped British POW. However, the situation deteriorated rapidly when the Japanese completely took over the country on 9 March. French citizens were to be rounded up for imprisonment. With a Frenchman named Trocoire, the crew fled north into Montegard country, stopping at Pie Tonal, sixty miles from Ttourane (Danang).

On 8 April Stevenson, Peterson, and Trocoire departed for Hue to arrange sea evacuation from Pleiku. Tragically, they were captured and killed. The circumstances of their deaths are unknown but it was rumored they were buried alive.

Crew 8 joined the French resistance and engaged the Japanese in firefights. While operating from PleTonan on 27 April, they were betrayed by an Indochinese sergeant and ambushed by eighty Japanese soldiers. The men fought the superior forces until they ran out of ammunition. Henry was wounded and died in the arms of Quinn, who had also been wounded. Purcell was away on a food search. In "Crew Eight," Capt. Melvin R. Schultz later wrote about the crew, saying, "they put up one helluva fight." Two hours later, six of the crew were executed gangland style, shot in the back of the head while kneeling, their hands and arms tied behind their backs. They were Barnes, McGowan, Douglas, Daley, Venditti, and Yates. They were eventually interred in a common grave in a military cemetery in India.

A few days later, Quinn and Grady were paraded along the main street of Kontum. Leading the procession was a portion of the victorious platoon followed by stretchers bearing six Japanese casualties. The Americans were bound at hands and elbows, convenient targets for rocks hurled at them by the populace. Both were tortured and questioned for days about the identities of underground members and then confined in a Saigon POW camp.

Following liberation, they were interviewed extensively before returning to the United States. Quinn testified at a War Crimes trial at which six Japanese were convicted of atrocities. Sadly, Grady was killed in an auto accident in October, within a month of repatriation.

In February 1945 VPB-25 was transferred to Jinamoc Island, Leyte, Philippines, under the operational control of FAW-10 to begin courier-flight service to Mindoro, Subic Bay, and Lingayen Gulf. After receiving and checking out its new Martin PBM-3D2 Mariners, the squadron transferred six aircraft back to Mangarin Bay on 25 February 1945, supported by *San Carlos* (AVP 51).

In March the squadron's Mangarin Bay detachment received orders to relocate to Manila Bay, off Cavite. Tender support was again provided by *San Carlos*. Daylight sector antishipping patrols were conducted from this site west of the Philippine coastline. The Leyte detachment conducted similar daylight sector searches to the east of Jinamoc Island.

On 24 June 1945 the Cavite detachment was relocated to Lingayen Gulf, relieving VPB-17. Tender support was provided by *Currituck*. Operations commenced with the squadron conducting Nightmare operations against enemy shipping on 28 June. The seven aircraft of the Leyte detachment flew to Cavite to take its predecessor's place, with three of the aircraft assigned to courier flights based ashore and the remaining aircraft assigned to *San Carlos* for antishipping patrols west of the Philippines.

The Cavite detachment was transferred on 9 July to Puerto Princessa, Palawan, Philippines, with tender support provided by *Barataria* (AVP-33) and partially by the shore establishment. This detachment was relieved on 23 July to rejoin the rest of the squadron at Lingayen Gulf assigned to *Currituck*.

On 20 August 1945 *San Pablo* arrived on station at Lingayen Gulf to relieve *Currituck*. One half of the squadron shifted to *San Pablo*, and the other half flew to Tawi Tawi, with tender support provided by *Pocomoke*. *Pocomoke* was relieved by *Orca*

(AVP-49) on 3 September, and the Tawi Tawi detachment shifted aboard the latter. During this period, the Lingayen Gulf detachment conducted numerous Dumbo missions. The Tawi Tawi detachment engaged in antishipping and surveillance patrols for convoys off the approaches to Borneo until the Japanese surrender on 3 September 1945.

VPB-28

VPB-28 was the last PBM squadron to be formed in World War II. It was commissioned at Harvey Point, North Carolina, on 1 July 1944. In January 1945 the squadron received its orders to report to FAW-17 at Leyte, Philippines, then on to Lingayen Gulf, where it would be based aboard *Tangier* (AV-8). The last VPB-28 aircraft arrived on 31 January, with night barrier patrols commencing immediately.

On 8 February VPB-28 was relocated to *Half Moon* (AVP-26) and began flying day patrols from Mindoro toward Indochina (Vietnam) and Hainan. Much shifting of crews from one tender to another took place during this period. On 13 February, the squadron moved back aboard *Tangier* and on 27 February, it was relocated to *Barataria* (AVP-33).

On 1 March it relieved PBY squadron VPB-71, and flew Nightmare missions while based aboard *Barataria*. From 1–13 March VPB-28 was aboard *Tangier* again. Hunting

was good, although most of these patrols were flown in poor weather over shores and coastal islands, battling antiaircraft fire from convoys, shore installations, and unescorted ships. When the Nightmare missions that began on 1 March were completed on 23 April, 76,910 tons of enemy shipping had been damaged on the forty-two vessels that were attacked. VPB-28 lost one man, a bow gunner, who was killed by a ship's 20-mm antiaircraft gun burst. Five attacks were made using the newest APQ-5 radar-bombing system and three torpedoes were launched. Adm. Thomas C. Kincaid, commander of the Seventh Fleet, sent the following message to the squadron:

> It is with the greatest satisfaction that I forward the following message from Commander Seventh Fleet. Quote: "Congratulations on the impressive total of enemy ships sunk and damaged during March. This is hitting the Japanese where it hurts the most and will eventually deprive him of the plunder he so badly needs from the South. Please express to all who have contributed my sincere appreciation of their accomplishments to all hands well done."

VPB-28 attacks on Japanese shipping continued into April 1945. Action was well recorded in squadron documents:

> April 1—Lieutenant (j.g.) P. J. Richert, USNR, attacked a destroyer escort 20

miles off-shore between the Pescadores and Tainan. In two runs, the pilot scored a hit amidships with a 500 pounder, a near-miss by the stem with a 250 pound bomb and with his last bomb, a 500 pounder, a near-miss that lifted the DEs [destroyer escorts] bow out of the water. The ship was dead in the water after the second run and was assessed as probably sunk.

April 8—Lieutenant C. E. Soderholm, USN, established radar contact with a five-ship convoy, consisting of two DDs [destroyers], one DE, a possible cruiser and a large merchant ship. Lieutenant Soderholm selected the cargo vessel as his target, but the ship was lost in the radar sea-return caused by high waves. Proceeding to Formosa, the pilot picked up an unescorted ship north of Takao, headed north. An APQ-5 radar attack was carried out, the target being virtually invisible under the 600 foot ceiling. Coming in at 350 feet, using APQ-5 for range and ASG [bombing system component] for deflection, Soderholm again lost the target on the scope in the "sea-return," but observed a light on the ship and homed on it. APQ-5 triggered the bombs for at least one hit. The ship blew up and sank. In the flash of the explosion, the vessel was identified as a 1,000 ton FFD [a Japanese merchant ship]. This attack represented the first use of APQ-5 gear by a PBM in an attack on a Japanese ship.

April 9—southeast of the Pescadores, Lt (jg) Dykins detected a five-ship convoy, consisting of two DEs, two large and one medium size merchant vessels. After one reconnaissance run under the 600-foot ceiling, Dykins attacked one of the DEs, dropping three bombs which fell 100 feet astern of the target. As the PBM circled for an attack on one of the larger ships, eight Japanese planes appeared from the direction of Tokyo. Forming a box, in pairs, 500 feet above the Mariner, they took turns in making bombing runs from different angles, dropping a total of eight bombs. All fell astern or to the side of the Nightmare. After three hours, Dykins shook off the Japanese, with the help of night fighters which rose from Laoag. This action marked the first occasion known to the squadron of night attempts at air-to-air bombing.

On 27 June 1945 VPB-28 was split into two detachments, with one remaining at Lingayen Gulf aboard *Barataria* (consisting of six planes and eight crews), and the other at the Jinamoc seaplane base, Jinamoc Island, San Pedro Bay, Leyte Gulf, Philippines. The Jinamoc detachment, with five aircraft and nine crews, began fly-ing two antisubmarine patrols daily east of Samar, Leyte, and Mindanao.

June 30—Lieutenant W. L. Hermanson, Crew 3, landed in a rough sea off the China Coast west of the Luichow Peninsula, and rescued a Navy officer, Lieutenant Scott, an Army officer, and the crew of an Army rescue PBY which had tried unsuccessfully to pick up the two offi-cers the day before. These two officers had parachuted from a C-47 in an effort to locate and aid in rescuing the crew of a Privateer (PB4Y-2) of Patrol Bombing Squadron 119, which had been shot down near Fort Bayard on 17 June. The survivors of this crew were subsequently rescued after two were killed by Japanese, as reported by natives. Another Privateer crashed on 24 June, presumably with the loss of all hands, in assisting their rescue. In the parachute landing Lt. Scott's leg was broken, but he and the Army officer with the aid of natives and supplies dropped by plane, reached the west coast of Luichow.

On 1 July 1945 the squadron had three additional aircraft assigned to Manila, based at Naval Air Base (NAB) Sangley Point, Philippines. One crew was assigned to ferry aircraft between Saipan and Manus.

The Lingayen detachment arrived at Manila on 4 July to relieve six VPB-25 air-craft from antisubmarine patrol responsi-bilities. VPB-28 moved aboard the tender *San Carlos* (AVP-51) until *Barataria* could arrive from Lingayen Gulf. The latter duly arrived at Manila Bay on 3 August, and the squadron switched its berthing. At the time of the Japanese surrender, the entire squadron was reunited at Jinamoc.

Another Mariner training squadron, VPB-99, was commissioned at NAS Alameda in January 1945.

The Bonins, February 1945

In his book *Combat Command,* Adm. Frederick C. Sherman explained the impor-tance of seizing Iwo Jima:

In November of 1944, Saipan-based bombers began hitting the Imperial home-land. The B-29 Superfortress was the only plane capable of making the round trip from Saipan to Tokyo, and to do so it was forced to reduce its bomb load by 70%. Moreover, fighter-protection was impossi-ble over such a distance. Directly en route from the Marianas to Japan were the enemy-held Volcano and Bonin Islands, the former group including Iwo Jima. From these islands the Japanese were able to warn Tokyo of the approaching American bombers, and were able to send up interceptor planes as they passed over. Possession of a base in that area would have aided B-29 operations greatly, as well as facilitated future amphibious campaigns at Okinawa and Kyushu. Iwo lay 660 nautical miles from Tokyo and 700 from Saipan. It was a "must."

On 19 February 1945 the invasion of Iwo Jima took place. Iwo was needed as a base for fighter escorts for the 20th Air Force B-29 operations against the Japanese homeland, and as an emergency recovery field for damaged aircraft that would otherwise be lost.

Capt. G. A. McLean was designated commander of Seaplane Base Group (CTG 51.9). The Seaplane Base Group's mission was to provide searches and antisubmarine patrols, conduct air-sea rescue missions, and furnish naval observers to accompany B-29's on their picket boat searches in advance of the fast carrier force. More specifically, the flying boats were to support and protect U.S. ships by attempting to locate the remnants of the Japanese fleet.

The searches were to be carried out by PBM-3D2s of VPB-19. These were the first jet-assisted takeoff (JATO)–equipped planes in the Pacific. VPB-26, based in Eniwetok and equipped with the JATO-capable PBM-5, was ordered to send a two-plane detachment to Saipan specifically for press and high priority mail flights to Iwo. PBYs of Rescue Squadron 2 also participated in the operation.

The first Mariners at Iwo were the VPB-26 "press planes." The first landed at Iwo on D-day, but was severely damaged in a rough water landing. The next day, 20 February, Lt. Howard L. "Sam" Cornish made a successful round trip. He repeated the trip on 24 February, this time flying out the film for the famous Iwo Jima flag raising photograph.

As at the Marianas, the first tender at Iwo Jima was a converted destroyer, the USS *Williamson* (AVD-2). It arrived at Iwo on 19 February. It was joined the next day by *Hamlin* and *Chincoteague*. Although the tenders were to establish a floating base for seaplanes, bad sea conditions and heavy gunfire from the beach prevented the immediate accomplishment of this task. With the capture of Mount Suribachi on 23 February, the seadrome was established the next day.

At 0743 on 24 February *Hamlin* anchored near berth 18, six hundred yards from shore, and began laying the seaplane moorings, working in very close to shore with a heavy sea still running. The site for the seadrome was assigned on the basis of a prevailing northwest wind. Unfortunately, the wind came from directions between east-northeast and south-southwest 50 percent of the time. Swells were almost always from the northeast or east. Because the seadrome was located on the southeast side of the island, it was unprotected.

Operations were hampered a great deal by the poor easterly weather. Other problems arose because the seadrome area was also used by the small boats supporting the amphibious forces. As a result of the congestion offshore, the PBMs taxied five to ten miles out to sea to takeoff in order to be clear of debris and boat traffic. Thus, nearly all operations were conducted under open-sea conditions.

A press plane alighted from the Marianas on 24 February. In preparing to receive the plane, boats swept the landing area continuously, clearing as much debris as possible. This was one of the major obstacles in operating at Iwo Jima. There was so much debris that only the larger items could be effectively removed. Rafts, timbers, ammunition cases, and other implements of amphibious landing continuously drifted through the seadrome, as well as corpses and blood plasma crates. The whole area was cluttered with floating wreckage, oil drums, gasoline cans, shell casings, and half-sunken barges. Nevertheless, the press plane landed, was serviced and loaded, and made a successful JATO takeoff. No patrol operations were possible for four additional days because of wind, weather, and congestion in the seaplane operating area.

The first patrol unit, consisting of three planes of VPB-19, arrived on 27 February 1945. Two searches were flown the following day, and additional planes were flown

in. From then until 6 March, the flying boats flew five-hundred-mile search flights to the north and west of Iwo every day except 2 March, when search flights were canceled because of seadrome conditions. Altogether, twenty-seven complete patrols were flown. When PB4Y Liberators were able to operate off the Iwo land strips on 6 March, the flying boats began their return to Saipan.

Okinawa, March 1945

The Okinawa campaign extended from 1 April until 21 June 1945. By March the Japanese had suffered serious defeats but they were not ready to surrender. One more major base was required to support the projected invasion of Japan proper; Okinawa would be that base. Again, facilities for land-based patrol aircraft were not available to permit the search coverage required, so the seaplane was again called upon to meet requirements. For the most complete protection of the U.S. forces involved, an extensive pattern of air searches was necessary. These searches would reach south to Formosa, west along the coast of China as far north as the coast of Korea, across Tsushima Straits, and along both coasts of Kyushu. The assigned missions of the patrol seaplanes was to patrol the sea-lanes; to provide long-range offensive search and reconnaissance, offensive antishipping sweeps, and block patrols; and to conduct antisubmarine operations and air-sea rescue services.

The flying boats would be based at Kerama Retto, a group of small islands lying ten to twenty miles southwest of Okinawa. The occupation of Kerama Retto by the U.S. Army's 77th Division occurred 25–26 March 1945. To establish the seaplane base, seven seaplane tenders—*Hamlin, Onslow, Yakutat, St. George, Bering Strait, Shelikof,* and *Chandeleur*—arrived on 28 March, four days before the landings on Okinawa itself were made. *Hamlin* immediately began the establishment of the seaplane base. *Chandeleur* laid eight seaplane mooring buoys in thirteen fathoms of water on 28 March. Runway markers were arranged. Then it became possible to call forward the seaplane squadrons. On 29 March thirty PBMs arrived and began operating from the floating base. By 1 April three large seaplane tenders (AVs) and four small seaplane tenders (AVPs) were tending fifty-four aircraft at Kerama Retto.

Two VPB-18 crews downed enemy fighters during the same patrol on 6 April 1945. Lt. Jorden B. Collins claimed a Nakajima B5N, Navy Type 97 Carrier Attack Bomber (Kate) over the East China Sea south of Kyushu. An hour later, Lt. Gerald Hooker and his crew spotted an Aichi D3A, Navy Type 99 Carrier Bomber (Val) over the East China Sea northeast of the Ryukyu Islands and shot it down.

On 7 April the Japanese decided to attack Okinawa with a fleet built around *Yamato,* the world's largest battleship. The task force consisted of *Yamato,* the cruiser *Yahagi,* and eight destroyers. The mission of the task force was to cause maximum damage to the U.S. forces on the island. Since the Japanese had only enough fuel for a one-way trip, this was truly a suicide attack. It was part of a planned massive kamikaze attack (*kikusui*) that included 355 kamikaze planes and the same number of conventional planes attacking Okinawa. The plan called for *Yamato* to fight its way to the beach at Okinawa, ground itself, and then destroy as much of the occupying force as possible with the ship's gigantic 18-inch guns. These guns could hurl a shell weighing more than a ton approximately thirty-five miles.

The Japanese task force sailed out of the Inland Sea and south toward Okinawa. Fortunately, two U.S. submarines spotted it and broadcast the alert. At 0957 two PBMs of VPB-21, piloted by Lt. Dick Simms and Lt. Jim Young, respectively, made visual contact. The two PBMs skillfully shadowed the battleship and its escorting task force using clouds and necessary distance for evasive cover, all the while leaving the Mariner's radio transmitting key open to aid the carrier planes in locating the targets.

The Japanese task force was decimated by the U.S. carrier aircraft. The *Yamato* sank with twenty-four hundred sailors on board. It was learned later that of the total 2,650-man crew, only about 250 survived! Another eight hundred to one thousand Japanese sailors died in the sinking of *Yakagi* and two destroyers. Two other destroyers were damaged enough so that they later had to be scuttled. Four destroyers were the only Japanese ships to escape.

The Mariner's activities were not limited to tracking the Japanese. They performed search and rescue (SAR) during the attack. While Simms acted as decoy to attract enemy gunfire, Young landed in the open sea to rescue a downed Avenger pilot, who was in the same water as hundreds of *Yamato* crewmen. The two pilots were awarded the Distinguished Flying Cross for their day's work.

On 16 April 1945 two VPB-18 crews shot down another Japanese aircraft. Lt. Jorden B. Collins and Lt. Paul D. Fitzgerald shared credit for the destruction of an Aichi E13A, Navy Type 0 Reconnaissance Seaplane (Jake) shot down over the Korean Strait.

Kenneth Whiting, Casco, Suisun, and *Norton Sound* arrived at Kerama Retto on 25 April. *Duxbury Bay* arrived from Ulithi on 29 April and began sweeping the seadrome area near the anchorage, as well as helping maintain VPB-27.

By 26 April a total of six VPB squadrons and one VH squadron had reached the area and gone into operation. Squadrons VPB-18, VPB-21, and VPB-27 (all PBM-5) had flown in on 29 March. VPB-208 (PBM-5) followed on 1 April, and VPB-13 (PB2Y-5) and VPB-26 (PBM-5) arrived on 26 April. VH-3 arrived on 29 March with the first three patrol squadrons. It was equipped with six PBM-3Rs and was based on *Hamlin* and *Bering Strait.*

On 27 April VPB-27 and VPB-208 each furnished three Mariners for an attack on a Japanese supply convoy in the East China Sea approaching the Philippines from an area not reachable by carrier planes. The night mission was commanded by VPB-208's executive officer, Lt. Comdr. Gaylord Lyon. It was a long, tough flight. The Mariners were to fly to within fifty miles of the convoy and then drop to an altitude of fifty feet to make their bombing run. When they were twenty-five miles out, the convoy started putting up antiaircraft fire. The tracers and antiaircraft bursts surpassed any Fourth of July fireworks display the aircrews had ever seen. The Mariners made the attack through a veritable hail of enemy light-, medium-, and heavy-duty antiaircraft fire. All the Mariners were badly shot up. Several men suffered minor wounds, but no one was killed. Every Mariner survived, although one was so damaged it was barely able to limp back

PBM-5 being
hoisted aboard
large seaplane
tender at
Kerama Retto,
Ryuku Islands,
1945.
*U.S. Navy via
Capt. Al Raithel*

to Okinawa. Severe damage was inflicted on at least two enemy ships.

Arriving back at base, the Mariners had to circle for quite some time because a Japanese air raid was in progress. The landing was anything but routine. There were no runway lights or landing lights. Also, the aileron cables on one of VP-208's planes were broken.

For their actions this night, the squadrons received the following message of commendation on 28 April:

> The task group commander takes the greatest pleasure in offering an enthusiastic "well done" to the pilots and crews of VPB-27 and VPB-208 who braved heavy enemy fire to strike at the well defended Japanese convoy last night. The admira-

tion of all hands for the valor of the act is exceeded by their gratitude for the safe return of all who participated. Confounding the silk purse-sow's ear principle, they manufactured excellent strikers out of ASP planes. In their hands, PBM's made history last night.

By 1 May 1945 five AVs and seven AVPs were tending seventy-eight planes at Kerama Retto. On 4 May VPB-18 Mariners claimed two more Japanese aircraft. Lt. Paul D. Fitzgerald and his crew claimed a Nakajima KI-27, Army Type 97 Fighter (Kate) while on patrol over the East China Sea east of Naha, Okinawa. Lt. (j.g.) John D. Martin and his crew shot down a Kate in the same general area eight minutes later.

As described in the official squadron history, in May VPB-18 was involved in an aggressive series of antishipping missions:

Three anti-shipping patrols met with extraordinary success despite the fact that one met with disaster. On the morning of May 5, two Mariners left Kerama Retto on a routine search into the Yellow Sea and through the islands forming the West coast of Korea. It was in the latter area that they succeeded in finding and sinking four ships; three small tankers and one small freighter, each in a different channel for a total of 7,500 gross tons. Effective AA [antiaircraft] fire was returned by all but one of the ships, and one of the Mariners was riddled although the crew was untouched.

However, on 6 May a kamikaze struck the crane on the seaplane deck of *St. George* while it was at anchor in Kerama Retto. The engine of the aircraft penetrated below decks into the VPB-18 area stateroom of Lt. Jorden Collins, killing him instantly and injuring his roommate, Lt. Peter Prudden.

In *Aces of the Rising Sun,* historian Henry Sakaida recounted an 11 May 1945 incident. Two PBMs of VPB-21 were attacked off the west coast of Kyushu by four Japanese "George" fighters of the 343 Air Group. This group was an elite unit commanded by Capt. Minoru Genda, the mastermind of the Pearl Harbor attack. Lt. Dick Simms and Lt. John Hook were the pilots. They were attacked by Lt. Shoji Matsumura, Chief Petty Officer (CPO) Yoshikazu Miyamoto, CPO Seiichiro Sato, and Petty Officer 1st Class (PO1c) Mahito Yoshihara. The Japanese planes were armed with air-to-air rockets and this was the first time they used the weapon. Matsumura's rockets failed to fire, but Miyamoto's and Sato's were successfully launched. Miyamoto's rockets failed to hit anything, but Sato's rocket exploded near Hook's PBM, causing extensive damage. The Japanese made some ineffective runs, then returned to base where they were lambasted by the squadron leader for not being successful. They did not realize that Simms had to make a ditching in the sea. Luckily, the crew survived and were picked up by a VH-3 PBM the next day. Bill Graves, the copilot, got a deep cut across his nose when a 20-mm shell detonated inside the cockpit. Seaman 1st Class Lavernus Cottrell, the starboard waist gunner on Simms's plane, was credited with a kill. However, all four Georges returned to base; none were hit in combat.

On 14 May two other VPB-18 Mariners returned to the vicinity of Pusan for a repeat performance on a smaller scale, sinking three sea trucks and three luggers. They probably sank a fourth sea truck, and seriously damaged three others. Two other

VPB-18 Mariner sinking after being shot down by Japanese fighters, 15 May 1945. *U.S. Navy via Don Sweet*

VPB-18 Mariners again engaged Japanese aircraft from the 343 Ku Fighter Kikotai 701 on 15 May. The Mariners were on an antishipping strike in the Tsushima Straits. They sank one ship along their return track. Four fighters took off after the two PBMs initially, with four more to follow. However, two of the later group missed forming up, and another from the later group had engine trouble and had to return. As such, five Japanese fighters attacked the PBMs multiple times.

The PBMs were commanded by Lt. (j.g.) Irving E. Marr and Lt. Marvin E. Hart. It was Hart's first patrol and Lt. E. C. Dixon was aboard as checkout pilot. In a short but vicious fight, both PBMs were shot down. Marr and his entire crew were lost. Hart was forced to ditch later on, but the crew was unhurt and all but three men were able to leave the plane in rubber boats. Before they went down, however, they did shoot down one Japanese aircraft, whose pilot was also lost.

After staying afloat for twelve hours and only two miles from the enemy shore, they were rescued by a courageous submarine, guided to the scene by another squadron plane. One man had his arm broken when the submarine's bow plane crashed down onto the rubber boat in the heavy seas. The three men left behind on the plane were not seen again, although there was a search for days for survivors.

At the time, the PBMs claimed two Zekes, one Tony, and one Tojo. Postwar U.S. Navy records show that all of the aircraft engaged were Kawanishi N1Ks (Georges).

On 11 May 1945 *Mackinac* joined the force. On 7 June *Gardiners Bay* arrived, giving a total of fourteen tenders servicing some ninety-five aircraft.

VPB-21 was also active in attacking Japanese shipping. A 16 May 1945 attack left a small Japanese freighter in a sinking condition. On 28 May, VPB-18's Lt. John T. Moore and his crew claimed a Nate fighter after being attacked while on patrol over the East China Sea north of the Ryukus.

VPB-26 was the first seaplane squadron to bomb any target on the Japanese homeland. On 15 June 1945 two of VPB-26's Mariners attacked a shipyard on Shikoku, taking the enemy completely by surprise. They left one ship sinking and a shipyard in flames. Continuing on their patrol, they found many more targets as they turned for home, including a number of ships, a passenger ferry, a radio station near the harbor, and another, smaller shipyard. They left all in flames.

Two days later, on 17 June, two more VPB-26 Mariners attacked a shipyard and adjoining railyards in the harbor area of

Susaki. Damage was quite extensive. The shipyard was left in ruins, a number of railroad cars were destroyed, and a total of seventeen Sugar Dogs were destroyed. One ferry boat was damaged and beached. Another ferry boat was strafed; badly damaged it was forced aground. Twelve new Sugar Dogs were strafed and left afire. Quite a two-day record!

Okinawa was declared secure on 21 June 1945 and preparations began for the invasion of Japan. On 12 July VPB-18 was withdrawn to Saipan for ten days of crew rest and aircraft maintenance. During its operational tour at Kerama Retto the squadron had claimed ten enemy aircraft shot down and had sunk forty-four ships during 422 combat missions. Six Mariners had been lost during this period, three from combat and three from accidents.

On 14 July the seaplane anchorage was shifted from Kerama Retto to the more protected seadrome at Chimu Wan, which later became known as Buckner Bay, on the east coast of Okinawa. From this seadrome operations by the seaplane squadrons continued until the end of the war.

Mariners aggressively went after Japanese shipping. Fleet Communiqué No. 455, dated 5 August 1945, reported: "Search seaplanes of Fleet Air Wing One on August 4, sank a small coastal cargo vessel and damaged a dredge, a pier, a radio station, a light house and other installations on the south coast of Shantung

Province, China." The mission was recalled in some detail by Lt. (j.g.) John Drover, patrol plane commander of crew 14, in Raithel et al.'s *Mariner/Marlin*:

VPB-21 had received orders to move to Eniwetok and was assigned one last combat patrol at Okinawa. Air Crews #4 (Lieutenant Floyd Harris, PPC) flying D-4, and Crew #14 were selected with Lieutenant Harris leading and my D-14 flew "wing." A basic plan for the flight was laid out the night before, and on the morning of the 4th the two planes checked their "rubbers" (IFF, radar identification) and headed for the south coast of China's Shantung Peninsula.

Approaching Lao Yao from the south, Harris led an attack on a radio station on a bluff south of the harbor, bombing and strafing the facility with my Mariner following and strafing, inflicting heavy damage. Our planes continued on up the coast, surprising the enemy by attacking from inland across the harbor, dropping down to 100' over the water. D-4 was close to the south shore with D-14 off its port quarter (looking for ships in the harbor). Harris dropped three bombs on a 150 foot dredge, destroying the dredge, and three more bombs on a pier.

There being no ships in port at that time, Crew 14 strafed targets of opportunity and harbor installations including a second dredge which both crews strafed extensively on the way out of Lao Yao Harbor. The planes sped across the harbor followed by heavy 40mm AA [antiaircraft fire] from the shore batteries. A large concrete building near the lighthouse received severe damage from direct hits by D-4 bombs.

The two planes continued up the coast and spied a small enemy coastal cargo vessel (sugar dog) at anchor. My plane attacked, laying 100 pound bombs on the stem, mid ship and forward. When the smoke cleared, the crew had abandoned ship and the starboard gunwale was awash.

We continued up the coast and upon approaching the outer Tsingtao harbor two large "sugar dogs" were spotted at anchor near what would have been the "sea buoy." The planes initiated an attack immediately with little change in heading needed, each plane taking a ship. As the planes closed, the ships opened-up with heavy 40mm AA. Both planes dove for the water at full throttle and headed out to sea, as the shore batteries on surrounding hills joined in with more 40mm AA. Our "sitting ducks" turned out to be well-armed picket ships and more than a match for the Mariner twin 50s in the bow, especially since by this time in the flight, D-4's bow guns were inoperative from the extensive strafing we had done.

As the planes advanced toward the open sea at an altitude of 100 feet using evasive maneuvers, I zigged when I should have zagged and was hit by three or four 40mm shots in the tail section. They took off 30% of the top of the port fin and rudder, damaged the port horizontal stabilizer and elevator, shattered the tail turret, wounded Thomas Granger, the tail gunner, and put 30 plus holes in the tunnel section. At a safe distance from the beach, the two aircraft climbed to 8,000' altitude to allow us some flexibility in case the damaged plane became unmanageable. Most patrols were flown much lower to stay below radar detection. With Crew 4 watching closely, I checked D-14's controllability carefully and except for noticeable vibration in the tail, it flew all right. Upon return to Okinawa, D-14 was immediately hoisted aboard the USS *Hamlin* for repairs.

On 7 August 1945 two of VPB-27's Mariners left the seadrome and headed for an antishipping sweep off Formosa. About two hours later they reported strafing three enemy patrol (PT) boats and driving the heavily damaged PTs onto the beach. That was the last word heard from the planes. Searches for the two planes continued for several days, but to no avail. About eleven days later, VPB-27's base was notified that the only trace of the two planes was a wing tip floating in the general vicinity of where the planes had last been seen. Nothing else was ever found.

The war with Japan was ended with the 6 August and 9 August atomic bombing of Hiroshima and Nagasaki, respectively. On 15 August VPB-27 received orders to stand down from combat operations, bringing its fighting phase of the war to an end. During the last months of the operation, the squadron lost eight aircraft: two shot down on a night mission, one shot down by a friendly night fighter, one from battle damage, one from detonation of bombs accidentally jettisoned, one from an emergency landing, and two damaged on reefs beyond economical repair.

The Rescue Squadrons at Okinawa, Spring–Summer 1945

Rescue Squadron 3 (VH-3) arrived at Kerama Retto on 29 March 1945 with the first three patrol squadrons. It had six PBM-3Rs and was based on *Hamlin* and *Bering Strait*. VH-3's PBM-3Rs had been hastily assigned from the assets of transport (VR) squadrons. A number of these aircraft had been sent as PBM-3Cs to Great Britain in late 1943 as part of the Lend-Lease Program. They had been returned by the Royal Air Force (RAF) with less than one

PBM-3R
demonstrates
JATO takeoff,
Kaneohe,
Hawaii, 1945.
*U.S. Naval
Institute Photo
Archive*

hundred flight hours. Since then, however, they had been converted to transports and seen hard service. They were no longer in tip-top condition.

Despite the limitations of the PBM-3R, VH-3 set a magnificent record during the Okinawa campaign. In Donald Sweet et al.'s *Forgotten Heroes,* VH-3 Combat Aircrewman Lee Roy Way recalled:

From March 29, 1945, until August 13, VH-3 made 77 rescues from Kerama-

Retto and Buckner Bay, rescuing 175 survivors in 77 open-sea landings and 74 takeoffs. (Three times, the aircraft was damaged so extensively on landing that they had to taxi back to base on the open sea: for 145 miles, for 154 miles, and for over 200 miles.) Also, during this time, over 54 survivors were rescued by surface vessels and lifeguard submarines, when sea conditions were too heavy for our Dumbos to effect the rescue. Every time survivors were sighted by VH-3 Dumbos, the rescue or assisted rescue was made.

Three other rescue squadrons also arrived at Okinawa: VH-4 on 24 June, VH-6 on 27 July, and VH-1 on 1 August. These squadrons operated PBM-5s. In his *Operational History,* Kammen notes:

> It was in this area in the concluding months of the war that the air-sea rescue work of the flying boat reached its climax. The spectacularly successful rescue operations for pilots and crews whose planes had been forced down were a vital part of the Okinawa campaign. Seventy percent of those airmen forced down in the open sea during March, April, and May were rescued.

From January 1944 to August 1945 Mariner squadrons had served in every major Pacific campaign, performing vital scouting and reconnaissance missions as well as attacking and sinking Japanese submarines, naval vessels, and merchant ships. In heroic open-sea landings Mariner Dumbos rescued hundreds of airmen and seamen. The Mariner and its crews established a glorious record of achievement. The aircraft would continue to serve the U.S. Navy well for another decade.

CHAPTER FOUR

THE MARINER BETWEEN WARS

Atlantic Drawdown, 1944–1946

VPB-202, VPB-205, VPB-208, and VPB-216, four of the eighteen Atlantic Mariner squadrons, had been transferred to the Pacific in 1944 and early 1945. After the surrender of Germany in May 1945 ten of the remaining fourteen squadrons were decommissioned by July. VPB-32 was transferred to the Pacific in September 1945. One more Atlantic squadron was decommissioned in May 1946. Finally, only VPB-74 and VPB-201 remained active in the Atlantic. Both were based in Panama for canal defense.

Pacific Occupation Duties, 1945–1947

Although seven of the Pacific operational squadrons, one of the training squadrons, and most of the rescue squadrons were disestablished soon after the Japanese capitulation, the remaining Mariner units in the Pacific stayed extremely busy after Victory over Japan (VJ) day. On 28 August 1945 seaplane tender *Cumberland Sound* (AV-17) arrived in Japan, part of the very first group of Allied warships to enter Tokyo Bay. PBM-5s of VPB-26 arrived on 30 August. It was the first squadron to be based in and operating from Japan. In September 1945 VPB-32 arrived from the Atlantic Fleet. It was homeported at Saipan, establishing mail and passenger flights to Truk and forming detachments as needed at Kwajalein; Truk; Eniwetok; Yokosuka, Japan; Tsingtao, China; Hong Kong; and Sangley Point in the Philippines. VPB-205 was relocated to Wakayama, Japan, to provide surveillance support during the disarmament of Japan and to provide courier/passenger service for the occupation forces. VPB-17 and VPB-20 operated from Jinsen (Inchon), Korea, and Shanghai and Taku Bar, China. They were supported by *Currituk* and *Barataria* (AVP-33). VPB-18 made fifty-one round trips from Saipan to Tokyo in the month following the surrender. VPB-21 was relocated from Eniwetok to Ominato, China, and then to Hong Kong. VPB-27 relocated to Sasebo, Japan, to perform courier and mail flights throughout Japan.

Eighteen Mariners were lost in operational accidents between VJ day and the end of 1945. Most of these accidents were the result of the primitive or nonexistent facilities at the operating sites. Planes were lost in Japan, China, the Philippines, and in the Marianas. Only two of these losses resulted in fatalities. Seaman 1st Class Robert C. Wensling died in September when a VPB-27 aircraft broke loose from its moorings during a storm. In October a VPB-205 aircraft disappeared during a patrol. The crew of eleven, including Rear Adm. W. D. Sample, the Fleet Air Wing 17 commander, was lost.

On 15 November 1945 a Mariner was involved in one of the first incidents that presaged the so-called "Cold War" era. On a routine patrol mission a Mariner was attacked by a Soviet fighter twenty-five miles south of Dairen (Port Arthur), Manchuria, while it was investigating six Soviet transport ships and a beached seaplane in the Gulf of Chihli in the Yellow Sea. The Mariner suffered no damage.

Even as Mariners in the Pacific were busy with occupation and disarmament tasks, the postwar drawdown continued. Six more patrol bombing squadrons were disestablished: VPBs 17, 20, 25, 26, 98, and 99. However, new missions were developed for the versatile PBM, including polar exploration and support of atomic testing.

Atomic Testing and Polar Exploration, 1946–1947

Operation Crossroads

Operation Crossroads was a nuclear weapon test series conducted at Bikini Atoll in the Marshall Islands in the summer of 1946. Its purpose was to study the effects of nuclear weapons on ships, equipment, and material. A fleet of more than ninety vessels was assembled in Bikini Lagoon as a target. This fleet was comprised of older U.S. capital ships; three captured German and Japanese ships; surplus U.S. cruisers, destroyers, and submarines; and a large number of auxiliary and amphibious vessels. Military equipment was arrayed on some of the ships as well as on various amphibious craft that were berthed on Bikini Island. Technical experiments were also conducted to study nuclear weapon explosion phenomena.

A support fleet of more than 150 ships provided quarters, experimental stations, and workshops for most of the forty-two thousand men of Joint Task Force 1 (JTF 1), the organization that conducted the tests. Additional personnel were located on nearby atolls such as Eniwetok and Kwajalein.

Two atomic explosions occurred during Operation Crossroads: Able and Baker. In the Able test, an airburst on 1 July 1946, the weapon was dropped from a B-29 *Superfortress* and burst directly over the target fleet. In the underwater Baker test on 25 July 1946 the weapon was suspended beneath an auxiliary craft anchored in the midst of the target fleet.

Fifteen Mariners were employed in Operation Crossroads as part of Task Unit (TU) 1.6.3, designated Seaplane Unit, Naval Air Base Ebeye Island, Kwajalein Atoll. The Mariners and crews were from two squadrons: Patrol Bombing Squadron 32 (VPB-32) and Air-Rescue Squadron 4 (VH-4). Combat Aircraft Service Unit (Fleet) 34 (CASU[F]-34) supported the Mariners.

VPB-32 had been homeported in Saipan, Marianas Islands. Its entire squadron of 9 PBM-5s, 30 officers, and 125 men was deployed to Ebeye to participate in Operation Crossroads. Because VPB-32's combat Mariners were to function as transports during Crossroads, the aircraft were stripped of deck turrets, guns, and armor plate. Their decking was strengthened with plywood to prevent damage from heavy loads. Provisions were made for two thousand pounds of mail and seats were provided for up to twenty passengers.

VH-4 contributed six PBM-5s for air-sea rescue coverage. The VH-4 aircraft were on airborne alert for both the Able and Baker tests.

The Mariners were supported by TU 1.6.4 (Seaplane Tender, Bikini) and USS *Orca* (AVP-49).

Except on Able and Baker days, *Orca* was stationed at Bikini as a terminal and service unit for the transport seaplanes. The ship maintained seaplane runways and furnished maintenance and fuel servicing for all seaplanes on their turn-around flights. Because there were no land-plane facilities at Bikini, the Mariners provided the only air transportation between Kwajalein and Bikini.

A typical Mariner schedule between Kwajalein and Bikini was two round trips daily, but extra flights were quite frequent. Throughout the operation, Task Unit 1.6.3 made 417 transport flights, carrying 3,512 passengers as well as 422,935 pounds of mail and 293,848 pounds of freight. The passenger list included the secretary of the navy, senators, congressmen, the president's evaluation committee, high-ranking military officers, and some of the nation's leading scientists.

The Mariners did about everything there was to be done to support operations during Crossroads. The big flying boats carried mail, supplies, and VIPs with such efficiency that the percentage of planes in operations was always over 90 percent and on both rehearsal and A-bomb test days 100 percent. Technical missions included photography, radiometry, radiological reconnaissance, and damage estimation.

On Able day VPB-32 had six Mariners performing photography and radiological reconnaissance missions. Some of the aircraft were equipped with automatic cameras that could be controlled from the ground and a rudimentary television receiver. Two VPB-32 Mariners performed radiological reconnaissance. The day after the Able blast, *Orca* was able to resume its station inside Bikini Lagoon.

On Baker day eight PBMs performed similar missions, again with two doing the dangerous but vital radiological reconnaissance after this underwater burst with its attendant radiation particles. The Mariners made numerous runs at various altitudes measuring radiation. The pilots of the two radiological reconnaissance aircraft, Comdr. Leslie E. Pew and Lt. Comdr. William Lower, were awarded Air Medals for their conduct during these missions. After Baker, *Orca* was not able to return to Bikini Lagoon because of the radiation danger, so the Mariners had to continue operations from the open sea, using the JATO system.

In Roland C. Friederichsen and Bill Lower's "Recollections of Crossroads," Lower states that VPB-32 was recommended for a special unit citation for its performance in Crossroads but no U.S. Navy records have been found that the citation was ever awarded. Operation Crossroads was considered a complete success, a success aided in no small measure by the utility and versatility of the Mariner under the most primitive of operating conditions.

Operation Nanook

After World War II, the Soviet Union began building up a long-range bomber force. Its aircraft was based on the TU-4 Bull copy of the Boeing B-29. U.S. strategists considered it wise to explore the possibilities of defensive air facilities in the Arctic.

On 12 February 1946 Congress approved Public Law 296, which directed the chief of the U.S. Weather Bureau to establish "an international meteorological reporting network in the Arctic regions of the Western Hemisphere." The Weather Bureau turned to the U.S. Army and the U.S. Navy. Together the three agencies came up with a plan to build reporting stations that summer at Thule, Greenland, and at the southern tip of Melville Island in the Canadian Arctic. The U.S. Atlantic Fleet commander, Adm. Marc A. Mitscher, selected a few ships, designated them Task Force 68, and appointed Capt. Richard H. Cruzen as commander of the Operation Nanook expedition. The operation was obviously named after Robert J. Flaherty's famous 1922 documentary film titled *Nanook of the North.*

Cruzen's first orders, issued 31 May 1946, called for a general plan with a sec-ond phase that consisted "of operations to establish weather observation and reporting stations of the U.S. Weather Bureau" in the Canadian Arctic and Greenland. Additionally, Cruzen ordered one ice-breaker, along with seaplane tender *Norton Sound* (AV-11), to operate "in the general vicinity of the southern limit of the ice pack which is expected to be encountered in the Baffin Bay area." With this project the navy began its effort to systematically expose man and machine to the rigors of polar life.

Task Force 68 was comprised of the seaplane tender *Norton Sound* as flagship, submarine *Atule* (SS-403), attack transports *Beltrami* (AK-162) and *Alcona* (AK-157), net tender *Whitewood* (AN-63), and U.S. Coast Guard icebreaker *Northwind* (WAG-282). Two Mariners from VPB-19, commanded by Lieutenant Commander Bannowski and Lieutenant Bounds, were loaded aboard *Norton Sound* in Norfolk, Virginia.

The crew of *Norton Sound,* which had returned to the United States from wartime and occupation duties in the Far East on 22 May 1946, was reportedly less than excited at the prospect of a deployment to the Arctic. Also, with the postwar demobilization, the ship was shorthanded. Personnel were shanghaied from other Atlantic Fleet units to man the ship. Fifteen junior officers joined the ship on a temporary additional duty (TAD) status from their permanent units. Lt. Andy Sinclair was one of them. Sinclair recalls that he had only been aboard VP-205 in Bermuda for about two weeks when the squadron's executive officer (XO) informed him he was being sent to *Norton Sound.* Sinclair thinks his selection was influenced by the fact that he and the XO were dating the same girl!

The Nanook task force arrived in the Arctic in early July 1946 and initially operated from Melville Bight, Baffin Bay. On 20 July a PBM surveying Thule Harbor had engine trouble and was forced to land in the harbor. Submarine *Atule* was dispatched to assist; it subsequently was joined by *Norton Sound* and *Whitewood.* From 22 July to 5 August activities of Operation Nanook centered around Thule. *Norton Sound* anchored in North Star Bay and serviced its two PBMs.

From Thule the Mariners flew polar navigation flights north of Greenland to within 450 miles of the North Pole testing navigation equipment suitable for these high latitudes. In his "Operation Nanook" article, Jim "Robbie" Robbins relates that when *Northwind* was left high and dry by a thirty-foot tide on Ellesmere Island north of the Arctic Circle in August 1946, a Mariner landed nearby. It was carrying the task force commander, who had come to survey the situation. A decision was made

to wait for the next high tide and *Northwind* floated off without damage.

A PBM aircrewman, Robbins also recalls:

> After we had been in full operation about 4 or 5 days another PBM-5 was sent up loaded with surveying equipment and the Army Engineers who were to survey an area just south of Thule to build the Air Force Base and landing strip which now exists there. I'm not certain where this plane initially departed from on [its] final flight to Thule, but they had been in the air for some 19 hours (as reported panically [*sic*] by the PPC [patrol plane commander]), were flying in ceiling zero and visibility zero conditions and could not climb above it. The PPC thought he was lost and had already flown over the North Pole. In a desperate attempt to lighten the plane, he felt it was necessary to ditch the U.S. Mail and keep what he believed was his primary mission, the surveying equipment, on board.

Bannowski took off immediately, made a rendezvous with the lost plane by radio homing and radar, and escorted it in to Thule and *Norton Sound.* Sinclair remembers all hands on the fantail of *Norton Sound* were ready to joyously welcome the lost plane. When it became known that the mail had been jettisoned, the welcome became less joyous.

Meanwhile, *Whitewood* and *Atule* conducted exercises and tests in the Smith Sound–Kane Basin area. On 5 August, *Norton Sound* and *Whitewood* headed for Dundas Harbor, Devon Island, to attempt air and surface operations there. Unfortunately the ships found the harbor iced over, with a belt of pack ice extending out three miles down the coast. *Northwind* later joined the two ships in the vicinity of Dundas Harbor. The ships searched for a suitable anchorage that could accommodate them and their attached aircraft. *Whitewood* succeeded in finding a small, ice-free anchorage at Tay Ray, off northwestern Bylot Island.

At Goose Bay, Labrador, on a mail run, Mariner BuNo 59076 was damaged and partially sunk on 5 August 1946 after striking the bottom while taxiing. Because it was impossible to make repairs at Goose Bay, classified material was destroyed and the aircraft was abandoned.

Operation Nanook was completed in September 1946. Sinclair recalls: "Although one of the objectives of the Task Force was to experience polar conditions, the weather in fact was quite pleasant with the air temperature hovering around 32 deg F.—the air [i]nvigorating. With the sun never setting, one's energy level was quite high, and little sleep was required." After completion of Operation Nanook, a number of Task Force 68's arctic-experienced personnel joined a new Task Force 68 for the Operation Highjump exploration of the South Pole area.

Operation Highjump

Soviet-American relations were rapidly deteriorating throughout 1946. If a another world war broke out, a strategic battleground would most likely be in the North Polar region. It was in the best interest of the United States to expose and prepare men, ships, and equipment to the extremes of polar regions as quickly and efficiently as possible.

At the instigation of famed polar explorer Rear Adm. Richard E. Byrd, on 26 August 1946 Secretary of the Navy James V. Forrestal, and Fleet Admiral Chester W. Nimitz, the chief of naval operations, established the Antarctic developments project. It would be carried out during the forthcoming Antarctic summer (December 1946–March 1947). The project was christened Operation Highjump.

On 15 October 1946 Adm. Marc A. Mitscher, the commander-in-chief of the Atlantic Fleet, appointed Capt. Richard H. Cruzen as commander of the operation, which was designated Task Force 68. Byrd would have the title "officer-in-charge," but he was more a consultant than a commander. Cruzen was one of the U.S. Navy's most experienced arctic sailors. He had participated in Byrd's U.S. Antarctic service expedition of 1939–41, and had just completed his command of Operation Nanook in Greenland. After Nanook, Cruzen was promoted to the rank of rear admiral.

With the exception of Rear Admiral Cruzen and some of his immediate staff, the cast of ships and men would be quite different from Operation Nanook. In order to expose as many men as possible to polar conditions, the commanders of the Pacific and Atlantic Fleets were to each designate six ships for the expedition.

From the Atlantic Fleet came the expedition flagship *Mount Olympus* (AGC-8), seaplane tender *Pine Island* (AV-12), fleet oiler *Canisteo* (AO-99), destroyer *Brownson* (DD-868), submarine *Sennet* (SS-408), new fleet aircraft carrier *Philippine Sea* (CV-47), and the U.S. Coast Guard icebreaker *Northwind* (WAG-282). The Pacific Fleet supplied the destroyer *Henderson* (DD-785), attack transports *Yancey* (AKA-93) and *Merrick* (AKA-97), seaplane tender *Currituck* (AV-7), fleet oiler *Cacapon* (AO-52), and the navy's icebreaker *Burton Island* (AG-88).

Tentative plans were to establish a base, to be called "Little America IV," on the Ross Ice Shelf near Little America III, which had been the home of Byrd's 1939–41 expedition. After Little America IV was established, a "systematic outward radial expansion of air exploration" would be performed by ship-based flying boats operating along the Antarctic coastline and land-based airplanes departing from Little America. A primary objective of Operation Highjump was the aerial mapping of as much of Antarctica as possible, particularly the coastline.

The expedition was divided into three groups: Central, Eastern, and Western. The Central Group (Task Group 68.1) would be joined by the aircraft carrier *Philippine Sea* (Task Group 68.4). The aircraft carrier would launch ski-equipped R4Ds, the navy version of the DC-3, for the risky six-hour flight to Little America IV. Little America IV itself was designated Task Group 68.5.

On either side of the Central Group and the *Philippine Sea* would be the Eastern Group (Task Group 68.3) and Western Group (Task Group 68.2). The Eastern Group, built around seaplane tender *Pine Island,* would rendezvous at Peter I Island. From there it would move toward zero degrees longitude (Greenwich Meridian). The Western Group would be built around the seaplane tender *Currituck. Currituck* would rendezvous with support ships at the Balleny Islands and then proceed on a westward course around Antarctica until, hopefully, it met up with the Eastern Group.

Each seaplane tender would be supplied with three PBM Mariners. The plan was to have the Mariners make daily flights to photograph as much of the coast and interior as possible. The crews of all six PBMs, drawn from operating squadrons, were assembled at the Naval Air Station Norfolk on 1 November 1946. They had only one month to prepare. Meanwhile, the PBMs were winterized and fitted out with some special navigational instruments, as well as the trimetrogon photographic equipment. Aerial photography for topographic mapping used one vertical camera and two oblique cameras. Photographs were taken simultaneously. Survival gear was gathered as the crews were quickly instructed in polar navigation. On 27 November three of the seaplanes flew from Norfolk to San Diego, California, and were lifted aboard *Currituck.* Back in Virginia, the other three planes were brought aboard *Pine Island.* In order to get *Pine Island* through the Panama Canal, the Mariners had to be off-loaded and flown across the Isthmus to the Pacific side.

CENTRAL GROUP (TASK GROUPS 68.1, 68.4, AND 68.5) ACTIVITIES

On 25 January 1947 *Philippine Sea* rendezvoused with *Northwind, Cacapon, Sennet,* and *Brownson* near Scott Island. Four days later the first two R4Ds successfully took off from the flight deck of *Philippine Sea* for the flight to Little America IV; Admiral Byrd

was aboard the first plane. By 30 January all six R4Ds had arrived safely at Little America IV. With its mission completed, *Philippine Sea* departed for the Canal Zone.

From Little America, several R4D photographic missions were flown, including a two-aircraft flight to the South Pole on 15–16 February. However, flights from Little America were hampered by the weather. A flight attempt was made on 22 February, but had to turn back due to poor weather. This terminated Little America–based flight operations for the expedition. Little America was evacuated by *Burton Island* on 23 February 1947. The R4Ds were left behind.

WESTERN GROUP (TASK GROUP 68.2) ACTIVITIES

The Western Group, commanded by Capt. Charles A. Bond, had rendezvoused at the Marquesas Islands on 12 December 1946. It arrived at the edge of the pack ice northeast of the Balleny Islands on Christmas Eve day. The *Henderson* and *Cacapon* fanned out to serve as weather stations while flight operations from *Currituck* began. The primary weather problem was fog.

A few flights were attempted but the fog continued until New Year's Day 1947. After the fog lifted the first mapping flight of about seven hours was flown successfully along the Oates coast. Whereas the pilots at Little America IV fought dense cloud formations rising to thirteen or fourteen thousand feet, the pilots of the Western Group, flying along Wilkes Land, found that even if the overcast was dense, "ordinarily you would break out in the clear soon. On the average the cloud layer wasn't any more than 4,000 or 5,000 feet thick with not too much icing . . . it would be absolutely clear on top."

Icebergs were encountered, but "[b]ergs were shown by radar with fidelity and the ship maneuvered in and out among them easily." Bond was pleased because significant air operations resulted in unquestioned successes. Flights from their staging area in the Balleny Islands were made on 2, 4, 5, and 6 January over the continent. "Operations were eminently successful and a substantial portion of the area assignment had been completed by this time." With the first assignment completed, Cruzen radioed from the Central Group instructing Bond to cease present operations and sail *Currituck* eastward to the vicinity of Scott Island in order to reconnoiter for *Northwind* and its bedeviled flock in the Ross Sea. *Currituck* reached Scott Island on the 10 January. Both patrol planes flew reconnaissance missions on 11 and 12 January, but no leads could be seen for their trapped colleagues in the ice below. *Currituck* next headed west again past the Adélie coast and on to Wilkes Land along the Sabrina, Knox, and Queen Mary coasts.

Unfortunately, no flights were possible between 13 and 21 January because of a huge northerly swell. On 22 January the swells moderated and the weather became acceptable for flights to resume. Over the next week, several long and successful photomapping missions progressed to the west.

On either 30 January or 1 February Lt. Comdr. David E. Bunger, a Mariner pilot, lifted from the bay and headed south for the continent some hundred miles distant. At this time *Currituck* was off the Shackleton Ice Shelf on the Queen Mary coast of Wilkes Land. Reaching the coastline, Bunger flew west with cameras humming. Suddenly the men in the cockpit saw a dark spot appear over the barren white horizon. As they drew closer, they saw what Byrd later described in "Our Navy Explores Antarctica" as a "land of blue and green lakes and brown hills in an otherwise limitless expanse of ice." Bunger and his men carefully inspected the region and a few days later returned for another look. Finding one of the lakes suitable for landing, Bunger carefully landed the flying boat. The water was actually quite warm for Antarctica, about 30°F, so some men dipped their hands in to their elbows. The lake was filled with the red, blue, and green algae that gives a distinctive color. The Mariner crew "seemed to have dropped out of the twentieth century into a landscape of thousands of years ago when land was just starting to emerge from one of the great ice ages," Byrd later wrote. Byrd called the discovery "by far the most important, so far as the public interest was concerned . . . of the expedition." Unfortunately, "the water in the bottle turned out to be brackish, a clue to the fact that the 'lake' was actually an arm of the open sea."

By the end of January, inclement weather forced the airmen to skip over the existing gap between 150° E and 145° E longitude. Later expeditions would have to complete the mapping data. Mapping missions continued day after day, covering a fifteen hundred mile long area between 141° E and 115° E longitude. According to Byrd, Wilkes Land proved to be a "featureless ice sheet that ranged from 6,000 to 9,500 feet above sea level. No mountains were lofty enough to thrust their heads into the frigid winds above this white blanket, although valleys and ridges in the ice surface up to 100 miles inland gave a hint of rough terrain underneath."

The weather turned typically Antarctic as the first week of February arrived. Seas became rough and snowstorms frequently occurred. Flight operations were limited to only three days during the month. During that time *Currituck* sailed hundreds of miles around the coastline, from 115° E to 40° E longitude, all around Wilkes Land, the American Highland fronting the Indian Ocean, and on to Queen Maud Land. When the planes were able to fly, outstanding results were the norm. These results

would be of significant importance in the selection of base sites some ten years later during the international geophysical year (IGY). On 12 February, when *Currituck* was off the Princess Ragnhild coast of Queen Maud Land, pilots W. R. Kreitzer and F. L. Reinbolt lifted off in their PBM for a routine photo mission to map three hundred miles of coastline. What had previously been drawn in as coastline now proved to be towering ice shelf rising high above the sea. As they turned south, they suddenly discovered a range of ice-crystal mountains, luminously blue against the dark sky, rising more than two miles into the air. Flying near the mountain peaks, Kreitzer and Reinbolt followed the range for nearly one hundred miles before turning back. One of them later told Byrd, "It was like a landscape on another planet."

On 1 March 1947 the final flights of the Western Group's Mariners were made in the vicinity of Ingrid Christensen coast. *Currituck, Cacapon,* and *Henderson* departed Antarctica on 3 March. All three ships sailed for a well-earned port visit in Sydney, Australia, before returning to the United States.

EASTERN GROUP (TASK GROUP 68.3) ACTIVITIES

Operations of the Eastern Group, commanded by Capt. George J. Dufek (who had accompanied Admiral Cruzen in Operation Nanook), commenced in the vicinity of Peter I Island, north of the Bellingshausen Sea, late in December 1946. The *Pine Island* reported a position near Swain Island on 23 December. On Christmas Eve the first iceberg was spotted. Without question, the Amundsen and Bellingshausen Seas experience some of the worst weather conditions in the world. To complicate matters for the Eastern Group, frequent foggy weather, howling blizzards, and stormy waters made aircraft launching and flight perpetually hazardous.

Heavy swells and frequent snow squalls plagued the *Pine Island* until the weather suddenly improved and cleared the afternoon of 29 December. The Mariner designated "George I" was lowered over the side and shortly after 1:00 PM the plane lifted off the water on the first Eastern Group flight to Antarctica with Lt. Comdr. John D. Howell as pilot and Capt. George Dufek as observer.

Within hours, George I radioed back that weather conditions were favorable for mapping operations over the continent. So PBM George 2 took to the air later that evening. When George I returned at 11:05 PM, a third flight was scheduled with an entirely new crew. Because it was daylight twenty-four hours a day at this time of year in the Antartica, the next flight left at 2:24 AM on 30 December with Lt. (j.g.) Ralph Paul "Frenchy" LeBlanc at the controls.

The copilot was Lt. (j.g.) Bill Kearns. The rest of the crew consisted of pilot/navigator Ens. Maxwell A. Lopez, Aviation Radioman 1st Class Wendell K. Hendersin, Flight Engineer Frederick W. Williams, Chief Photographer's Mate Owen McCarty, Aviation Machinist's Mate 2nd Class William Warr, Aviation Radioman 2nd Class James (Jimmy) H. Robbins, and the skipper of the *Pine Island,* Capt. Henry H. Caldwell.

As George I flew southwest at four hundred feet above the ice, the weather "looked anything but promising," as Kearns later recalled in Owen McCarty's "Dead Men's Diary." The plane flew for three hours before picking up the coastline of Thurston Island (then called the Thurston Peninsula). Kearns took over the controls from LeBlanc and took the plane up to one thousand feet in altitude. Unfortunately, the plane began picking up a great deal of ice. The bow station Plexiglas (acrylic plastic) froze and the cockpit windows frosted despite all efforts with the on-board de-icing equipment. The plane suddenly entered an "ice blink": streams of sunshine trapped beneath the clouds, bouncing off the snow "in a million directions, as if each ice fragment were a tiny mirror." To make matters worse, a fine, driving snow obstructed the surface below, the altimeters began giving different readings, and the wings began to ice up.

Kearns turned to LeBlanc and said, "I don't like the looks of this. Let's get the hell out of here!" LeBlanc nodded in agreement and as Kearns gently banked the plane, all on board felt a "crunching shock" that "reverberated all along the hull." The plane had obviously grazed something. Kearns immediately applied full power and both Kearns and LeBlanc pulled back hard on the yoke.

The next thing the crew knew, the Mariner blew up. The hull gasoline tank exploded because of the impact and the plane had literally blown apart. Lopez, Hendersin, and Williams were killed. The others crawled into what was left of the fuselage to lay stunned and bleeding.

Rescue operation preparations began as soon as the aircraft was overdue, but search flights from *Pine Island* were hampered by the weather. On New Year's Day 1947 George II was lifted over the side but a dense fog suddenly rolled in. The plane was tied up to the stern by a three hundred foot line. At two the next morning, disaster struck. The swells swung the plane around and thrust it into the side of the ship, extensively damaging a wing tip, de-icing boot, and aileron. By 5 January George II had been repaired and George III assembled for backup. Both planes were lowered over the side but once again the fog rolled in. Finally, the weather cleared and a test flight was ordered in the afternoon. It went off without a hitch. Later in the evening a

search was made over the last reported position of George I. The aircraft returned to the ship when the weather deteriorated. The following day surface conditions allowed a second flight, but the mission was scrapped due to fog and snow. Snow, fog, and heavy swells continued to plague the search efforts until 9 January, but even the search that day was turned back due to "very unfavorable weather."

Good fortune would finally smile on Dufek and his men on the morning of 11 January 1947. At 4:30 AM, George II, flown by Lt. (j.g.) James Ball and Lt. (j.g.) Robert Goff, was hoisted over the side. It lifted from the water at 7:00 AM and flew off in the direction of the continent. Later, at the crash site, Kearns suddenly sat up and shouted, "Airplane!" The men struggled out of their tents. On the horizon was Ball's PBM. Everything that could burn, especially the raft, was dragged out of the plane. They waited and waited. Two hours after the first sighting, Caldwell cried, "There she is, lads!" Robbins dropped a match on the pile of debris. A tall column of smoke rose high into the sky. The PBM rocked its wing and the men on the ice shelf went hysterical, dancing and jumping in the snow. However, their ordeal was not yet over.

Supplies, including food, clothing, cigarettes, bedding, a rifle and ammunition, and even two quarts of whiskey, came floating down by parachute. The survivors next wrote a large message on the blue wing of the plane, letting those above know that Hendersin, Lopez, and Williams had been killed. Meanwhile, George II copilot Goff looked to the north for a landing spot. A few minutes later, George II returned and dropped a message in a sardine can, "Open water ten air miles to north. If you can make it on foot, join hands in a circle. If not, form straight line. Don't lose courage, we'll pick you up." "Let's go," Kearns said, and all but LeBlanc joined hands.

Ball and Goff, still overhead, getting low on fuel, needed to return to *Pine Island*. Lieutenant Commander Howell was already on his way in George III. Soon Howell was overhead. He began dropping additional supplies to the men below. George III then went back to the shore and landed some two miles out. Aircrewmen Conger and Howell loaded a sled and supplies into a life raft and gently lowered themselves into the sea for a brisk row to shore. Once ashore, they loaded the sled with supplies and headed off into the interior. It was difficult going. As the two men trudged onward, the weather got colder and colder. Fog rolled in and the possibility of disaster loomed larger and larger.

Meanwhile, the George I survivors had pushed their way along through huge snowdrifts. As the fog drifted in ever closer, they dropped to the snow in exhaustion. Suddenly, all heard a pistol shot. Robbins stood up and saw two figures moving

toward them, dragging a sled. As Howell and Conger made their way to the six men, they could not believe what they saw. Exhausted, bearded, battered men stood before them, overcome with pain and emotion. Howell quickly got the men moving. By this time, the fog had engulfed the rescue plane. To make matters worse, it started snowing. The return trail was not visible. The earlier sled marks and footprints were now covered. But fate stepped in at the last moment. The party suddenly arrived at the edge of the shore. They now would wait impatiently for the fog to lift. Eight hours later the fog lifted enough for George III to be guided in. All were rowed out to the plane and several hours later the PBM was carefully hoisted aboard the *Pine Island*. Everyone recovered but LeBlanc's legs had to be amputated two weeks after the rescue.

On 18 January 1947 *Pine Island* rendezvoused with *Brownson* and transferred the crash survivors. The survivors were then taken to *Philippine Sea* for transfer back to the United States. Further photographic flights from *Pine Island* were initiated on 23 January, covering the Getz Ice Shelf to the vicinity of Thurston Island. Early in February the ship moved to the northeast of Charcot Island. Flights were made to Charcot and Alexander Islands and Marguerite Bay. Intentions were to land a party at Charcot Island but the shifting pack ice prevented any possibility.

Vessels of the Eastern Group were ordered to proceed to the Weddell Sea on 14 February, but unsatisfactory weather prohibited any worthwhile photographic flights. On 4 March the Eastern Group departed Antarctic waters. It returned to the United States via Rio de Janeiro, Brazil.

HIGHJUMP ACCOMPLISHMENTS

Operation Highjump may have been a rush job, with minimum preparation and training in order to place men and ships south into polar training conditions as quickly as possible, but the expedition overall was a huge success. It was the precursor of modern day scientific exploration on the icecaps.

The greatest achievement of Operation Highjump was the gathering of approximately seventy thousand aerial photographs of the coast of the Antarctic and selected inland areas. This task would have been impossible without the Mariner. The success of Operation Highjump was in a large part due to the versatility and performance of the Mariners and their crews, along with supporting seaplane tenders *Currituck* and *Pine Island*.

Postwar Squadron Redesignations, 1946–1948

On 15 November 1946, as part of the postwar fleet rationalization, the remaining Mariner squadrons were redesignated from patrol bombing squadron (VPB) to patrol squadron, medium seaplane (VP-MS). Further redesignation took place on 1 September 1948 when all Mariner squadrons became simply patrol squadrons (VP). (Designation development is shown in the table on page 82.)

MARINER SQUADRON EMPLOYMENT, 1946–1950

Postwar missions for Mariner squadrons usually included occupation and disarmament tasks, search and rescue, shipping reconnaissance, and antisubmarine warfare.

Former PBY squadron VPB-71, stationed at Norfolk, Virginia, after World War II, was redesignated Patrol Squadron, Medium Amphibian 3 (VP-MA-3) in 1946. The squadron was equipped with the PBM-5A amphibians in August 1948 and redesignated VP-33 on 1 September 1948. VP-33 was disestablished on 15 December 1949.

On 1 September 1948, a former PBY squadron, VP-MA-4, homeported at NAS Norfolk, was redesignated VP-34 and equipped with new PBM-5A amphibians. Because the weight and volume of the landing gear reduced the operational capability of the PBM-5A, the amphibian was withdrawn from patrol service and the squadron was re-equipped with PBM-5S flying boats in June 1949.

Squadron Designations

Pre–15 November 1946	15 November 1946	1 September 1948
VPB-19	VP-MS-9	VP-49
VPB-21	VP-MS-11	VP-41
VPB-22	VP-MS-2	VP-42
VPB-27	VP-MS-7	VP-47
VPB-28	VP-MS-3	VP-43
VPB-32	VP-MS-6	VP-46
VPB-71 (PBY)	VP-MA-3	VP-33
VPB-73 (PBY)	VP-MA-4	VP-34
VPB-74	VP-MS-10	VP-40
VPB-201	VP-MS-1[1]	—
VPB-204	VP-MS-4	VP-44
VPB-205	VP-MS-5	VP-45
VPB-208	VP-MS-8	VP-48

[1] VP-MS-1 received P2V Neptunes and was redesignated Patrol Squadron, Medium Landplane 8 (VP-ML-8) on 5 June 1947.

VP-40 was homeported at NAS Coco Solo, Canal Zone, beginning in September 1945. It was disestablished on 25 January 1950.

VPB-21 remained active in the immediate postwar period, relocating from Okinawa to Eniwetok to Ominato, China, to Hong Kong to Sasebo, Japan, to Tsingtao, China. In November 1947 VP-MS-11 was assigned a homeport at San Diego. In September 1948 the squadron, now redesignated as VP-41, deployed to Tsingtao, China. It returned to San Diego in March 1949. VP-41 was disestablished on 23 April 1949.

By early 1946 VP-MS-2, the former VPB-22, was assigned a homeport at San Diego. In late 1947 the squadron performed a split deployment to Buckner Bay, Okinawa, and Tsingtao. The squadron returned to San Diego in April 1948 and was redesignated VP-42 in September.

VPB-28 was homeported at NAB Jinamoc, Philippines, and made a deployment to Japan for occupation duties in 1948. When it was disestablished on 31 March 1949 its designation was VP-43.

VPB-204 had been assigned a homeport of NAS Coco Solo, Canal Zone, in

July 1945. Even after its redesignation to VP-44 in 1948, it remained at Coco Solo, maintaining search and rescue detachments at NAS Guantánamo Bay, Cuba, and with various seaplane tenders in different parts of the Caribbean. In January 1950 the squadron was relocated to Norfolk, where it was disestablished on 20 January.

VPB-205 returned to the United States from the Pacific in November 1945. It was homeported at Bermuda in April 1946. The squadron was redesignated VP-45 in 1948. In 1950 the squadron was relocated to Norfolk.

In September 1946 VPB-32 was assigned to Saipan, Mariana Islands. Homeported at Saipan until mid-1949, the squadron operated detachments at Kwajalein; Truk; Eniwetok; Yokosuka, Japan; Tsingtao, China; Okinawa; Hong Kong, and Sangley Point. It participated in Operation Sandstone, the nuclear weapons testing done in 1948 at Eniwetok. The squadron, now redesignated VP-46, was assigned a new homeport at San Diego on 1 July 1949.

VPB-27 performed occupation duties from Sasebo, Japan, until reassigned to NAS Kaneohe, Hawaii, in March 1946. In March 1949 the squadron, now redesignated VP-47, was assigned a new homeport at San Diego. In January 1950 VP-47 was deployed to Saipan with detachments at Yokosuka and Sangley Point. Its scheduled return to San Diego was interrupted by the outbreak of the Korean War.

After occupation duty in Tokyo Bay, VPB-208 was homeported at Norfolk and Jacksonville until being assigned to NAS Trinidad, British West Indies, in September 1946. Redesignated VP-48 in 1948, the squadron was disestablished on 31 December 1949.

Upon its return from Eniwetok in the Pacific theater in early 1946, VPB-19 was assigned to a homeport at Norfolk. In 1948 the squadron was redesignated VP-49.

The PBM-5A Amphibian, 1948–1954

Amphibious aircraft are capable of operating from both land and water. Such aircraft are extremely versatile military vehicles. They can be completely waterbased, receiving service from seaplane tenders. Where adequate facilities are available, they can be completely land based and free of the servicing difficulties inherent in tender basing as well as the operational limitations of rough or freezing water. They also can be supported from very minimal shore facilities and use natural waterways for takeoff and landing.

During World War II, the amphibious version of the PBY Catalina, the PBY-5A, demonstrated that versatility time and time again. In the North Atlantic land-based PBY-5As replaced seaplanes unable to operate because of weather conditions. In the South Pacific water-based PBY-5As were supported by ships or by easily constructed minimal island bases close to operational areas.

Toward the end of the war, the U.S. Navy issued a requirement for an amphibious version of the Mariner. A PBM-5 Mariner flying boat, Bureau Number (BuNo) 59349, was converted at the Glenn L. Martin Company factory to the prototype XPBM-5A amphibian. It was delivered to the Naval Air Test Center in April 1946. Testing was satisfactory and thirty-six PBM-5A patrol bombers (Bureau Numbers 122067–122086, 122468–122471, and 122602–122613) were ordered. Deliveries began in March 1948. Some early Mariner reference material discusses four additional conversions, Bureau Numbers 59253–59256. However, there is absolutely no indication in official U.S. Navy aircraft history cards that any such conversion of these four aircraft occurred. Having flown with BuNo 59255 during the Korean War, I can state categorically that it was never an amphibian. In fact, BuNo 59255 later served with the Uruguayan navy as A-811. Total PBM-5A production was one single prototype and thirty-six production aircraft.

Although the production PBM-5As were considered "new-built" aircraft, by design and construction they were essentially conversions of the PBM-5 flying boat. They even retained unnecessary, but sometimes useful, beaching gear fittings. About the only new features on the PBM-5A were power-assisted elevators and reversing propellers. The reversing propellers were extremely useful in taxiing on both land and water. They were especially welcome in rough-water landings.

The first new PBM-5As were assigned to Patrol Squadrons 33 and 34 (VP-33 and VP-34), homeported in Norfolk, Virginia. Comdr. Robert G. Wilson, who served with VP-34 during this era, recalled that the squadrons were assigned the task of evaluating the PBM-5A for patrol bomber use.

The squadrons found that as a patrol bomber the PBM-5A amphibian suffered in comparison with the PBM-5 flying boat. The landing gear added twenty-three hundred pounds to the basic weight. The provisions for its retraction and internal storage reduced fuel capacity by six hundred gallons. Its combat range was therefore approximately 1,500 miles, about 430 miles less than the PBM-5.

Because of the loss of operational capability, the squadrons recommended that no more PBM-5A patrol bombers be procured. VP-34 was re-equipped with PBM-5S flying boats in June 1949; VP-33 was disestablished in December 1949.

One PBM-5A, BuNo 122067, was evaluated by the U.S. Coast Guard. It was damaged beyond repair during open-sea testing on 18 November 1949. Even though the PBM-5A was attractive to the coast guard from an operational utility and from a support and maintenance standpoint, it was deemed "too heavy" for that service's use because the footprint of its single-wheel main landing gear was too high for existing coast guard ramps and aprons.

The PBM-5A, however, provided many more years of useful U.S. Navy service. With guns, armor, and turrets removed, it proved to be a dependable and versatile utility and fleet logistics support aircraft. Although U.S. Navy PBM-5As were lost and damaged in operational accidents, there were no casualties in any of these incidents.

PBM-5As were assigned as support aircraft to bases at Trinidad, British West Indies; Guantánamo Bay, Cuba; Port Lyautey, Morocco; Midway Island; Kwajalein Atoll; Agana, Guam; Sangley Point, Philippines; and Yokosuka (Oppama), Japan. PBM-5As were also used at the U.S. Naval Academy in Annapolis, which has no land plane facilities, for midshipman aviation indoctrination.

PBM-5As were assigned to the Atlantic Fleet's Air Transport Squadron 24 (VR-24) and to the Pacific Fleet's Air Transport Squadrons 23 and 21 (VR-23 and VR-21). The mission of these squadrons was to provide on-demand service to the fleet and the versatile amphibian accomplished missions otherwise impossible in those pre-helicopter days.

Richard Palmer served with VR-21 and VR-23 from 1949 until 1952. In his "That Maverick 'Mariner'" article, he provided a wealth of colorful firsthand information on some Pacific PBM-5A activities. In 1949 Palmer joined VR-23 in San Diego while PBM-5As were being reconfigured for the transport role by Fleet Aircraft Service Squadron 110 (FASRON-110). Four of the reconfigured aircraft went in pairs to VR-23 detachments in Guam and Kwajalein. Palmer was assigned to a group of two destined for the VR-23 Philippine detachment. One of these was flown from San Diego to the Philippines; the other made the San Diego–Hawaii leg of the journey aboard seaplane tender *Salisbury Sound*. On 5 November 1949 Palmer's aircraft reached Kwajalein, where it was tasked to join with another VR-23 PBM-5A in carrying a congressional touring party to several Pacific trust territory islands.

After World War II, the United Nations had named the United States the trustee of the "Trust Territory of the Pacific Islands," the former League of Nations Japanese mandates that included the Caroline Islands, the Marshall Islands, and Marianas (except Guam). The commander in chief of the Pacific Fleet was also the high commissioner of the trust territories. The U.S. Navy was charged to support this trusteeship. The PBM-5A became an essential part of this operation. BuNo 122469 was the only loss during these support flights. It was lost during a takeoff from Maleolap Atoll on 23 May 1950.

Some of the exotic Pacific Island trust

territories flights of the PBM-5As were recalled by "Moose" Welch in Palmer's "That Maverick 'Mariner.'" A plane commander stationed at Kwajalein, Welch visited Ponape, Kusaie, Majuro, Wake, Ronelelap, Ailinglapalap, Rongerik, Eniwetok, Wotje, Bikini, and Roi. Welch also recovered two English pilots who had ditched their Canberra jet at Ailinglapalap; they had been stranded for ten days.

At Agana, Guam, Palmer's crew was again pressed into local service. BuNo 122606 suffered an engine failure on 19 December 1949. The crew was forced to jettison mail, cargo, and spare parts but made a successful single-engine night landing in an unmarked bay at Koror Island. The aircraft was ramped at a former Japanese seaplane base lighted only by jeep headlights.

When Palmer arrived at Clark Air Force Base (AFB) north of Manila on 9 January 1950 he found that VR-23 had been merged into VR-21. VR-21's flight operations were directed by Commander Fleet Logistics Air Wings, Pacific and generally paralleled those of the Military Air Transport Service (MATS). Missions, however, were oriented toward unique navy requirements. The squadron's assigned mission was logistics support for the Seventh Fleet and Commander Naval Forces Philippines. It transported personnel, mail, and material throughout the Philippines

and the Western Pacific, including Saigon, Singapore, Taiwan, and Japan.

Most PBM-5A missions were routine flights from Clark AFB, the terminus of MATS transpacific flights, to the naval bases of Sangley Point and Subic Bay. One notable break in the routine was a survey flight over the Cubi peninsula for Adm. Arthur W. Radford, who wore triple hats: Commander in Chief, Pacific; Commander in Chief, Pacific Fleet; and High Commissioner, Trust Territory of the Pacific Islands. Cubi is hilly and heavily forested and appeared to be a difficult spot for the construction of an airfield. Yet Radford was able to see firsthand its strategic potential to the navy and approved the construction of what became the Cubi Point Naval Air Station.

The outbreak of the Korean War on 27 June 1950 brought new missions for the Pacific Fleet's PBM-5As. Almost immediately, one of the Philippine-based aircraft was ordered to report to Commander Fleet Air Japan and arrived at Haneda AFB north of Tokyo on 11 July. From then on, the Mariners were busy transporting passengers, mail, and high priority cargo to airfields and harbors in Japan and Korea.

By September 1950 the Mariners had transferred their base of operations to Naval Air Facility (NAF) Oppama, a former Imperial Japanese Navy seaplane base in Yokosuka Harbor. From Oppama, the

Mariner transports flew varied missions to support the fluid tactical situation in Korea. A few examples follow. In early September 1950 a PBM-5A delivered classified material to the naval command ship of the Inchon landings. On 25 September 1950 BuNo 122470, after having loaded fourteen combat casualties in Sasebo Bay, lost power on both engines due to contaminated fuel. Luckily the aircraft was able to make a safe deadstick landing in Fukuoka Bay. It returned to service the next day. On 25 October 1950 BuNo 122077 carried classified documents from Itazuke AFB to the commanding general of the U.S. Army's 1st Cavalry Division at K-23 airfield, Korea.

BuNo 122077 was lost on Thanksgiving Day 1950 when the nosewheel door gave way during a hard landing in Sasebo Bay. Although the men were recovered from the water, the aircraft was too badly damaged for repair. It was stricken from navy inventory.

In early December 1950 the PBM-5A and the PBM seaplane patrol squadrons in Japan were ordered to prepare for a water-based operation to evacuate marine combat casualties from the Chosin Reservoir. The preparation came to naught, however, when the reservoir froze over!

VR-21 Mariners continued to provide unique service to the U.S. Navy in the Far East and the Pacific Islands throughout the Korean War era. BuNo 122610 was damaged on 19 May 1952 while on a rescue mission from Midway Island to pick up a critically ill crewman from USS *Wiltsie* (DD-716). Damaged during the open-sea landing, the aircraft required a major overhaul. It was towed back to Midway by USS *Chevalier* (DD-805).

In the Atlantic VR-24's PBM-5As covered the Mediterranean from the base at Port Lyautey, Morocco. A typical VR-24 Mariner mission was described in the aircraft accident report (AAR) of BuNo 122604. Damaged during a landing at Genoa, Italy, on 1 June 1952, BuNo 122604 had departed Port Lyautey with 4,058 pounds of cargo and one passenger. It was en route to Genoa and Nice, France, with a scheduled refueling stop at Algiers, Algeria. On arrival at Genoa, the pilot found the harbor crowded with small boats so he elected to make an open-sea landing approximately one-half mile offshore. During the landing, repairable damage was suffered by the starboard stabilizer.

Additional Atlantic Fleet PBM-5A activity is inferred from other AARs because there are few surviving operational records. On 11 January 1952 BuNo 122608, assigned to FASRON-108 at the U.S. Naval Academy, suffered minor damage during landing practice at the Naval Air Station, Coco Solo, Panama Canal Zone. On 1 February 1952 BuNo 122074, assigned to Utility Squadron 10 (VU-10), water-looped at the naval station at Guantánamo Bay, Cuba. It then caught fire and burned.

Known to thousands of midshipmen of the era, the PBM-5A was used at the U.S. Naval Academy for aviation indoctrination. Many future navy pilots received their first exposure to naval aviation with a flight in the lumbering Mariner. Some PBM-5A aircraft were permanently based at the academy; others were brought in from other bases during the summer training season.

By 1954 the PBM-5As were beginning to be declared surplus. They were being replaced by the new and more economical Grumman UF-1 Albatross amphibian. In 1955 seventeen surplus PBM-5As were purchased by the Dutch navy. They were completely overhauled and refitted as patrol bombers for service in Netherlands New Guinea.

Another surplus aircraft, BuNo 122071, was purchased on 11 July 1958 for $2,251.02 by Frontier Flying Service of Visalia, California. After passing through a number of owners, it was acquired in 1972 by the National Air and Space Museum and subsequently placed on loan to the Pima Air and Space Museum in Tucson, Arizona. In 2001 the Mariner/Marlin Association finished restoration of the aircraft. It is currently the only example on display, out of a total of 1,367 Mariner flying boats and amphibians produced.

CHAPTER FIVE

THE MARINER IN THE KOREAN WAR AND AFTERWARDS

Pre-Korea Mariner Squadrons

In June 1950 only six Mariner squadrons of nine planes each remained in service. The Pacific squadrons—VP-42, VP-46, and VP-47—were based at San Diego. The Atlantic squadrons—VP-34, VP-45, and VP-49—were based at Norfolk. Most of the Mariners in service were the PBM-5S version that had been especially configured for antisubmarine warfare (ASW) with the installation of sonobuoy equipment, electronic countermeasures (ECMs), a magnetic anomaly detector (MAD), radar bombing gear, and a searchlight. The top deck turret was removed, but the bow and tail turrets and single .50-caliber machine guns at each waist station were retained. ASW armament included 500-pound

The final Mariner configuration, designated PBM-5S2, 1952. This version was optimized for anti-submarine warfare. Note the new AN/APS-31 radar in a teardrop radome. *U.S. Navy*

bombs, depth charges, and the Mark 24 homing torpedo. Later, the squadron allowance was increased to twelve aircraft. The final Mariner modification, the PBM-5S2, came into service in 1951. The PBM-5S2 had APS-31 radar in a teardrop radome, which gave the aircraft a more pleasing appearance. The PBM-5S2 had gone through a weight reduction program. Some armor plate and the MAD and radar bombing equipment had been removed. The capability to carry the Mark 37 hom-

ing torpedo had been added. The primary mission of PBM squadrons by 1950 was surface and subsurface search with a secondary mission of aerial mining.

Pacific Operations

From Routine Deployment to War, 1950

The three Mariner squadrons stationed in the Pacific were supported by the large seaplane tenders *Pine Island* (AV-12), *Salisbury*

Sound (AV-3), and *Curtis* (AV-4) and the small tenders *Gardiners Bay* (AVP-9), *Floyds Bay* (AVP-40), and *Suisun* (AVP-53).

In January 1950 VP-47 began a routine six-month deployment to Saipan with detachments at Yokosuka, Japan, and Sangley Point in the Philippines. The squadron conducted ASW exercises with British naval forces in March and with VP-28 in Japanese waters in April.

When the Korean War broke out on 27 June 1950, VP-47 aircraft, having completed their routine deployment, were strung across the Pacific en route back to the United States. Homebound aircraft were held up at Pearl Harbor, Guam, and Sangley Point and sent back to Yokosuka to begin operations in the forward combat areas in Korea. By 7 July the squadron was reunited and relocated to Iwakuni, Japan, with support from *Curtiss*. Advance bases at Inchon and Chinhae, Korea, were supported by *Gardiners Bay*. One of the squadron's first tasks, starting 15 July, was antisubmarine coverage of the convoy carrying the U.S. Army's 1st Cavalry Division from Japan to Korea. By 31 July the squadron began combat patrols of the Tsushima Strait, mine reconnaissance around Inchon and Wonsan, and antisurface patrol (ASP) over the Sasebo to Pusan shipping lanes.

The strategic situation in the Far East developed into two major parts: the Korean War "police action" and the confrontation between Red China and Taiwan. In addition to its participation in the Korean conflict, the United States established a Formosa Straits patrol to provide early warning of any Red Chinese attempt to invade Formosa. The Mariner–seaplane tender team was ideally suited for this mission.

On 15 June 1950 VP-46 had begun its routine deployment to replace VP-47. On 31 July the squadron instead was tasked to establish the Formosa Straits patrol. Initially this was with combat aerial patrols of the China Coast and Formosa Straits flying from the Pescadores Islands based on board *Suisun*. Later the squadron was redeployed to Sangley Point with a detachment on board *Salisbury Sound* at Buckner Bay, Okinawa. VP-46 was tasked to conduct twenty-four-hour reconnaissance of the China Coast from south of Swatow north to the Saddle Islands. On 5 November BuNo 84769 was declared missing when it disappeared on a patrol from Sangley Point to Buckner Bay. The entire crew of twelve men was lost.

VP-42 departed San Diego on 14 July 1950 for Iwakuni to augment VP-47 in the Japan/Korea area. Upon arrival on 21 June, the squadron was transferred to Yokosuka to conduct twenty-four-hour antisubmarine patrols of the shipping lanes between Japan and Korea. At the end of August VP-42 was assigned back to Iwakuni. From Iwakuni the squadron patrolled the Korean coastline and conducted searches for mines near the shipping lanes.

Malcolm Cagle and Frank Manson, the authors of *The Sea War in Korea,* state,

One of the most unusual tasks performed by the patrol squadrons during the Korean War was the spotting and destruction of mines. This task commenced in late September 1950 and became increasingly important. After the amphibious assault at Inchon, two PBM aircraft from VP-42 were flown to Inchon harbor and tendered there by the USS *Gardiners Bay.* Their task was to fly low over the approaches to Inchon and Chinnampo, and to spot the anchored mines for the surface sweepers.

The two VP-42 aircraft arrived at Inchon on 2 October and commenced mine search operations the next day. Many minefields were located and reported, as well as numerous drifting and floating mines. A number of these were sunk or destroyed by gunfire by the PBMs. This initial operation was successful because low tide left the mines exposed or "watching."

In anticipation of the amphibious landing at Wonsan, VP-42 changed its operating [location] to Wonsan in early October, joining with the aircraft of VP-47 in the search for mines. In this task, the Mariners teamed with helicopters and

surface ships to clear a path through the minefields for the amphibious forces. During this period, VP-42 was credited with the destruction of eight mines.

Mine hunting was hazardous. In Capt. Albert Raithel et al.'s *Mariner/Marlin,* R. Orton Rudd, a pilot in VP-42 during this deployment, described some mine hunting operations:

We flew most of our missions from Iwakuni where we were supported by shore facilities augmented by seaplane tenders. Our crew flew PBM side number SA-5. In October 1950 we were sent to operate with the small seaplane tender, *Gardiners Bay* (AVP-37), which was anchored in Inchon harbor. Our mission was to search for and attempt to destroy anti-shipping mines deployed by the North Koreans.

The most successful hunting ground for finding "floaters" (those mines which had broken loose from their moorings or had been purposely released to float into detonation range with an Allied ship) was in the tidal line. With tides up to 33 feet off the west coast of Korea, the tidal line was sharply described. Most of the mines found off the Korean west coast were of the Russian Mark V type with 550 lbs of explosive. When these detonated, the flume from the explosion would extend up to about 500 feet.

Our crew was the first to blow-up a mine from a fixed-wing aircraft. We received a "Letter of Commendation" from Commander Fleet Air, Japan, for mines destroyed on October 6, 7 and 8, 1950.

The first time we located a floating mine, we requested and were given permission to "attempt to destroy" by Task Force Ninety Five (TF-95), the area commander. We approached the mine and commenced firing our 50 caliber machine guns from about 500 feet altitude using in sequence the bow turret, deck turret, waist guns and tail turret. We had expended almost 2600 rounds (of about 2800 on board) and we were feeling frustrated that nothing had happened. So we kept getting closer to the mine. We were down to under 100 feet altitude and offset from the mine only about 150 feet when the mine finally exploded. The concussion was pretty severe at that range. Over the intercom the tail gunner screamed: "The tail is coming off!" He probably thought it was: the flexible Mariner was wiggling like a worm and flapping like a bird. Needless to say we did not fire from so close a range again.

Crew 5 continued to lead the squadron in mines destroyed so we nick-named our plane "Minnie the Miner" and one of our more artistic crew mem-bers painted our crew emblem on the nose of the PBM.

During the antimining operations, the versatile Mariner also performed naval gunfire spotting. On 12 October 1950, while searching for mines in Wonsan harbor, a VP-47 Mariner flown by Lt. Comdr. Randall Boyd was present when the sweepers *Pirate* (AM-275) and *Pledge* (AM-277) were taken under fire by Wonsan shore batteries. In attempting to dodge the gunfire, *Pirate* struck a mine and sank. Before *Pledge* could move out of range, it suffered the same fate.

Boyd flew over the stricken vessels to give support and to draw the fire of the Wonsan batteries. Air support from the carriers was requested. Meanwhile, the PBM continued to circle the area, attacking blockhouses and trenches as well as directing the gunfire of *Endicott* (DMS-35). The enemy's surface batteries were effectively silenced.

Three U.S. Naval Reserve squadrons were activated in 1950 and equipped with Mariners: VP-892 (Seattle, Washington) in August; VP-661 (Anacostia in Washington, D.C.), and VP-731 (Grosse Ile, Michigan) in September. VP-661 was assigned to the Atlantic Fleet. The complement of all Mariner squadrons was also increased from nine planes to twelve. VP-892 arrived in Iwakuni in December and flew its first mission on 18 December 1950.

Gearing Up and Continuing Patrols, 1951

In January 1951 two more new Mariner squadrons were established: VP-40 in the Pacific and VP-44 in the Atlantic. *Curtiss* was withdrawn from seaplane tending duties and began conversion to be a base for scientific work, including atomic testing.

The six Mariner squadrons now stationed in the Pacific were tasked to maintain a two-squadron presence in the Far East. One squadron was based at Sangley Point under Fleet Air Wing 1 with tender-based detachments in Okinawa and the Pescadores to cover the Formosa Straits. The other squadron was based at Iwakuni, Japan, under Fleet Air Wing 6 to cover the Korea/Japan theater. The Mariners were joined at Iwakuni by a detachment of Royal Air Force *Sunderlands* of the Far East Flying Boat Wing. The squadrons were rotated back and forth from the United States in a systematic fashion. Additional seaplane tenders were also added to the fleet in 1951. The small tender *Corson* (AVP-37) was recommissioned in February, the large tender *Kenneth Whiting* (AV-14) in October, and the small tender *Orca* (AVP-49) in December.

Mariners suffered tragic losses due to operational accidents during 1951. On 11 January a VP-46 aircraft (BuNo 84662)

water-looped while attempting to land at Amani O Shima, resulting in the loss of seven men. On 22 April VP-892's BuNo 84663, flying out of Iwakuni, lost an engine and had to ditch at sea with the loss of five men. On 14 June VP-731's BuNo 85148 crashed into Manila Bay on landing. Three men were lost.

VP-40, which had been established in January, was deployed to Iwakuni and flew its first missions in June. On 19 June BuNo 84691 hit a mountain on Okurokami Shima with the loss of the crew of twelve. VP-46's BuNo 84622 crashed on landing at Iwakuni on 25 November. Four were lost. A VP-47 aircraft (BuNo 84682) crashed on takeoff from Hong Kong on 31 December. Four were lost.

After the Wonson invasion, Mariner operations in the Pacific became fairly routine. Although the official missions of Mariner squadrons in the Far East during the Korean conflict were all-weather antisubmarine operations and aerial minelaying, surveillance of surface ship activity along the coastlines became the principal focus of their patrols.

Korean War patrols were long, generally nine to thirteen hours, and there was enough work aboard to keep the crew busy. The three, and sometimes four, pilots spent long hours on the flight deck. They appreciated the roomy Mariner. They were able to stretch their legs because they could stand

and walk erect throughout much of the aircraft. All crew officers were pilots. The most junior officers spent most of their time at the navigation table. Generally two radiomen shared the radio circuit and two electronic technicians operated the radar and ECM equipment. Three aviation mechanics divided the duty of manning the flight engineer's panel, which required considerable attention to the monitoring of engine performance, as well as watching the aircraft's fuel consumption and electrical and mechanical systems. One of two ordnance men usually did the cooking, and they were often accused of using gun oil for cooking eggs. Mariner patrols often required that unprepared flight rations for three full meals be carried. With only a two-burner electric stove, much time was spent preparing the food to feed the normal crew of twelve. Often a photographer's mate would be along to operate the K-16 or K-25 aerial camera. Anyone not on duty was free to nap in one of the four bunks.

Enemy naval units were seldom encountered, but many commercial vessels were. Because the vessels were often headed to or from Red China, they received close attention. An identification process, termed "rigging," was used to record the type of vessel. The name, nationality, deck cargo, shapes of the bow and stern, and the sequence of masts, funnels, and kingposts were logged. The vessel's course, speed, and position were recorded. Many merchant ships were identified as British. They were obviously trading with mainland China at the same time British troops were fighting Chinese forces in Korea.

Another Mariner patrol activity was passive (listening) electronic countermeasures (ECMs). Enemy electronic emissions were monitored to gain intelligence about capabilities, equipment, and locations. Radarscope photographs were taken of Chinese and Korean installations as well as cities in case they were needed for possible future attack by carrier aircraft.

Many patrols were flown at night. In the Korean theater, Mariners would fly a night antisubmarine (ASW) patrol around the carriers off the east coast and also fly north to collect weather data needed for the carriers so they could plan the next day's strikes. Mariners would also fly ASW cover for British carriers operating off the Korean west coast. In the Formosa Straits, night patrols kept watch for possible armadas of small ships that might indicate an invasion of Formosa (Taiwan). The night patrols in the straits were particularly grueling. External navigation aids were almost nonexistent, and onboard equipment was limited to loran and manually plotted radar. The patrols were flown at low altitude to enable searchlight identification of surface traffic. Autopilot "altitude hold" was an unknown concept in the early 1950s and the barometric altimeter was not precise enough for flight below one thousand feet. Fortunately, the Mariner was equipped with the accurate and reliable APN-1 radar altimeter. It was able to safely descend to as low as two hundred feet for searchlight runs. Searchlight runs were sometimes exciting. I remember illuminating a target that turned out to be a British cruiser; its antiaircraft guns were calmly tracking my lumbering Mariner! Numerous rock pinnacles rose from the ocean along the Chinese coast. They presented a radar target that was similar to that of a large ship. Because some pinnacles rose to four hundred feet, it was vitally prudent to offset from the target when making a searchlight run at two hundred feet!

Attacks and Disasters, 1952

The routine nature of patrols was broken on 11 May 1952 when a VP-42 Mariner (BuNo 85155), flown by Ens. Hugh Marlin, was attacked by Red Chinese MiG-15s over the Yellow Sea near the Korean Coast. Although the Mariner was hit several times by cannon fire, there were no injuries to any members of crew 3. The aircraft returned to base safely.

In his "VP-42 MiG Attack" article, crewman Frank J. Nelson recalled:

We were heading back to Base at 8000 feet when we were jumped by a flight of two MiGs. Our position was well off shore and we were surprised when they fired on us. Mr. Marlin later wrote to me "I went up to climb power and pushed over into a dive with a view to reach 200 feet as soon as possible." He also said that he reached the airframe red line just before leveling off. We might have taken a hit on the first pass but the major damage happened on our way down to the deck. Ed Handley was in the bow turret and he said that the tracers were going past him down into the water. All of the attacks came in from the tail with the MiGs breaking sharply away to either side before the bow or waist could get a shot at them. Joe Young in the tail returned most of the fire. He shot off most of the ammo in the tail and ended up warping one of the barrels. I stuck my head out of the hatch to see if I could spot where they were coming from and I could see the brass from the tail in the slipstream but no MiGs.

When we got down on the deck, Mr. Marlin took evasive action and they didn't hit us again. On the last pass I got off one short burst at one as he broke away but he was gone in a flash.

The MiGs broke off the attacks with no apparent damage but I wouldn't be surprised that with the amount of lead Joe Young threw at them that they brought a few holes home with them.

Two British Sea Furies answered our Mayday but the MiGs were long gone. They stayed with us for a while and were able to give our PPC damage estimates.

There were hits in the wing and starboard engine and a big hole in our rear end. That shell hit us dead on the sternpost and we later measured the hole at 12″ wide and we assumed it was a 37mm hit. Crew-6 (Bless them) kept a plywood equipment box in the after station between the waist hatches and it stopped the shrapnel from coming up into the waist. We stuffed a mattress into the hole for our landing. We also found a neat round shell hole in the starboard spoiler board that left a 3 foot crease along the hull before glancing off. The hit on the starboard engine came the closest to doing us in. It was probably a 23mm round and it went into the cowling, hit the engine mount and barely missed the main oil line.

I think it was truly remarkable and a tribute to Hugh Marlin's flying ability that we were able to return to base safely without any injuries to the crew.

Crew 3 was back on the line in their own aircraft within days.

On 31 July 1952 a VP-731 PBM-5S (BuNo 59277), flown by Lt. E. E. Bartlett, was attacked by two Chinese MiG-15 fighters while on a reconnaissance mission over the Yellow Sea. Two crewmen were killed in the attack: Aviation Machinist's Mate Harlan G. Goodroad, the tail gunner, and Airman Apprentice Claude Playforth. Aviation Ordnanceman 3rd Class R. H. Smith and Airman Apprentice H. T. Atkins were seriously wounded. Bartlett was able to escape the MiGs and landed his damaged aircraft at Paengnyong-do, South Korea. After temporary repairs, he flew the Mariner back to Iwakuni.

VP-892 had deployed to Sangley Point in March 1952. The squadron performed Formosa Straits patrols from the Pescadores and were supported by small tenders *Corson* (AVP-37) and *Floyds Bay.* The squadron suffered the loss of two aircraft in widely separated accidents in August.

On 7 August BuNo 84774 departed Sangley for a daylight China Sea patrol. Being the typhoon season, Sangley Point was beset by high winds and low clouds. About an hour after takeoff the aircraft suffered engine failure due to a propeller malfunction. Unable to maintain a safe altitude, and with the heavy precipitation interfering with the aircraft radar, return to Manila Bay was attempted in instrument conditions with no navigational aids except the low-frequency Manila radio range. The aircraft hit Santa Rosa Mountain on the Bataan Peninsula. Thirteen men were lost.

Early in the morning of 8 August aircraft SE-2 (BuNo 84782) took off from

Iwakuni, Japan, in darkness. It was vectored into a mountain by radar ground control. Investigation revealed that a U.S. Air Force ground controller, unfamiliar with the extremely slow climb performance of a loaded Mariner, had assumed SE-2 had reached an altitude to clear the hills. Fourteen men were lost in the two disasters.

In November 1952 VP-47 began its third deployment to the Korean theater. It was based at Iwakuni, supported by *Kenneth Whiting* and *Gardiners Bay*. A detachment was maintained at Fukuoka, Japan, supported by *Corson*. BuNo 84787, on patrol off the coast of Korea, experienced an engine failure on 26 December. The aircraft ditched and exploded, with the loss of ten men.

From Korea to the Cold War, 1953

The former U.S. Naval Reserve squadrons were given new, regular Navy designations to reflect their permanence in the fleet for the cold war era on 4 February 1953. VP-731 was redesignated VP-48, VP-892 redesignated VP-50, and VP-661 redesignated VP-56. The phaseout of the Mariner in the Pacific began in April, when VP-40 began conversion training for the new P5M Marlin.

As the cold war heated up, Mariner Pacific deployments were expanded to include Alaska. VP-42 was deployed to Kodiak from July to November. They also operated two planes from a tender at Port Clarence, north of Nome, for the one ice-free month. BuNo 85158 was lost at sea on 2 July. It was forced to ditch in the Alaskan fog after an in-flight fire.

A Mariner was on patrol when the Korean armistice was signed on 27 July 1953. The contribution of the Mariner was well summarized in Cagle and Manson's *The Sea War in Korea:*

Of the three elements of naval aviation in Korea——carrier, Marine aviation, and patrol——the patrol squadrons had the most routine operations. This does not mean that their operations were without contribution or significance to the war effort. Patrol squadrons increased the effectiveness of the blockade by their reconnaissance flights, the search for and the destruction of mines, and the surveillance of enemy fishing activity. Patrol squadrons furnished up-to-date weather information for the carrier forces which was always helpful and frequently vital. . . . They obtained reconnaissance of the coastal areas of Korea, and kept surveillance over merchant shipping in the immediate area of Korea. The seaplane squadrons provided certain logistic and transport functions which could not be supplied by landplane types. The mere presence of highly trained, antisubmarine squadrons in the Korean area discouraged the use of submarines by the enemy. Lastly the patrol squadrons minimized the danger of any invasion of Formosa by the Communists.

The Korean armistice did not reduce Mariner activity. Emphasis for the Japan-based aircraft shifted from carrier task force protection and weather reconnaissance to shipping surveillance and passive electronic monitoring. The Formosa Straits patrols continued.

The escalating cold war involved VP-50 in a series of attacks by Red Chinese MiG-15 jet fighters in October and November 1953. Members of the Mariner/Marlin Association, a crewman from each of three incidents provide first-hand accounts of the attacks. In Raithel et al.'s *Mariner/Marlin,* Dave Rinehart recalled:

> During the early morning of October 2, 1953, a PBM of VP-50 departed the seadrome at Iwakuni, Japan, for a Fox Red Patrol. This patrol track took the air-craft westward across the southern por-tion of Honshu Island, south of the Korean Peninsula, and on a direct line toward Shanghai, China.
>
> The PBM was "9-boat," officially SE-9 [BuNo 84713], but the crew was mixed. Crew 3 had been assigned this

patrol, but was shorthanded so the buoy watch already on the plane was pressed into service. Ray Cook, Charley Fix, and I were that buoy watch. We were in the wrong place at the wrong time.

Until 1200 hours, the patrol was as all others before. Flying along the Red Chinese coastline, picking up surface ves-sels on radar and intercepting them for identification purposes. We were about 30 miles east of Tsingtao and had just made several low passes on a British freighter that was inbound. We were climbing back to our patrol altitude of 1000' when I heard what sounded like metal being ripped from the top of the flight deck. I looked at the copilot, Ens. Paul Rutan, and he was looking back over his right shoulder and his lower lip started to trem-ble. Instantly, I knew what was happening. We were being fired upon.

Although we had machine gun ammo aboard, the guns were not loaded nor the bow or tail turrets manned. ADAN [Airman (Aviation Machinist's Mate)] Billy McGill had just been relieved at the flight panel, as I had on the radar. Bill also knew what was happening and I was right behind him as we started aft. We hollered at those men in the bunks and aft as to what was happening. Bill ran all the way to the tail turret. I stopped in the after station to man one of the two .50-caliber machine guns there. I opened the port waist hatch and immediately saw a pattern of shell fire strike the water just abaft of us, the shells making splashes considerable more than did our own .50s. This was immediately followed by the shooter, a silver-colored MiG-15, streak by the port side of our plane and it opened out to turn for another firing pass. I swung the machine gun up and out, secured it to the hatch sill, attached the chute for the ammo belt and began feeding the ammo down to the gun. I charged it, pulled the trigger, but it would not fire. The third man to come back was Charley Fix, AO3 [Aviation Ordnanceman 3rd Class], who was loading the starboard gun. I hollered at him, "Charley, this gun won't fire, trade places with me." I then continued loading the starboard gun. The 4th man to immediately appear in the after station was Ray Cook. We told him to go back to the tunnel to run the ammo belts from the boxes back to the tail turret so Bill could return fire. Bill was in the turret with nothing to do but the important duty of telling the PPC [patrol plane commander], Lt. [M. N.] "Moe" Hansen, which side a MiG was attacking from so Moe could make steep banking turns into him, foiling his firing pass. We believed there were two MiGs attacking us.

At this point, the rigorous training that Mariner crews received probably enabled the crew to continue functioning during the combat. Rinehart's account continues:

For those of us in the after station, this maneuvering meant alternately looking straight down at the water, perhaps 100 feet away, or straight up at the sky. We never had time to get the safety belts on us.

Charley and I never did find the "sight leads" that supplied power to the electric sights for the waist .50s. That did not deter me from just pointing the gun at a MiG just as he was beginning a pass and squeezing off 20 rounds or so. The MiG immediately swerved up upon seeing my gun flashes and apparently left the area with his cohort.

The bow turret was manned by AO3 Scoville from the start of the affair and its guns were loaded immediately. I don't believe Scoville ever got a chance for a shot since the MiGs did not make any bow-on passes. The tail turret never fired a shot since loading was not complete before the MiGs broke off.

We had been hit twice by 37-mm cannon shells. The MiG-15s carried two 23-mm cannon (they made the large pattern of splashes I saw) and one 37-mm cannon. One 37-mm round penetrated the port wing beavertail just aft of the bomb bay. It did not explode, but left a perfect hole about one and one-half inches in diameter going completely through the wing. The other 37-mm round exploded in the starboard fin, tore a hole perhaps 8 inches in diameter and shrapnel from this made another 200 holes in the horizontal stabilizer and tunnel areas of the plane.

Several firing passes were made by these jets and it's incredible that they could not knock us down. I believed that they would and I recall thinking I would end up in a raft in the Yellow Sea, with $110 cash in my pocket that I was unable to send home. Our PPC, Lt. Hansen, was quoted as thinking, "I'll be captured and paraded through the streets of Shanghai in a bamboo basket!"

Fortunately, no one was hurt and the aircraft made it back to Iwakuni. I think we did very well considering we were unaware of the MiG's presence until they fired and that we got away without injuries. Most of the credit must go to Mr. Hansen whose air combat maneuvering saved our bacon. It's interesting that the navy never publicized this attack but thirteen of us were there and we have pictures!

Hansen thought that Airman McGill, for his calling of the MiG firing passes, should receive special recognition. The squadron recommended him for an Air Medal, but Fleet Air Wing 1 disagreed.

Lt. Richard (Dick) I. Erb, also of VP-50, was the patrol plane commander during the second MiG attack. He vividly describes the events of 6 November 1953 in his "Attack by Chinese MiG-15" article:

I was scheduled to take my Patrol Plane Commander check ride on 6 November and it would be a Fox Blue Patrol. Lt. R[obert] D. Robbins, our operations officer would be the check pilot, and our aircraft would be SE-2 (BuNo 84747).

Fox Blue was a patrol that departed Iwakuni and proceeded westbound to the point where the Shimonoseki Straits entered the Inland Sea. Crossing the Sea of Japan we would fly south of Korea to the Yellow Sea, then north along the west coast of Korea to Dandong at the border of Korea and China. Turning southbound at that point we would follow the Chinese coast past Tsingtao on to Shanghai and then return to Japan via the Shimonoseki Straits.

Flight departure was 0600. At our 0400 preflight intelligence briefing, our squadron intelligence officer said we would be looking for a Soviet V-beam search radar that had been installed, during the war, on an island north of the 38th parallel. It had been used to monitor F-86 flights as they departed U.S. bases. It would then vector MIGS to intercept.

We took off at exactly 0600, using four JATO units because of our heavy weight. After the empty JATO cylinders were jettisoned and all stations reporting normal we climbed to five thousand feet and started down the prescribed track over the Shomonoseki Straits. The flight went as planned with the only action being the identification and photographing of three freighters northbound to the Port of Darien, Manchuria.

As we passed abeam Dandon at the border of Korea and China we turned south to explore the China coast. At that point I had all the guns test fired and followed the contour of the Chinese coast about fifteen miles off shore at one thousand feet.

Erb's description thus far typifies normal patrols. Usually, most patrols return to base without incident. However, the situation changed for BuNo 84747. Erb continues:

As we approached the Shantung Peninsula my electronic counter measures technician informed me he had picked up the signal from the V-band radar we had been briefed on. Frequency, PRF [pulse repetition rate], and power were exactly as briefed. With the old equipment we had, the only way to get a line of position (LOP) was to home directly toward the transmission.

We did this, took a reading and then turned right angle to that heading and proceeded to a point I considered to be 30 degrees from the previous LOP and then turned inbound to get another LOP. I repeated this one more time. We now had three lines that intersected on the island of Lingshan Dao 15 miles east of Tsingtao.

The V-band radar had been sector scanning us for some time, so I told Robbie, "Let's get out of here" and cautioned the crew to keep a sharp lookout for aircraft as I made a descending turn to exit the area.

Just as I did this the tail gunner reported aircraft approaching and as I looked to port I observed tracers first going over the wing and then under the wing. They seemed to be just floating by and as they hit the water they would splash and ricochet.

At this point I saw a MIG-15 pass by so close I could see the pilot's face in the cockpit as he turned to look at us. There were no markings on the aircraft except a red ring around the nose.

I continued the descent to about 100 feet. If there was one MIG there could very well be several and I was beginning to think that we were in serious trouble. The MIG-15 had one 37-mm cannon and two 23-mm cannon.

The waist hatches were open and guns deployed and I instructed the gunners to fire at any target within range. Tail gunner had tracked the MIG that fired on us to a point aft and high on the port side. As he commenced the next run I cranked the aircraft into a 60 [degree] port turn. My altitude was about 100 feet and as I looked up I could see tracers going over the top of us but the MIG couldn't pull through to get the proper lead.

As he passed us I turned back to an outbound heading. The same aircraft made three other passes at us and the tactic of turning into him produced the same result except that on the last pass he pressed too hard and actually went below my 100 foot altitude.

I was sure he was going into the water and the turret gunner had a perfect shot at him but he missed. With the throttle bent over the stops we exited the area and I called for a damage report. Rough air, our guns firing, and the scent of cordite in the air made me think we had taken some hits. When the report came back, no damage, I was almost disappointed. No battle scars!

When we reported the attack to Commander Naval Forces Far East, the reply came back: "Continue patrol." We landed at Iwakuni and made the buoy 10.2 hours after takeoff. Of course, Lieutenant Robbins gave me an "up" on my Patrol Plane Commander check!

Lt. (j.g.) Virgil J. Hoffman was on board the third VP-50 aircraft that was attacked by Chinese MiG fighters. In a 2001 letter to Dick Erb he recalled:

On November 18, 1953, while on Fox Green Patrol we were jumped by two MiGs.

Events leading up to the incident as best as I can recall were something like this: Fox Green Patrol was a daylight patrol. Our aircraft was a PBM-5S2 BuNo 84747 SE-2 assigned to Patrol Squadron 50. Pilots were Lt. Hank Shotola, Lt. (j.g.) Bill Easton, Ens. John Ireland, and myself. Departing from Iwakuni our track was to Fukuoka, north of Cheju Island, and then on a direct course toward Shanghai, north in the Yellow Sea, then over to the west coast of Korea and south returning back to Iwakuni. Things were normal as we headed in a direction southwesterly from North of Cheju Island. Very strong northeasterly winds of about 35–40 knots were observed.

We were flying at a low altitude to avoid any radar detection by the Chinese. Only occasionally would the radar be turned on and only then to pick up any targets for navigation. As can be expected with the strong northeasterly wind, we were rapidly advancing along the track. On the final "power on" of the radar we had contact with the islands just off the coast of Shanghai. Much earlier and closer than we had planned. I was flying in the left seat and we did a one-eighty and headed for the deck, all hands were ordered to man their battle stations. No more than about 10 minutes had passed when the tall gunner reported that he had two targets at six o'clock advancing rapidly. Lt. Shotola requested the tail gunner give us an alert when the MiGs started to make a run on us. When they did we made a turn to meet them head on and give the bow gunner the better shot at them. We were at a low enough altitude to keep them from flying below us. On the third firing run by the MiGs a smoke stream was noted coming from one of the MiGs. They were last observed flying formation above and about a mile off the port side. They never made another run. By this time we had the protection of a cloud cover and broke off the patrol to return to base. During an inspection of the aircraft after returning to Iwakuni, no holes or other damage was found.

The success of the lumbering Mariner in escaping destruction by modern jet fighters was due in a large part to the training and skill of the pilots. Mariner crews used the effective tactic of flying as close as possible to the surface of the ocean and making sharp turns into the attacker.

VP-50 may have escaped the MiGs, but the squadron did not escape tragedy on this deployment. On 10 November 1953

Lt. Paul Nielson with crew 11 departed Iwakuni in BuNo 85152 on a Fox Green Patrol. The merchant vessel SS *Swordknot* reported seeing "dense fire and smoke" in the vicinity of Cheju Island. *Swordknot* proceeded to the scene and recovered two wing floats and other debris. Although a malfunctioning cabin heater was suspected, no cause for the accident could be determined. Fourteen men were lost.

VP-50 was relieved by VP-47 in December. During 1953 replacement of the Mariner by the new P5M Marlin was completed in three Pacific squadrons: VP-40 in April, VP-46 in September, and VP-42 in November.

Although the primary Mariner activity in the Korean War was naval air patrol or reconnaissance, Mariner crews performed many varied tasks: destruction of floating mines, antisubmarine screening for carriers, strategic shipping observation, passive electronic intelligence gathering, weather observation, invasion early warning in the Formosa Straits, and logistic, mail, and passenger flights. Mariners were equipped to lay mines in enemy harbors and shipping lanes if necessary. Although Mariners were attacked five times by Red Chinese MiG jet fighters, the only direct combat casualties were the two VP-731 crewmen lost on 31 July 1952. However, operational casualties due to weather or equipment problems were heavy. Fifteen aircraft and 132 lives were lost during the Korean War era.

Pacific Deployments, 1954–1955

The remaining two Pacific Mariner squadrons, VP-47 and VP-50, continued their Far East deployments in 1954. VP-47 suffered a loss on 9 June. BuNo 84779 was en route from Iwakuni to Hong Kong on a rest and recreation (R&R) flight when it hit a mountain on Yaku Shima Island with the loss of seventeen men. This was the last Mariner casualty crash in the Pacific theater.

On 17 September 1954 a VP-50 aircraft was near the end of a Tsushima Straits patrol when a fire in the port engine caused the aircraft to be ditched at sea. Fortunately there were no casualties and the story of the incident is truly a flying boat saga. In "PBM Ditching," Al "Shippy" Schipporeit tells the tale:

> At 0900 PBM-5S2 BuNo 85141 (SE-7) of VP-50 stationed at Iwakuni, Japan flown by Lt. Cmdr. Wardall and Lt. (j.g.) Easton as copilot departed on a routine patrol of the body of water between Japan and Korea called the Tsushima Strait. At approximately four hours into the patrol, a crewmember in the after station called to the plane commander that the port engine was trailing vapor and or smoke. The sighting was confirmed and

the flight engineer opened the hatch on the fuselage that gave access to the wing in order to observe the engine to determine the source of the smoke. He concluded that there was an oil leak and when the drops of oil came in contact with the hotter parts of the engine it created the smoke that we were seeing. It was also concluded that the rate at which the oil dripping there would be no danger of consuming the 15 gallons of oil carried in reserve before the mission was completed.

> At about 1630 the patrol was completed and all seemed well, the port engine was operating normally and the volume of smoke coming from it had not changed noticeably. At 2500 feet, while climbing to 7000 feet in accordance with ATC [air traffic control] clearance there a sudden, relatively severe shaking of the aircraft followed immediately by severe and continuous buffeting of the control column. It was observed that [the] port engine was burning with heavy flames coming from the cowl flap area. Plane Commander Wardall immediately applied full power and full low pitch to both engines, activated the CO2 [carbon dioxide] purging system, actuated the feathering switch, placed the IFF on emergency, cut the mag [magneto] to the port engine and called for the flight engineer to secure it.

When the oil on the engine ignited, the entire plane filled with dense, black, choking and eye watering smoke. In the darkness the first instinct was make way to the nearest hatch and hit the silk but within 2 minutes the fire burned itself out and the smoke vented itself out through the two open cargo doors in the aft section of the plane. It was a relief that the plane was still intact and continuing to fly. The port engine was stopped and feathered but a considerable area of the cowling and bomb bay doors were burned away.

The aircraft controls continued to buffet severely and the maximum power that could be obtained from starboard engine was 52" of manifold pressure and only 1600 RPM [revolutions per minute]. The pilot could not maintain single engine flight and we were losing altitude. The crew managed to jettison approximately 1000 pounds of gear before the call came on the intercom for all hands to prepare for ditching.

At the time the oil on the engine ignited we were out 15 miles SW [southwest] of Mi-Shima Island and seven minutes later the actual ditching was made about 3 miles off shore. Final landing was achieved after three bounces, each successively more severe. The crew was checked and found to have suffered no injuries, the aircraft was inspected for watertight integrity and found to be completely intact. The port engine had drooped downward at about 25–30 degrees and inboard such that one [propeller] blade had pierced the hull.

Schipporeit next describes the rescue operations.

Within 15 minutes a plane arrived over the scene, we were able to establish communications with the pilot and ask him to relay to Fukuoka Control and VP-50 that we had effected a safe open sea landing.

Several Japanese fishing boats approached the aircraft to offer assistance but they were waved away. With the approaching darkness we were concerned about other vessels running into us since we had no running lights or power for further communications because of a now dead electrical system. A watch schedule was organized, two crew members at a time would go on top of the aircraft to watch for approaching ships and hope that the two flashlights on board would be sufficient to get their attention and warn them of our presence. Several other crew members took inventory of the supplies in the galley carried for just such an emergency. They came up with one loaf of bread, peanut butter, jelly, several cans of pork and beans and some canned fruit. Many of the crewmembers climbed out on top of the plane to get away from the smokey interior to enjoy their dinner, the cool air and the setting sun.

At approximately 1930, a crashboat from Ashiya Air Force Base arrived on the scene to stand by until a sea plane tender the USS *Grapple* could arrive sometime later in the night. The beginning effects of an approaching typhoon was causing the sea to get rougher by the hour and a decision was made to tow the plane to the nearest Japanese mainland and the safety of a bay or cove some 30 miles away. While members of the crew changed off tending to the duties of the towing procedure, others opened their now useless parachutes and tried to get some sleep.

The pace was slow and tedious, the match up between the crash boat and a 25 ton aircraft was not the best but any faster speed in this sea condition would cause the plane to sway wildly. At 0645 we reached land, a safe haven and another day.

The story was not yet over. Schipporeit continued:

The plane was anchored and with the coming of daylight a [U.S.] Coast Guard plane located us and relayed the information to the USS *Grapple*. They had reached our crash location but could not find us so they chose to shut down, wait for daylight and hopefully a new fix on our whereabouts. It was a welcome sight to see the ship come over the horizon and stop just outside of the cove. The ship's crew lowered a boat over the side to come in and pick us up from the plane. The time was 1400 hours and after having been on the plane now for 30 hours we were tired and hungry. The ship's galley crew had prepared a banquet and a pack of cigarettes was placed at each setting and did we ever enjoy.

After the meal the authorities determined that because of the rough seas the ship could do nothing further for the welfare of the plane, it would have to seek safety from the storm for itself so we headed for Ashiya, leaving the plane behind and hopefully sufficiently anchored to weather the storm.

Later that evening the USS *Grapple* docked at Ashiya and the PBM crew was met by a bus to transfer us to the Air Base. A C-119 was being serviced to fly us back to Iwakuni while we enjoyed still another meal in the base mess hall. Touch down was made at Iwakuni at 22:30 with one dog-tired crew.

The next day, Iwakuni and the rest of southern Japan braced itself for the storm. The anchors on SE-7 could not hold up against the wind and crushing waves, it slowly drifted up on the beach by the high tide and was completely dashed to pieces. After the storm subsided, a crew was dispatched to remove items and equipment of value from the plane and the remainder was sold to a local salvage company for scrap metal.

VP-48 transitioned to the Marlin in June 1954. VP-47 made the transition in October. VP-50 was now the only remaining Mariner squadron in the Pacific Fleet.

Last U.S. Navy Mariner in the Pacific, 1956

The Mariner presence in the Pacific had begun with the Naval Air Transport Service's PBM-3Rs in 1942. The U.S. Navy's final use of the Mariner in the Pacific was VP-50's deployment from January through June 1956. In June 1956 a Mariner flew its last patrol and VP-50 converted to the Marlin. The saga of the Mariner in the Pacific Fleet was over.

Atlantic Operations

Tom Willli, who flew Mariners in VP-56 and VP-661, provided a fine overview of PBM deployment in the Atlantic Fleet in Raithel et al.'s *Mariner/Marlin*:

> At the end of 1949, there were three PBM squadrons in the Atlantic Fleet. These were VP-34, 45 and 49, and were supported by Fleet Aircraft Service

Squadron (FASRON) 102. All of these squadrons were based at Breezy Point, Norfolk. Each squadron, other than the FASRON, was equipped with nine aircraft of the PBM-5S type, although a few straight "fives" were still in use as spares.

All the major East Coast Air Stations maintained seadromes; overseas seadromes were maintained at Bermuda, Argentia, San Juan and Coco Solo. Naval Station Trinidad had closed in 1948. The only large tender in the Atlantic Fleet was the USS *Currituck* (AV-7). AVPs in service included the USS *Greenwich Bay* (AVP-41), USS *Timbalier* (AVP-54), and USS *Valcour* (AVP-55). The PBM squadrons could set up shop virtually anywhere in the Atlantic Command.

Redeployment and Buildup, 1950–1951

The increasing tensions of the Cold War caused a buildup and redeployment of Atlantic Fleet patrol squadrons. VP-661, a U.S. Naval Reserve squadron, was called to active duty on 15 September 1950 and homeported at Norfolk. VP-34 was relocated from Norfolk to the reopened base at Trinidad, British West Indies, in October.

A new Mariner squadron, VP-44, was established in January 1951. It was based at Norfolk. In April VP-45 was relocated to NAS Coco Solo, Panama Canal Zone. From May through August VP-44 deployed to

Bermuda with detachments at San Juan, Puerto Rico, aboard *Timbalier* (AVP-54) and at NAS Argentia, Newfoundland. In July VP-49 was permanently assigned to Bermuda.

By mid-1951 the Atlantic Mariner squadrons had been deployed to best meet the growing Soviet submarine threat. Based in Norfolk, Bermuda, Trinidad, and the Canal Zone and capable of advanced base operations supported by the recommissioned *Currituck* (AV-7) as well as *Timbalier* (AVP-54) and *Duxbury Bay* (AVP-38), the Mariners concentrated on convoy protection and antisubmarine warfare missions.

Transitions and Operation Mainbrace, 1952

From January through March 1952 VP-44 operated from Cuba supported by *Duxbury Bay*. VP-44 began the transition to the new Marlin in April, the first Atlantic squadron to be so equipped.

In September and October VP-49 and VP-661 participated in Operation Mainbrace, a massive exercise held in the vicinity of Denmark and Norway in which all combined navies of the North Atlantic Treaty Organization (NATO) joined in a hypothetical defense of Western Europe. Units from eight NATO nations and New Zealand participated. The operation included eighty thousand men, one thousand planes, and two hundred ships.

Directed by Britain's Adm. Sir Patrick Brind, Operation Mainbrace was the largest NATO maneuver held up until that time.

From their Norfolk and Bermuda bases, the Mariners flew to Argentia, Newfoundland, for refueling. The aircraft then crossed the North Atlantic to Rejkjavik, Iceland, where they were serviced by *Timbalier* (AVP-54). These were probably the first Mariners to operate from Iceland since VP-74's PBM-1s in 1941.

VP-661's aircraft flew several operational flights from Trondheim, Norway. They were tended by *Currituck* (AV-7). Several aircraft also operated from Lerwick in the Shetland Islands, again tended by *Timbalier*. Aircraft of both squadrons then operated from *Currituck* at Skogn, Norway, where *Currituck* also serviced Royal Air Force Sunderland flying boats of 201 Squadron.

Apparently the exercise went well. Surviving U.S. Navy records relate no unusual incidents relating to the Mariners. Mainbrace is mostly remembered in Mariner lore because of Shetland ponies. In the Shetland Islands, some Mariner crews had become enamored with the smallest of all the ponies. The famous Shetland ponies stand only about forty-two inches high at the withers. Some were purchased for the kids back home. The ponies fit nicely in the after station. The men thought that all the ponies needed was a little hay and

Three VP-45 Mariners being refueled from *Timbalier* (AVP-54), Guantánamo Bay, Cuba, 1953. *U.S. Navy*

water for the day or two flight back to Norfolk. The "Pony Express," however, did not go quite as planned.

The returning Mariners were forced to wait in Rejkjavík for several days awaiting favorable winds. One VP-49 aircraft sank during its taxi as the result of an open tunnel hatch. The difficulties of transporting live animals was apparent by the time the squadron arrived in Norfolk. In Raithel et al.'s *Mariner/Marlin,* VP-661 crewman Paul Legg described Operation Mainbrace events: "The planes that had the ponies ran into trouble with the authorities at Norfolk. The ponies had to be quarantined for weeks at a price until they were cleared. What a mess! To say nothing of the interior of the planes." For years afterwards it was said that a pony-carrying Mariner could be recognized by the smell! In December 1952 VP-49 transitioned to the Marlin.

Atlantic Deployments, 1953–1956

In January 1953 VP-34 employed all twelve of its aircraft in patrol and training flights between Trinidad and Corpus

Christi, Texas. VP-661 was redesignated VP-56 in February and began transition to the Marlin in May. In March VP-34's aircraft were tender-based on *Currituck* at San Juan, Puerto Rico, for the amphibious training exercise PHIBEX II-53. VP-34 lost one aircraft (BuNo 85151) on 22 March when it disappeared during a night search mission.

In May 1953 VP-45 deployed a three-plane detachment to Guantánamo Bay, Cuba, for advanced base tender operations with *Timbalier*. In June VP-34 deployed all twelve of its aircraft for patrol and training flights at NAS Corpus Christi, Texas, in support of the midshipmen's summer training program. During this period VP-45 deployed six planes and crews from Coco Solo to Naval Station (NS) Trinidad to cover the sector. VP-45 made a two-week deployment to the Galápagos in September, tended by *Currituck* in support of the Office of Naval Research's Operation Churchy, tracking "Skyhook" balloons instrumented to conduct cosmic ray research.

VP-45 began to convert to the Marlin in April 1954, reducing Atlantic Fleet's Mariner squadrons to one: VP-34 in Trinidad. In June and July VP-34 and the remaining PBMs of VP-45 participated in Operation Hardrock Baker, an exercise to assess the fleet's capabilities in locating potential weapons-carrying ships destined to support a communist takeover attempt in Guatamala.

In June 1955 VP-34 was relocated from Trinidad to Coco Solo. The U.S. Navy's last Atlantic Mariner casualty occurred on 31 October 1955 when BuNo 59232 suffered an engine failure on takeoff and hit a rock seawall. Eight men were lost.

In June 1956 NS Coco Solo reverted to caretaker status and VP-34 returned to Norfolk for disestablishment. The U.S. Navy's operational history of the Mariner in the Atlantic, which had begun with the 1940 deployment to Iceland, was over.

Final Mariner Activities, 1956–1964

A few Mariners continued serving the U.S. Navy at the flying boat advanced training unit at Corpus Christi until 1958. That same year, the U.S. Coast Guard flew its last Mariner flight from San Diego. Mariners continued in service with the Dutch, Argentine, and Uruguayan navies. The last operational Mariner flight was that of Uruguayan A-811 on 3 February 1964, nearly twenty-five years after the first flight of the XPBM-1 in 1939.

CHAPTER SIX

THE MARINER IN THE COAST GUARD

Coast Guard Ocean Rescue Pioneers

From 1943 until 1958 nearly eighty different Mariners were operated by the U.S. Coast Guard. Although the use of seaplanes for ocean rescue by the coast guard dates back to the 1930s, the Mariner became the best known and most widely used, performing dozens of rescue missions in the postwar years.

The U.S. Coast Guard had been formed in 1915 by combining the U.S. Lifesaving Service with the Revenue Cutter Service. In 1916 an act of Congress established an "aerial coastal patrol" as part of the service and appropriations were made to establish ten coast guard air stations along the Atlantic and Pacific coasts, the Gulf of Mexico, and the Great Lakes. In

U.S. Coast Guard PBM-5G makes jet assisted takeoff (JATO), circa 1950. *Glenn L. Martin Museum*

that same year, two coast guard pilots began training with the navy. The new U.S. Coast Guard immediately entered discussions with the Glenn L. Curtiss Company about the design of a "flying life boat." World War I interfered with the completion of this design, but in 1920 the U.S. Coast Guard received six Curtiss HS-2 flying boats on loan from the navy. The U.S. Coast Guard involvement with the operation of flying boats began.

Because of budgetary limitations, the HS-2s were returned to the navy after about a year and coast guard aviation lay dormant until Prohibition and the "rum wars." In 1926, to enable the U.S. Coast Guard to efficiently perform its expanded antismuggling mission, Congress appropriated funds for the purchase of aircraft and for the construction of the air stations that had been authorized in 1916. All the air stations were to be equipped to handle seaplanes.

In 1931 the U.S. Coast Guard commissioned the first of its Dolphin amphibians, designed and manufactured by the Douglas Aircraft Company. The service received five purpose-built General Aviation (successor to the North American Fokker Company) PJ-1 flying lifeboat (FLB) flying boats in 1932.

The Dolphin and the FLB both had very low landing and takeoff speeds. Because impact force is proportional to the square of the velocity, these low speeds permitted safe operation in rough water. Almost immediately after receiving these aircraft, the U.S. Coast Guard began to develop a reputation as the world's premier aerial ocean rescue service.

The new FLB Arcturus performed a spectacular ocean mercy mission in 1932. Flying out three hours from its Miami base, it landed in darkness on a rough sea and picked up a critically ill passenger from the U.S. Army's transport *Republic*. After a night takeoff, Arcturus delivered the patient safely to Miami.

In January 1933 Arcturus landed in very rough seas to rescue a boy adrift in a skiff. Damaged in the landing and unable to take off, Arcturus was eventually blown ashore. All were saved and Arcturus was salvaged, remaining in service until 1941.

Dolphin ocean missions are first noted in 1933. Sirius, piloted by Coast Guard Commander Elmer Stone (Coast Guard Aviator #1 and one of the pilots of the U.S. Navy's NC-4 on the first transatlantic crossing), landed off the coast of New Jersey to recover the body of the commanding officer of the crashed blimp J-3.

Coast guard open-sea rescue missions became almost commonplace during the 1930s. A new aircraft of greater range was needed. In 1936 seven new PH-2 flying boats were ordered from the Hall Aluminum Company. Although the PH-2 was based on the design of an earlier navy patrol bomber, it was optimized for the coast guard ocean rescue mission. The PH-2 biplane flying boat had the slow landing speed and short takeoff run necessary for rough sea operation. It was so successful that seven more of an improved PH-3 type were ordered in 1938.

On 11 November 1938 an urgent radio message was received from the freighter *Commercial Bostonian* in the Gulf of Mexico. A crewman was seriously ill and in need of medical attention. A PH-2 (V-165) was dispatched to provide aid, with Lt. C. F. Edge as pilot. Arriving on the scene two hours later, Edge landed the flying boat in the choppy Gulf waters. The patient was transferred from the freighter via lifeboat, and V-165 began its takeoff. During the takeoff run, the aircraft hit a large swell and the left wing pontoon was torn off. Two men rushed out onto the right wing to counterbalance the plane to keep it from capsizing, but a second large wave ripped the entire lower left wing off the aircraft. It began to capsize. The patient was put into a rubber inflatable life raft and the aircraft was abandoned just before it rolled over. The lifeboat from *Commercial Bostonian* rescued all hands. Thankfully, no lives were lost, but the U.S. Coast Guard lost one-seventh of its PH-2 Hall boat fleet when V-165 sank in over one thousand feet of water. The patient made a full recovery in a Tampa hospital.

Despite the inherent danger of open-sea flying boat operations, the only fatal loss recorded in such operations of any Dolphin, FLB, or Hall boat was that of V-164 on 15 July 1939. After receiving an ill crewman from a ketch, V-164 lifted off and then dived into the sea with the loss of two crewmen and the patient. The U.S. Coast Guard's accident board concluded it had hit a swell and had been thrown into the air in a stalled condition.

World War II Rescue Service

During World War II the U.S. Coast Guard became part of the U.S. Navy. To its life-saving mission were added the military tasks of coastal security patrol, convoy escort, and antisubmarine warfare. PBY Catalinas and Grumman's Goose and Widgeon amphibians joined the coast guard inventory. With the exception of Patrol Squadron 6 (Coast Guard), which operated in Newfoundland and Greenland, coast guard aircraft were not organized into squadrons, but operated as units of the coast guard shore stations.

In his *My Life in the Coast Guard,* Capt. David Oliver, USCG (Ret.), described typical coast guard wartime operations:

In early 1943 I was ordered to San Diego, California for anti-submarine warfare (ASW) duty against the Japanese. We car-ried depth charges in case we ran across a sub. We patrolled down to Lower California and all the way to a number of islands where submarines had been hidden in the past. When the threat waned, we turned our attention away from ASW. Rescue work became our main challenge. Several times I piloted a PBY in a rescue.

In December 1942 the U.S. Coast Guard had participated in the establishment of the first U.S. air-sea rescue unit, which was organized at San Diego. The increasing number of military and naval flights in that area demonstrated a real need for a well-organized agency whose primary function would be rescuing flyers forced down at land or sea. It had become apparent that independent rescue activities by the different services—army, navy, marine corps, and coast guard—were resulting in confusion and duplication of effort. Acting on the coast guard suggestion that a single agency coordinate all efforts, the secretary of the navy established an air-sea rescue agency in March 1944. It would be headed by the commandant of the U.S. Coast Guard. Army, navy, marine corps, and coast guard representatives were members of this agency, which was charged with coordinating operations; conducting joint studies; recommending methods, procedures, and techniques; and disseminating information. By 1945 Air Sea Rescue was responsible for 165 aircraft and 9 air stations. During that year, the agency responded to 686 plane crashes.

Initially, the amphibious PBY-5A and high-speed rescue craft were the agency's rescue vehicles. In late 1943, however, the U.S. Coast Guard was allocated thirty-seven PBM-3s, which were assigned to the various coast guard air stations. San Diego received four in December and one more in August 1944. In mid-1944, Comdr. Donald B. MacDiarmid, who had commanded VP-6 (CG), became commanding officer of Coast Guard Air Station, San Diego. The PBMs under MacDiarmid's direction began a new era in ocean rescue.

MacDiarmid observed that many of the crashes happened outside the range of crash boats. He felt that the newly assigned PBM would be a wonderful long-range rescue vehicle if it could be safely landed in rough water and take off again. It was a big "if."

MacDiarmid saw that the first step was to know how to land seaplanes safely at sea. Although the U.S. Navy and Pan American Airways had always landed seaplanes into the wind, he thought that was not necessarily the way it should be done in the ocean. Like many coast guard pilots, MacDiarmid was also an experienced seaman with a healthy respect for the movement of the ocean's surface. He sent his pilots to the Scripps Institution of Oceanography to learn about the physics of the surface of the sea.

The pilots learned that the topography of the ocean surface was comprised not only of local wind-driven waves, but, more important for seaplane operation, by a primary and often a secondary swell system. Swells are nonbreaking waves generated by distant storms. Because they are nonbreaking, they are difficult to see from the air. However, with experience and practice they can be identified and mapped.

At Scripps the pilots also learned that ocean swells can travel at up to seventy-five miles per hour (mph). Simple physics state that if a landing was made directly into these swells the aircraft would most probably be "thrown out" in a stalled condition and crash.

The Ultimate Rescue Plane: PBM-5G

In late 1944 the U.S. Coast Guard began to be assigned the more powerful, JATO equipped PBM-5. Most of these aircraft were configured as PBM-5Gs that had been optimized for rescue missions. All unnecessary weight was removed and the aircraft were fitted with reversing propellers to shorten the landing run.

MacDiarmid was assigned a specially instrumented PBM-5G. With volunteer crews, the aircraft made over two hundred open-sea landings. From these tests, conducted in seas up to eighteen feet and in winds of up to twenty-five knots,

Comdr. Donald B. MacDiarmid, USCG, makes an open-sea landing in coast guard PBM-5G, 9 January 1947. *Glenn L. Martin Museum*

MacDiarmid developed the concept of an accurate "sea evaluation," emphasizing the recognition of the primary and secondary swell systems and the interplay of these systems with the wind in selecting a safe landing and takeoff direction. In general, this was parallel to the primary swell system. He also developed the pilot techniques for safe operation. In landing, the pilot was to fly a semi-stalled approach. When at the desired landing point, the aircraft would be stalled, power would be cut, and (if available) full reverse power applied. The elevators would be manipulated to follow the contour of the swell. For takeoff, which is the most dangerous part of the flight, the aircraft would start a slow taxi in the take-off direction. If the pilot felt comfortable on this heading, full power was applied and four JATO bottles were fired. Even with JATO, takeoff remained the most dangerous phase of open-sea flying.

In the years that followed, a small band of MacDiarmid's followers used his research to develop emergency and ditching procedures for land planes that were forced down in the ocean. The result was the saving of passengers and crews of several large aircraft. These same procedures are taught today and are a permanent part of the *Airman's Information Manual.* For his work, MacDiarmid received two awards: his second Distinguished Flying Cross and the 1951 Octave Chanute Award, which is given annually to the person making the greatest contribution to aviation. He was posthumously inducted into the Naval Aviation Hall of Honor at Pensacola.

After World War II ended, the PBM-3s were returned to the U.S. Navy and the PBM-5G became the workhorse of coast guard aviation. Flown using MacDiarmid's techniques, PBM crews made spectacular rescues at sea far outside the very limited range of the early helicopters.

One PBM-5A amphibian (BuNo 122067) was evaluated by the U.S. Coast Guard but was "damaged beyond repair" during open-sea testing by MacDiarmid on 18 November 1949. Although the amphibian was attractive from an operational utility and from a support and maintenance standpoint, it was deemed "too heavy" for coast guard use because the "footprint" of its single-wheel landing gear was too high for existing coast guard ramps and aprons.

Although any open-sea seaplane mission is extremely hazardous, many were done by coast guard pilots as a matter of routine; no complete catalog of all of these missions is known to exist. Fortunately, some routine missions were documented and serve as an illustration of Mariner rescue work performed by the U.S. Coast Guard.

On 11 July 1947 the coast guard air station at Salem, Massachusetts, received an emergency call for immediate medical assistance. A young sailor on the Norwegian freighter *Cypria* had fallen thirty-five feet into the vessel's hold, breaking "almost every bone in his body." He was unconscious and desperately needed medical attention. Initially the injured Norwegian seaman was transferred to the U.S. Army troop ship USS *Willard Holbrook*. Medical staff on *Willard Holbrook* quickly determined that the seaman required treatment that could only be done on land. They requested help in transporting the injured man to an appropriate medical facility.

With eleven crew members, John A. Weber and his copilot, John Redfield, set out on the longest sea rescue mission attempted up to that time. In a PBM-5G (BuNo 84686) Weber flew 623 miles from Salem to pick up the injured man. Weber landed in eight-foot seas, buffeted by treacherous crosswinds, using the "old catapult scout plane technique of landing at sea on the slick of the wake from the ship." The seaman, still unconscious, was quickly transferred to the plane, which then took off with the help of JATO despite being hit by a large swell. A big wave "hit the starboard wing float 'heavy,' but we were able to get airborne without any trouble," Weber recalled in a 2000 article for the Augusta, Maine, *Capital Weekly*.

By the time the plane landed back in Salem, after a round trip of more than twelve hundred miles, the patient was barely alive. He was taken to the Chelsea Naval Hospital outside Boston where he spent the next five months recuperating. Seaman Knut Thorso completely recovered, became a U.S. citizen, and was finally able to thank Weber in person at an emotional reunion in 1999.

Other successful rescues were documented in contemporary newspaper accounts. The 22 February 1952 *St. Petersburg Independent* recounted: "A crew of U.S. Coast Guardsmen out of St. Petersburg flew approximately 1,000 miles late yesterday on an air-sea rescue mission. The Coast Guard made the trip to bring a seaman, Clarence Olsen, 37, to Mound Park Hospital. Olsen suffered an attack of appendicitis while aboard the disabled fishing vessel *Providence*."

The *St. Petersburg Times* of 28 February 1952 carried two stories describing different missions. One article read: "Local Coast Guardsmen, busy rescuing people all over the Gulf area, took time out Tuesday night to give a hand to one of their own. Seaman Douglas Bedsole, 20, attached to a CG unit at Dry Tortugas Island, was flown to St. Petersburg by PBM plane for hospital treatment for an apparent case of appendicitis." The second article read:

Coast Guardsmen raced nightfall yesterday to pick up an ailing seaman from a sea-going barge and return him here for treatment at Mound Park Hospital.

A PBM plane dropped down beside the barge *Cape of New Orleans* to transfer Seaman Howard T. Kennedy, 25, Nashville, Tenn. Kennedy has been ill for the past four days with a 102–104 fever and leg pains.

Coast Guardsmen picked up Kennedy off Cuba. Taking off from the local air base at sunset, they reached the *Cape of New Orleans* just before dark.

But success also had its price. In his *Rescue at Sea*, Capt. John M. Waters recounted that Ira McMullan, one of the coast guard's finest seaplane pilots, was attempting to land eight hundred miles off San Francisco. Part of his elevator was torn off by the sea, and the aircraft crashed, breaking the fuselage in two. No casualties are recorded for this incident.

On 11 January 1946 PBM-3S (BuNo 01663), piloted by Lt. (j.g.) H. C. Ledbetter from U.S. Coast Guard Air Station (USCGAS) South San Francisco, landed at sea to remove a stretcher case from a ship. The plane hit hard, waterlooped, and sank. Fortunately, there were no casualties.

A PBM-5 (BuNo 45431), piloted by Ens. F. T. Merritt from USCGAS Elizabeth City, made an open-sea landing ninety-five miles east of Cape Hatteras to remove a

Damage suffered by rudder of coast guard PBM-5G (BuNo 59012) during open-sea rescue, April 1948.
Glenn L. Martin Museum

Damage suffered by wing and aileron of coast guard PBM-5G (BuNo 59012) during open-sea rescue, April 1948. *Glenn L. Martin Museum*

medical case from a ship on 29 April 1946. The aircraft bounced during jet assisted takeoff (JATO) in high winds and rough seas. The pilot managed to get the aircraft airborne and was able to safely return to base. However, the aircraft was considered damaged beyond repair (DBR).

In March 1948 Andy Cupples was landing to pick up a sick sailor from a submarine off Cape Hatteras. He dropped heavily into the trough after missing the swell crest. Both engines tore loose from their mounts. Fuel sloshed freely in the hull from broken lines, and the crew abandoned ship. Three days later they arrived in Charleston aboard the submarine, wearing submarine dolphin insignias!

On 7 April 1948 an explosion and fire on board the British merchant vessel *Wilcox* in the Gulf of Mexico three hundred miles south of Miami left a crew member with severe burns. A PBM-5G (BuNo 59012), with Lt. Charles MacDowell as pilot, was tasked to provide a medical evacuation "mercy mission."

The open-sea landing was rough, but the patient was taken on board safely. As the JATO rockets fired during the takeoff, the aircraft lurched to the left and a loud noise was heard. Although the PBM became airborne, the pilots had problems trying to get the aircraft to climb in a straight and normal attitude. The control surfaces were extremely difficult to move. A

crewman climbed to the aft position up between the twin rudders. Using a flashlight he could see that the left rudder appeared damaged and jammed out of alignment. Checking the left side of the wing, he discovered the left wing tip float was missing along with about five feet of the left wing tip. The left aileron had also been damaged!

The pilots maintained control of the aircraft with sheer muscle power. The aircraft managed to return to Miami for a hazardous night landing in Biscayne Bay. As the aircraft slowed, three crewmen scrambled out on the right wing to keep the damaged left wing from dipping into the water. BuNo 59012 was then taxied onto a sand spit and came to rest with all hands safe. The aircraft was later considered DBR and had to be scrapped.

In November 1951 Harry Solberg, landing in the ocean off Bermuda, was on his runout after landing when the bombardier's nose door gave way. The plane went under without getting its way off. Solberg's shoulders provided a step so the flight deck crew could climb out and then Solberg himself managed to escape.

In January 1953 Lt. Comdr. John Vukic, flying a PBM-5G (BuNo 84738) out of U.S. Coast Guard Air Detachment, Sangley Point, Philippine Islands, landed in twelve-foot seas close to the Red China coast to rescue the crew of a P2V Neptune that had been shot down by Communist antiaircraft guns. On the takeoff, just as the plane cleared the water, one engine failed, and the PBM crashed. Although four navy men and five coast guardsmen were lost, the others were rescued by a navy destroyer after a miserable cold night in the water.

On 30 July 1953, a Sangley Point coast guard PBM piloted by Lt. G. F. Thometz Jr. rescued five survivors of a navy PBM that had gone down sixty miles off the coast of Luzon. BuNo 84743, based out of Sangley Point, was lost at sea during an offshore rescue mission on 14 October. Lt. Comdr. Franke landed off the coast of Luzon at 127°16' E, 12°58' N to pick up a seriously ill crewman from a merchant vessel. The PBM dropped in from fifty feet, bounced three times and finally came to rest with both engines drooping in their mounts. The aircraft was unflyable. It was abandoned and the coast guard crew and the navy doctor rode the merchant ship back to Manila.

U.S. Coast Guard records show that of the nineteen PBMs lost in coast guard service, fourteen were lost in open-ocean operations. Miraculously, the only fatalities suffered during the open-ocean operations were during the 1953 China Sea rescue.

The loss of seaplanes in open-sea landings brought a predictable reaction from headquarters. In too many cases, after a plane was lost, the intended evacuee recovered very nicely without help. Officials felt the price being paid was too steep. A policy was established that before landing the pilot would have to obtain permission from the shore-based district commander. This would enable the commander's staff to check on the availability of other means, such as surface vessels, to do the job. A prudent policy, it served as a restraint on possible rash action by an overeager pilot. In practice, however, it sometimes bogged things down. Communications were often slow, so the pilot had to circle endlessly awaiting permission to land, complaining all the while about the indecisiveness of the brass.

The policy was later modified to allow the pilot to make a landing if the pilot considered it necessary to save a life, but this policy put the burden of being right on the pilot. Of the dozens of hazardous rescues accomplished by U.S. Coast Guard PBM pilots, only a handful of those pilots received any official recognition or award, perhaps a not-so-subtle attempt to discourage open-ocean landings.

The Helicopter Arrives

In the 1950s the helicopter began to come of age. Its crews began to rescue people close in to the shore. As the performance and range of the helicopter improved, the requirement for seaplane ocean landings became less frequent, although they were still necessary at long distances offshore or when large numbers of survivors were in the water.

The PBM began to be supplanted in the U.S. Coast Guard inventory by the Grumman Albatross amphibian in 1951 and by the P5M-1 and P5M-2 Marlin flying boat in 1954. Although the Albatross was not nearly as rough water capable as the PBM, it was a versatile machine and was extremely useful in the search phase of a rescue operation. The Marlin was designed to be an even better rough water boat than the Mariner, although some pilots said the Mariner was unsurpassed. Seven P5M-1s and four P5M-2s served with the U.S. Coast Guard. All the Marlins were returned to the U.S. Navy in 1961, ending coast guard flying boat operations.

The last coast guard Mariner to fly was BuNo 59148, temporarily retained at CGAS San Diego after the station was re-equipped with P5M Marlins. Scheduled for scrapping, the old bird was employed to train young P5M pilots in open-sea work. On 22 April 1958, with Lt. Comdr. John "Muddy" Waters as instructor pilot, several landings and takeoffs were made in the ocean off Point Loma.

The 7 June 1959 *Chicago Tribune* carried a story about a "big white flying boat" that had been moored for six weeks in Lake Michigan near the navy pier. According to the *Tribune,* the plane was one of nineteen ex–U.S. Coast Guard Mariners purchased from navy surplus by Stanley Layne of Dune Acres, Indiana. An August 1959 *Tribune* article recounted how the plane broke loose from its moorings and crashed into the inner breakwater near the Chicago filtration plant. The U.S. Coast Guard pulled it off the breakwater and moored it to the navy pier where it later sank. This aircraft was possibly BuNo 84732, which carried the U.S. civil registration N4247A. The final disposition of this aircraft and the eighteen others is unknown.

An ex–U.S. Coast Guard Mariner (BuNo 59148) was shown at a North Island Armed Forces Day open house in 1961. This same aircraft was used as a hulk in "sea stilt" experiments by Convair General Dynamics in 1961–62. It was probably scrapped shortly thereafter.

CHAPTER SEVEN

THE MARINER IN FOREIGN SERVICE

In addition to its years of service with the U.S. Navy and U.S. Coast Guard, the Mariner was used by the armed forces of Great Britain, Australia, the Netherlands, Argentina, and Uruguay.

Mariners in the Royal Air Force

In 1940 the British government sought to purchase 150 PBMs from the United States. Due to U.S. Navy requirements, no aircraft could be released until 1943. In that year, a group of PBM-3s were allocated to the British under the Lend-Lease Program. A 31 December 1943 document from the U.S. Navy Department's Bureau of Aeronautics, entitled "Production Program Naval Aircraft, PBMs Delivered to the British," indicates that the total allocation was forty-one aircraft that consisted of twelve PBM-3Cs, twenty-two PBM-3Ss, and seven PBM-3Ds. However, Ken Meekcoms's *The British Air Commission and Lend-Lease* allows a correlation of Royal Air Force (RAF) to the U.S. Navy's bureau numbers and indicates the allocation was in fact forty-two aircraft: twelve PBM-3Cs, six PBM-3Ss, and twenty-four PBM-3Ds. The British designated all of the aircraft "Mariner G.R.1" and assigned the RAF serial numbers JX100 to JX141. This British use of the name "Mariner" was adopted by the U.S. Navy and the PBM became known as the "Mariner" for the rest of its service. Actually, only thirty-four of the forty-two Mariners, RAF serial numbers JX100 through JX133, were turned over to British custody.

Transfer of the RAF Mariners began in May 1943 with six PBM-3Cs being turned over to the British. Six more PBM-3Cs were transferred in June. All probably were ferried through RAF Ferry Command Staging Post 82 at the U.S. Naval Air Station, Elizabeth City, North Carolina, to the RAF flying boat base at Darrell's Island, Bermuda, for mechanical inspection and crew training before crossing the Atlantic Ocean.

A British Air Ministry's aircraft movement card (Form 78) shows that one of the Mariners "crashed after export." Although

Form 78 did not indicate the RAF serial number, the aircraft involved was JX101. JX101 was the first Mariner to arrive in Bermuda on 9 July 1943. It carried out a number of local flights to provide Bermuda ground crews with PBM beaching and launching practice. On 19 July, as it was preparing to depart for Boucherville, Quebec, it sank during taxi, probably due to the tunnel hatch being left open. One passenger, Leading Aircraftsman (LAC) L. L. Scott, RAF, drowned. The aircraft was salvaged the same day, but so much damage occurred during the salvage operation that the aircraft was scrapped. Scott is buried in the Royal Naval Cemetery, Ireland Island, Bermuda. A survivor of the JX101 accident, Mr. Jack Durbin, formerly of British Overseas Airways Corporation (BOAC), ended up as a neighbor of the author in California and shared his recollections of the accident. Durbin said Scott, who could not swim, lost his life jacket when he exited the aircraft.

During the 1943 summer, the Mariners were flown from Bermuda to Gander Lake, Newfoundland, and then on to Largs in Scotland. The first aircraft to arrive in the United Kingdom was JX103. Piloted by Squadron Leader W. E. M. Lowry, it arrived at Largs on 19 August 1943. Lowry would later be posted as commanding officer of No. 524 Mariner Squadron. JX103

Royal Air Force's Mariner (JX-117) moored at Middle River near Martin's factory, awaiting delivery to the RAF, 1943. *Glenn L. Martin Museum*

was processed by the Saunders-Roe facility at Beaumaris, Fyrar's Bay, Wales. On 6 September it was assigned to the Marine Aircraft Experimental Establishment (MAEE), Helensburgh, Scotland. Although twenty-three Mariners that reached the United Kingdom were returned to the United States, JX103 was one that was not returned.

Acceptance processing of the RAF Mariners was performed by Scottish Aviation at Greenock; the 57 Maintenance Unit (57 MU) in Wig Bay, Scotland; or Saunders-Roe at Beaumaris. Inasmuch as Greenock was quite close to Largs, aircraft destined for Greenock were towed rather than flown.

Fifteen more Mariners arrived in the United Kingdom in late September and October 1943. Form 78s show that JX102,

Royal Air Force Mariners at Bermuda en route to Great Britain, 1943.
Colin Pomeroy

JX104, JX108, and JX109 had been forced to return to Canada with engine problems before successfully crossing the North Atlantic. In his *The Flying Boats of Bermuda,* Colin Pomeroy recounts that JX104 had returned to Bermuda after engine failure en route to Gander.

In November and December eleven more Mariners reached the United Kingdom. Seven did not travel the winter North Atlantic route. Form 78s show that JX129 staged through Gibraltar and JX118, JX119, JX121, JX125, JX131, and JX132 staged through "West Africa." The usual winter itinerary was from Bermuda to Largs via San Juan, Puerto Rico; Trinidad, British West Indies; Belem and Natal in Brazil; Bathhurst (now Banjul) in Gambia; and Gibraltar.

The British Air Ministry has documentation for twenty-eight delivered aircraft. Form 78s were not located for the six Mariners with RAF serials JX120, JX124, JX126, JX128, JX130, and JX133. It is possible that these aircraft never reached the United Kingdom. According to Pomeroy, orders were received in December 1943 to suspend Mariner deliveries from Bermuda. Those awaiting departure were flown back to Elizabeth City except for JX133, which did not depart Bermuda for Norfolk, Virginia, until January 1944. The returned-from-Bermuda aircraft must be the six "non-delivered" aircraft.

Four of the aircraft that had arrived in

the United Kingdom in October 1943 were assigned to RAF No. 524 Squadron under command of No. 15 Group Coastal Command for operational evaluation. Excerpts from Form 540, the operational record book (ORB), of No. 524 Squadron provide a snapshot of the squadron's Mariner involvement:

1943

Sept 23

Information has been received that No. 524 Flying Boat squadron, equipped with Mariner aircraft, would commence to form at Oban under No. 15 Group, but as a lodger unit at RAF Station, Oban on 20 October.

Establishment of aircraft: 9 + 3 Mariners (War/CC/337).

It was decided that in the initial stages of [its] formation, the Squadron would be allocated 6 Mariner aircraft, with a view to gaining experience operationally on this type of aircraft. These aircraft were to be modified to absolutely minimum of standard essential for operational trials. Dependent upon the results obtained in these operational trials, the Squadron was to be expanded to its full establishment with a possibility of depatch [sic] overseas at a later date.

Establishment of Personnel for the Squadron was as follows:

43 Officers

111 Senior NCO's [noncommissioned officers]

118 Corporals and A.C.'s [aircraftsmen]

15 WAAF [Women's Auxiliary Air Force]

This provided an establishment of 14 air crews. . . .

Oct 19

Sqn Ldr W.E.M. Lowry, Squadron commander, posted in.

Oct 20

Six complete crews arrived. . . .

Oct 25

First aircraft arrived.

All Mariner aircraft were received into this country through Messrs Sanders-Roe, Beaumaris, who carried out modifications on these aircraft prior to delivery to this Squadron. During the time the aircraft were in use by this unit, considerable difficulty was experienced in obtaining relevant publications and spares.

The Squadron took possession of four aircraft only no's JX100-JX105-JX106-JX110.

No. 524 Squadron began evaluation of the four aircraft assigned, but that evaluation was short-lived.

Dec 13

Information was received from Headquarters, Coastal Command, under reference CC/S.9304/60/org that No. 524 Squadron was to be disbanded with effect from 7 Dec 1943.

Dec 20

The following signal (ref.0.99), received from Headquarters Coastal Command: "All flying of an instructional nature to cease on Mariner aircraft now with 524 squadron. Aircraft to be given a 40 hour inspection and prepared in all respects for overseas transit flight. This Headquarters and D.P.C.A. (M.A.P.) to be informed when aircraft ready for disposal.

"M.A.P." refers to Ministry of Aircraft Production. The last entry in the ORB is dated 29 January 1944 and states:

Squadron Commander W/Cdr W.E.M. Lowy posted to No. 8 OTU. Remainder of crews posted to Oban, No. 302 FTU and No. 131 OTU.

Two aircraft left the Squadron about the middle of January 1944 and the remaining two about the end of the same month. No aircraft had done more than 90 hours flying.

Although available information does not provide the definitive reason why the Mariners were not integrated into the RAF, inferences may be drawn from some ORB statements. The phrase "depatch [*sic*] overseas at a later date" could indicate that the RAF Mariners were originally intended for service in the Pacific, but that strategy had changed. The most probable reason can be inferred from the phrase "considerable difficulty was experienced in obtaining relevant publications and spares." This statement highlights the problem of supporting a relatively small number of complex aircraft and may have been part of the reason for the RAF decision not to use the Mariner. Furthermore, about the time the RAF Mariners were reaching squadron-level numbers, the Battle of the Atlantic was well in hand and an additional antisubmarine warfare [ASW] aircraft was not required.

Three Mariners had become unserviceable while in RAF service. JX111 was damaged beyond repair (DBR) and JX117 was struck off charge (SOC) in November 1944. JX118 was SOC in January 1945. The loss of JX117 is described as a flying accident in the ORB. In his *Flying Cats,* Andrew Hendrie relates that a Mariner was occasionally "run-up on the step" on Loch Ryan. The aircraft was abandoned and sank after the auxiliary power plant (APU) caught fire during one of these run-ups.

Twenty-three of the twenty-seven Mariners that reached the United Kingdom were returned to the United States. During

1944, JX106, JX121, and JX123 were returned in February; JX115, JX127, JX129, JX131, and JX132 in March; JX122 in April; JX109 in May; JX102, JX108, JX112, and JX119 in June; JX104, JX107, and JX114 in July; and JX110 and JX116 in November. JX100, JX105, JX113, and JX125 were returned in January 1945.

The log of the return itinerary for JX131 shows that it departed Gibraltar for Bathurst on 3 March 1944 and arrived in Norfolk, Virginia, on 18 March. It had made stops in Natal and Belem in Brazil; Trinidad, British West Indies; San Juan, Puerto Rico; and Banana River, Florida.

At least two Mariners were used by the RAF in a utility or transport role before being returned to the United States. According to Peter Berry's "Transatlantic Flight" article, "[S]everal RAF PBM Mariner (JX110/116) transport flights from Stranraer (Wig Bay) to Dorval, Quebec were made during October 1944 for No. 45 Group, RAF."

JX103, the MAEE aircraft, remained in the United Kingdom and was sold as scrap in August 1947. A photograph was taken of it as it sat on the ramp at Wig Bay as late as 1948. At some subsequent point, it was broken up.

Ex-RAF Mariner Service

Although it seems logical that all of the twenty-three near-new Mariners would be put into U.S. Navy service after their return from the RAF, documentation of this from the U.S. Navy records was difficult to find. Meekcoms's *British Air Commission,* however, provided information that allowed a correlation of RAF serials with the U.S. Navy's bureau numbers. Knowledge of the U.S. Navy's bureau numbers permitted the determination of the Mariners' U.S. Navy assignment after their return from the RAF.

BuNo 6741 (JX109) served with VPB-215, a patrol bombing squadron, after its return to the U.S. Navy. BuNos 6742 and 01694 (JX110 and JX116) were assigned to VPB-2's operational training unit (OTU).

Almost all the other returned Mariners were converted to the PBM-3R transport configuration and used by transport (VR) squadrons. Later eleven of the returned aircraft and five of the "not delivered" aircraft were assigned to rescue (VH) squadrons.

In Donald Sweet's *Forgotten Heroes,* Lee Way, a VH-3 combat aircrewman, stated: "In mid-December [1944] we left Kaneohe, flying west to Eniwetok Atoll" in six PBM-3Rs that had originally been sent to England early in the war on the Lend-Lease program "and then on to Saipan, an island in the Marianas, where our rescue operations began early in January 1945." Way later says: "Six crews returned to Kaneohe, where six more

RAF Serial Number	USN Bureau Number	Aircraft Type
JX100	6667	PBM-3C
JX101–JX105	6686–6690	PBM-3C
JX106–JX111	6738–6743	PBM-3C
JX112–JX117	01690–01695	PBM-3S[1]
JX118	48143	PBM-3D[2]
JX119–JX121	48145–48147	PBM-3D
JX122–JX133	48152–48163	PBM-3D
JX134–JX141	48185–48192	PBM-3D[3]

[1]The PBM-3S was a modified version of the PBM-3C for South Atlantic antisubmarine service with all power turrets removed. However, all photos of the RAF Mariners show power turrets. Probably these six RAF Mariners came from a PBM-3S contract, but were fitted as PBM-3Cs.

[2]The PBM-3D differed from the PBM-3C by having uprated R-2600-22 engines of nineteen hundred horsepower, self-sealing tanks, and improved armor and armament.

[3]Although slated for delivery to the RAF, these eight aircraft had never been turned over to British custody.

PBM-3Rs were available and flew them back to Saipan."

At least three of the returned Mariners have been documented as being involved in daring and spectacular rescue missions with VH-3: BuNo 01693 (JX115), BuNo 48145 (JX119), and BuNo 48162 (JX132). During April 1945 alone, VH-3 rescued thirty-nine airmen, the majority of the rescues occurred using ex-RAF aircraft.

Two ex-RAF Mariners were operational losses while they were in service with VH-3. BuNo 6689 (JX104) was lost on a search mission on 17 January 1945 after engine failure. On 20 January 1945 BuNo 6687 (JX102) went down after an engine failed during a search for a B-29 Superfortress

crew. The crews of both PBMs were rescued by the destroyer USS *Cassin* (DD-372), a ship that had been heavily damaged and originally considered lost in the Japanese attack on Pearl Harbor on 7 December 1941.

Five more ex-RAF Mariners were operational losses while in service with the U.S. Navy in the Pacific. BuNo 48155 (JX125), which was never assigned to a rescue squadron, ran aground and sank at Espiritu Santo Island in the New Hebrides as a unit of VR-2 on 9 August 1944. BuNo 01692 (JX114), another aircraft that was never assigned to a rescue squadron, force-landed at sea and sank on 17 October 1944 as a unit of VR-6.

BuNo 48159 (JX129), serving with VH-5, was on an operational search mission on 25 January 1945. With an engine on fire, it made a forced landing at sea at 30°30' N, 130°00' W. Although the aircraft was badly damaged it had to be sunk by gunfire, the entire crew was rescued by a ship. BuNo 48160 (JX130), serving with VH-1, was on a survivor search when an engine failed. It made a forced landing at sea on 12 July 1945. The plane capsized and sank but the crew was rescued four hours later. BuNo 48146 (JX120), which had served with VH-3, was sunk at Sangley Point in the Philippines on 30 August 1945 after being hit by a rearming boat.

The story of the RAF delivery and return of the Mariners may at first glance seem to have been one of a waste of valuable assets, but it is important to remember that the scenario developed because of changing wartime requirements. The former RAF aircraft performed extremely valuable service after they were returned to the U.S. Navy. Not only were they used extensively in a transport role, their availability allowed the rapid formation of the famous Dumbo rescue squadrons that saved hundreds of U.S. Navy and U.S. Army Air Force crewmen during the final Pacific campaigns.

In an official 1959 U.S. Navy study, Michael Kammen succinctly described the work of the Dumbo squadrons:

The greatest World War II successes in air-sea rescue operations were achieved during the months following the initiation of the campaign for Okinawa. From April to August 1945 the percentage of survivors rescued was higher than at any previous time during the war. The PBM Mariner was brought into full use during his period: it was able to complete rescues which its predecessors would have shied away from or found impossible. From April 1 to May 17, there were 132 men rescued out of 186 possible survivors. Of these, 63 were picked up by PBM "dumbos," 44 by ships, 18 by PBM squadron aircraft, five by VOS [scout/observation squadron] aircraft, and one by land forces; one made shore unassisted. Thus the PBMs rescued almost twice as many downed aviators as any other agency. The most successful group was the six twin-engined flying boats of VH-3. Flying missions from Kyushu to Formosa, VH-3 made 33 rough open-sea landings, of which 21 were made within ten miles of enemy-held land, and seven while under fire from shore batteries.

Mariners under the Southern Cross

In 1943 twelve Mariner PBM-3 aircraft, Bureau Numbers 6512, 6528, 6546, 6549, 6566, 6526, 6506, 6565, 6575, 6622, 6664, and 6538, were allocated under the

Lend-Lease Program for logistic and air-sea rescue service by the Royal Australian Air Force (RAAF). All originally had been delivered to the U.S. Navy as PBM-3C patrol bombers and assigned to operational squadrons. Because of the urgency of the Australian requirement, the aircraft were withdrawn from U.S. Navy squadrons and converted by the Glenn L. Martin Company to the PBM-3R transport configuration. The U.S. Navy's aircraft history cards continued to carry the aircraft as PBM-3Cs until they were turned over to the RAAF. Australian aircraft record cards (Form E/E88) carried them simply as "Martin Mariners." In order by bureau number, the RAAF Mariners were assigned the serials A70-1 through A70-12, with corresponding registrations VHC-PA through VHC-PL.

Delivery of the Australian Mariners began in October 1943. RAAF crews first underwent PBM transitional training at the U.S. Naval Air Station (NAS), Banana River, Florida, and then took delivery of their new aircraft at NAS Norfolk, Virginia.

From Norfolk the usual routing across the United States was to NAS Jacksonville, Florida, to NAS Corpus Christi, Texas, and from there to NAS San Diego, California. One of the Australian pilots, Flying Officer (FO) Philip Mathiesen, who made the delivery flights of A70-3 and A70-9, commented that the leg from Corpus Christi to San Diego was a strange route for a flying boat: eight hours and thirty minutes over a sandy desert! From San Diego the RAAF Mariners went up to NAS Alameda, California, to await favorable winds for the eighteen-hour flight to NAS Kaneohe, Hawaii. Mathiesen recalled that at Kaneohe the "extra hull tanks" were removed and shipped back to Alameda for the next aircraft.

The only problem recorded for any of the aircraft on the Alameda-Hawaii leg was for A70-3. At the point of no return, an engine failed. The aircraft was too heavy to maintain altitude. If fuel was dumped to reduce weight, A70-3 would not have enough fuel to reach Hawaii. Finally, the engine was restarted and A70-3 arrived safely at Kaneohe.

From Hawaii to Australia the Mariners staged through NAS Palmyra Island, Naval Air Facility (NAF) Canton Island, Suva in Fiji, and Nouméa in New Caledonia. From Nouméa the Mariners flew on to Townsville in Northern Queensland or to Rathmines in New South Wales north of Sydney. All twelve Mariners arrived in Australia between late November 1943 and mid-January 1944 and were issued to 1 Flying Boat Repair Depot (1 FBRD) at Lake Boga, Victoria, in preparation for operational service with No. 41 Squadron, RAAF.

While No. 41 Squadron's future Mariner pilots were receiving a fifty-hour transition course at Lake Boga, some of the Mariners almost immediately began service with 3 Operational Training Unit (3OTU). Reportedly, in February or March 1944 two of the Mariners were flown to Perth, Western Australia, because of reports of a Japanese fleet in the area. The twenty-five hundred mile flight to Perth was in two segments entirely over land: Rathmines to Adelaide and Adelaide to Matilida Bay (Perth).

The Mariner had been assigned to RAAF No. 41 Squadron to replace the German-designed Dutch Dornier DO 24K three-engine flying boats. Thirty-seven DO 24s had been with the prewar Netherlands East Indies Naval Air Force. Twelve had survived the Japanese invasion and were evacuated to Australia, but one was lost enroute. On 3 March 1942 five were destroyed in a Japanese raid on Broome, Western Australia, along with ten Catalinas and two Short C–class Empire flying boats. Five of the remaining six DO 24s were then assigned to No. 41 Squadron to fly cargo from Australia to Goodenough Island, Milne Bay, and Port Moresby, New Guinea. The DO 24 was a versatile and sturdy aircraft; versions served with the Spanish Air Force until the mid-1960s. In Australian service, however, the DO 24 suffered from a lack of spares support and the RAAF's Dash 1 version had a cargo capability of only two thousand pounds. (908 kg).

No. 41 Squadron was a flying boat transport squadron with a primary mission of carrying personnel and freight. The squadron had been formed in August 1942 at Townsville, Queensland, with a complement of two Short-class Empire flying boats. This complement was expanded in June 1943 by the addition of the ex–Dutch DO 24s. In July 1943 the Empire flying boats were returned to Qantas Airlines and service continued with the Dorniers alone. By May 1944 Mariners had completely replaced the Dorniers. In July, after an earlier move from Townsville to Rathmines, the squadron's headquarters and primary base was established at Cairns, Queensland, where it remained for the duration of the war.

No. 41 Squadron's first Mariner route was directed to be Brisbane–Cairns–Milne Bay and return two days out of three. However, when a survey flight by the squadron's commanding officer, Squadron Leader S. R. C. Wood, later the wing commander, found unsuitable seadrome conditions at Milne Bay, the northern terminus of the route was changed to Port Moresby. By August 1944 Mariners had carried over 350,000 pounds of cargo and also performed extended flights along the north coast of New Guinea to Madang in Hollandia and Woendi Island, including full load flights over the Owen Stanley

Mountains. By September regular flights to Hollandia were being made with a facility established at Lake Sentani. In October 1944 a new thrice-weekly schedule was given the squadron: Cairns-Moresby-Madang-Moresby-Madang-Morseby-Cairns. Proving flights showed that this schedule involved an inordinate amount of time at climbing power and the crossing of the New Guinea mountains in the afternoon when the weather was quite violent. Therefore, it was changed to Cairns-Moresby-Madang and return.

Not all Mariner flights were along scheduled routes. The squadron also operated to and from Darwin and Hollandia. Three aircraft carried personnel and stores to Espiritu Santo in the New Hebrides where HMAS *Australia* was being repaired after combat damage. As the Allies moved north, so did the Mariners. Departing from Cairns, Mariner A70-8 picked up senior air force and army officers at Madang and Salamaua, and then proceeded to Jacquinot Bay in New Britain. Thereafter, Jacquinot Bay became a regular stop as well as Manus Island north of New Guinea and Bougainville in the Solomons.

Most of the facilities at Australian terminals were minimal: a few squadron crewmen, a buoy, and a handling boat. Most places did not have refueling although some had a wharf originally built for surface craft.

Mariners also participated in tactical operations. In January 1945 A70-10 carried a special commando troop from Madang. The troop was to be put ashore at Aitape; that meant a three-hour run along the enemy-occupied northern coast of New Guinea. The pilot, Flying Officer Mathiesen, landed in the surf off the beach. Shortly after takeoff for his return, he experienced an engine failure. Faced with a single-engine flight along the Japanese-occupied coast, Mathiesen elected to return to Aitape where he knew there were friendly forces. The aircraft was towed to Seveo Island. Work crews discovered that a new engine would be required. Ten days later the new engine arrived by boat and was installed using the Mariner's self-contained engine crane.

In January 1945 A70-2, commanded by Flight Lieutenant L. G. Weber, was tasked to evacuate three radar stations on the southern New Guinea coast: Amorep, Mappi, and Kombies. In addition to evacuating the personnel of these stations, the Mariners brought out a number of generators weighing six hundred pounds each and Bofors guns. On 13 January Squadron Leader G. M. Mason in A70-9 lifted 36 A.I.F Infantry troops from Madang to Annanberg while on a mission station situated on the Ramu River. The troops were rushed reinforcements for a patrol that was being hard pressed by the Japanese. The versatility of the Mariner was demonstrated on 20 January when Mason departed Cairns to convey an advanced party of thirteen English Wrens (Women's Royal Naval Service) from Espiritu Santo to Brisbane.

The Mariner proved to be a sturdy airframe well suited for the Pacific's unique and primitive environments. While the aircraft was on the water, there were a number of cases of serious hull damage, but Australian ingenuity prevented the loss of any damaged aircraft. On 27 August 1944 A70-5 struck a submerged object when it landed at Cairns. At the time there was no seaplane ramp at Cairns so continuous pumping for eighteen hours by a bucket brigade was required to keep the aircraft afloat. It was flown off the next day for repairs at Bowen. On 14 September at Cairns A70-6 was holed below the waterline and was barely kept afloat by the combined efforts of its own pumps, bucket gangs, and pumps borrowed from the army. Unserviceable at the time of damage and unable to fly off, A70-6 was towed to a carefully selected mud flat at high tide. Repairs were done when the aircraft was high and dry at low tide.

In March 1945 A70-3 and A70-9 became unserviceable due to taxi accidents. A70-3 lost an argument with a Liberty ship in the Brisbane River. A70-9 ran around on a reef at Gasmata, New Britain. Perhaps the most spectacular waterborne incident

involved A70-2 in June 1945. It struck an unlit channel marker. In Brett Freeman's *Lake Boga at War,* Squadron Leader G. M. Mason, the pilot, recounted:

> There were a series of multi-piled channel markers, as big as houses, out from Cairns. Having passed the last lit marker, preparatory to take-off, I had just given my Mariner the gun when the flying boat crashed into the final unlit beacon. With an unholy crunch our bow collided square on and concertinaed almost to the cockpit bulkhead. The bow had acted a perfect shock absorber. Remarkably, we were able to taxi back to our mooring. Subsequently sheets of galvanized iron were affixed to the bow and the aircraft successfully flown to Lake Boga for repair.

A70-2 was never returned to service because the war ended before repairs were complete.

The most serious problem during the RAAF service of the Mariner was the reliability of its Wright R2600-12 engines. The time-between-overhaul (TBO) experienced by the RAAF was only 360 hours. The squadron commander repeatedly stated that the lack of replacement engines was the major factor affecting Mariner availability. Engine failures were common. Fortunately, most flying was done in daylight. All aircraft suffering engine failure were able to make safe landings. Some engine failures occurred close to servicing facilities. A70-6 suffered an engine failure and fire just after takeoff from Brisbane with twenty-two U.S. Army WACs (Women's Army Corps) aboard. Other engine failures put the aircraft in remote areas where repair was more challenging. A70-7 experienced an engine failure enroute from Brisbane to Cairns. Because the fuel jettison system did not function, the aircraft was too heavy to maintain altitude. An emergency landing was made in a bay at Quail Island. The next day A70-8 arrived with a new cylinder, repairs were made, and both aircraft departed safely. Complete engine changes often had to be done at locations where there was no seaplane ramp and very little support equipment. In these situations the Mariner's built-in work stands and self-support crane provisions were invaluable. An engine was also changed on A70-8 at Madang, where at least there was a pier.

The main problem with the engine was broken valves. Samples of faulty valves were sent to Australia's air board and queries concerning these valves were sent to the United States. In February 1945 No. 41 Squadron was visited by Mr. Walter G. Tomlinson, a representative of the Wright Aeronautical Corporation. Tomlinson concluded that the engine problems were caused by the use of an obsolete valve type

that had caused similar problems for the U.S. Navy. New valves were ordered and operating procedures were modified to reduce engine strain. TBO increased to the six hundred hours that was being realized by the U.S. Navy.

As the Allies moved north through the Philippines and Okinawa, the need for the Mariners to support Australian operations in the Southwest Pacific diminished. On 10 May 1945 No. 41 Squadron was slated to be disbanded. The date was first delayed until 10 June and then "until further notice." In June six of No. 41's Mariners were transferred to No. 40 Squadron and its attached 114 Air Sea Rescue Flight (ASRF). No. 41 Squadron continued service with daily service to Madang and a biweekly service to Brisbane until it was finally disbanded at Cairns on 27 September 1945. During its service with No. 41 Squadron, Mariners had carried 24,702 passengers and 2,148,177 pounds of cargo, flying a total of 5,745 hours.

Mariners continued their Australian service with No. 40 Squadron after the war ended. They transported released prisoners of war and other troops back to Australia, with 114 ASRF monitoring the redeployment of fighter aircraft and small craft.

All twelve RAAF Mariners survived the war. They had performed a vital function in an area without an aviation infrastructure and with a minimum of support. The

Hull of Royal Australian Air Force (RAAF) A-70-3 Mariner as a car trailer, 1972.
RAAFA (Royal Australian Air Force Association) Aviation Heritage Museum of Western Australia

last RAAF Mariner operation occurred on 8 February 1946. A70-7 rendezvoused with the destroyer HMS *Grenville* to fly a sick rating to Cairns.

Movement of the Mariners to Lake Boga for storage and disposition began in May 1945 and continued until the arrival of A70-8 on 30 April 1946. All were declared for disposal on 25 March 1948. Because the Mariners had been acquired through the Lend-Lease Program, they could not be sold while still capable of further operation. Eventually, wingless and without engines, they were sold as scrap for a few hundred dollars each. A70-2 and A70-3 had the forward portion of their hulls converted to caravans. A70-3 is on display at the Aviation Heritage Museum of Western Australia in Bull Creek.

Mariners in the Marine Luchtvaart Dienst

One of the most interesting episodes in the history of the Mariner was its employment in Netherlands New Guinea by the Netherlands Naval Air Service, the Marine Luchtvaart Dienst (MLD).

Most information published in the United States about the service of the Mariner contains a sentence or two noting that Mariner amphibians were used by the Netherlands in New Guinea. Few details of that service were known until the Netherlands Ministry of Defence published "The Freaked Flying Boat" (originally published in the May 1998 issue of *Alle Hens* magazine) on its Web site.

Although the Netherlands had granted independence to most of the Indonesian Archipelago in 1949, Holland retained sovereignty over the western half of the island of New Guinea, called at that time the Netherlands New Guinea (NNG) (now the Indonesian province of Irian Jaya). By the early 1950s the Republic of Indonesia was threatening military action to annex NNG so the Dutch began a military buildup.

One of the Dutch requirements for the defense of the island was for an aircraft capable of operating without an infrastructure of developed airfields. The aircraft had to be able to provide an armed defense against infiltration of commandos from small boats or submarines. An armed amphibian seemed to be the solution, but the MLD's Catalinas were old and few in numbers.

In the United States, the Martin P5M Marlin was replacing the Mariner PBM-5 patrol plane flying boat. The Grumman UF Albatross was replacing the amphibious Mariner derivative, the PBM-5A, which had been used mainly as a utility transport and for midshipman aviation indoctrination at the U.S. Naval Academy. By 1954 the U.S. Navy had declared its remaining twenty-three (of thirty-six built) PBM-5A amphibians to be surplus. The PBM-5As seemed ideally suited to meet the Dutch requirements.

Under a mutual defense assistance agreement concluded on 24 November 1954, the Netherlands agreed to purchase fifteen of the surplus U.S. Navy PBM-5As. The agreement included overhaul of the airframes and engines, refitting of armament that had been removed for the U.S. Navy training and transport missions, provision of ten spare engines, and a supply of spare parts, tools, and test equipment for two service tours and one major overhaul. The aircraft were assigned the Dutch numbers P-300 through P-314.

Under a second contract, the Netherlands also purchased two additional aircraft (assigned the Dutch numbers P-315 and P-316) for airframe spares, as well as fourteen more engines and an additional quantity of spare parts. Total cost of the seventeen aircraft and the engine and airframe spares came to a total of 20,170,000 DFL (about $5,239,000 in U.S. currency) including excise taxes and freight charges.

Aircraft P-300 through P-303 received major overhaul prior to delivery at U.S. Naval Air Station, Norfolk, Virginia. Work on P-304 through P-314 was performed at U.S. Naval Air Station, Pensacola, Florida.

Dutch crews received transition flight instruction at NAS Norfolk and NAS Pensacola before the delivery and transfer of the aircraft. Further flying instruction and crew training was carried out by MLD No. 8 Squadron based at Valkenburg Naval Air Station in the Netherlands. Operational training was carried out at Biak, Netherlands New Guinea, by No. 321 Squadron.

The first four aircraft—P-300 (BuNo 122075), P-301 (BuNo 122081), P-302 (BuNo 122085), and P-303 (BuNo 122608)—were ferried to the Netherlands by Dutch crews in December 1955. From Norfolk the PBM-5As were flown to NAS Argentia, Newfoundland, then to Lajes in the Azores and on to Valkenburg. The same transatlantic routing was followed later by P-304 (BuNo 122070), P-305 (BuNo 122072), P-307 (BuNo 122603), P-310 (BuNo 122602), P-313 (BuNo 122079), and P-314 (BuNo 122604). No particular problems were recorded for any of these flights.

Five of the Pensacola-overhauled aircraft—P-306 (BuNo 122084), P-308 (BuNo 122078), P-309 (BuNo 122611), P-311 (BuNo 122613), and P-312 (BuNo 122470)—were flown directly to Netherlands New Guinea via the arduous Pacific route during 1956–57. From Pensacola the Mariners went to NAS Alameda, California, for staging for the leg

to NAS Barbers Point, Hawaii. Two of the aircraft, P-309 and P-311, had mechanical problems enroute to Barbers Point and were forced to return to Alameda for repairs. From Barbers Point all the aircraft were flown nonstop to Kwajalein. This leg of the journey was almost as long as the leg from Alameda to Barbers Point, and showed the professionalism of the Dutch crews. U.S. Navy Mariners normally stopped at Johnston Island on this route. From Kwajalein the Dutch Mariners flew on to the Biak New Guinea Naval Air Station to join No. 321 Squadron, commanded by Lt. Cmdr. A. Bruinsma.

Dutch records do not show whether P-315 (BuNo 122082) and P-316 (BuNo 122086), the "spare parts" aircraft, were delivered to Holland by contractor flight crews or by ship. A photo of P-316 arriving at the Aviolanda Papendrecht maintenance facility appears to indicate that they had alighted on the River Meuse after being flown from the United States. P-315 was immediately designated for scrap/spare parts supply, but P-316 was given a major refit at Aviolanda and deployed to New Guinea for operational service.

In New Guinea the Mariners were used for transport flights to remote military stations and for aerial reconnaissance. The mission of the reconnaissance flights was to locate Indonesian infiltrators using small wooden ships. These infiltrators hid in the forests during daylight and moved by ship at night. Needless to say, they were extremely difficult to find. The native Papuan people were quite friendly to the Dutch and acted as "coastwatchers." A simple signal system was developed using tree trunks arranged in specific patterns. When the Mariners patrolled over Papuan villages and noticed "unsafe" signals, Dutch marines were sent to the area.

P-312, which had arrived in NNG on 27 June 1957, became the first Mariner loss. On takeoff from the Merauke airstrip on 12 August 1957, it failed to clear some trees. It crashed and burned, killing the crew of seven and two Papuan policemen.

Conditions in New Guinea were primitive. Off the beach at Tamisa Village, P-316 hit a reef in Fak Fak Bay on 3 August 1959 and damaged its bottom. It had to be barged five hundred miles back to Biak, arriving on 30 August. Permanent repairs at Biak were accomplished using "sheet metal and bacon grease."

Because an aviation industrial infrastructure in South East Asia was nonexistent, heavy maintenance and overhaul of the Mariners had to be done in Holland. The flight itinerary back and forth from NNG to Holland is a litany of exotic ports-of-call. Although specific flights varied with the overflight and landing rights that could be obtained, a typical trip from Holland might be to Malta and then on to

Naples or Athens, next stopping at Basra, Iraq; Karachi, Pakistan; Negumbo, Ceylon; Singapore; Labuan, Brunei; and finally Biak. Another typical trip might be through Malta; then Beirut, Lebanon; Baghdad; Abadan; Bahrain; Karachi; Katanuyake, Thailand; Singapore; Labuan; and Biak. The itinerary from New Guinea to Holland was similar, but occasionally included fuel stops at Dubai from Abadan, Iran; at Mauripur from Negombo, Catania; at Sicily from Beirut; or at Istres, France, from Athens.

The next two losses of Dutch Mariners were aircraft attached to No. 8 Squadron in the Netherlands. On 11 October 1957 P-307 crashed at Valkenburg while peforming "unauthorized one engine flying." There were no casualties. Reportedly, the hulk of P-307 served as an instructional airframe with the Airport Fire Brigade of Rotterdam-Zestienhoven until the mid-1960s.

On 22 November 1957 P-305 was practicing touch-and-go landings on the Haringvliet River in poor visibility. On a takeoff, a fishing boat was observed ahead and the pilot lowered a wing to turn and avoid the boat. The wing tip float caught the water and the aircraft broke up. No casualties were reported.

However, casualties were suffered in the loss of a fourth aircraft. P-303 was being flown to Holland for overhaul. Enroute it began to experience high oil temperature in the port engine. After reaching Abadan, Iran, and with mountainous terrain ahead, the patrol plane commander (PPC) requested an alternate route from Dutch navy headquarters. Headquarters' only answer was to send out a new PPC, Lt. Comdr. T. M. A. Hoebink. Hoebink made a night takeoff from Abadan, but the aircraft was not able to climb and the port engine oil temperature became dangerously high. By the time the pilot started a return to the airport for an emergency landing, the airport had closed and the runway lights had been turned off! The pilot had no alternative but to continue to the airport. While maneuvering to avoid oil refineries, the aircraft was reported to have hit the water twice. About one mile out the runway lights came back on, and although touching down fifty meters short of the runway, Hoebink effected a safe landing. The original crew was then sent back to Holland to ferry the newly overhauled P-316 to New Guinea. A repair crew and two new engines were sent to Abadan. On 20 August 1958 Hoebink and the repair crew departed for Holland. After takeoff, a severe oil leak developed in the port engine and the pilot requested an emergency landing. About one hundred meters before reaching the runway, P-303 made a violent turn to the right and crashed in an inferno of flames, killing all on board. The investigating commission concluded that the starboard propeller had gone into reverse pitch.

Less than a year later, the ill fortune of the Dutch Mariners continued with the loss of P-306. Like P-303, P-306 was on its way to Holland for a major overhaul. On 10 June 1959, between Nagumbo, Ceylon, and Karachi, Pakistan, an engine failed and the pilot opted for an emergency landing at Portuguese Goa. According to former crewmen of No. 321 Squadron, an attempt to jettison the two 350-gallon bomb-bay tanks failed. The heavy aircraft, making an approach in poor visibility to an airport located on top of a hill, hit a low wall near the end of the runway. The Mariner overturned and caught fire. Four of the eight crewmen were pulled from the wreckage alive but did not survive. A monument to the lost crew was erected in Goa in 1997.

The loss of this fifth Mariner was crushing to aircrew morale. In Dutch eyes, the Mariner had become a "crew killer." Several crewmen turned in their wings and others found excuses not to fly.

Corp. Gerhard De Bruyn was a flight engineer normally assigned to P-309. Sent by ship because of the experiences with P-303 and P-306, P-309 was in the Netherlands for overhaul later in the year. De Bruyn was asked by the No. 321 Squadron commander, Lt. Cmdr. J. Adriaanse to join the crew of P-302 on a four-day visit to all villages displaying "safe" signals. Adriaanse had assumed command of No. 321 Squadron on 1 October 1959, relieving Lt. Cmdr. P. N. Versteeg. P-302 departed Biak on 16 December 1959 and flew to the Island of Jeffman where No. 321 Squadron had a detachment. The next day P-302 arrived at Fak Fak in the Patipi Bay with Lt. H. K. Bertram, a pilot under instruction, at the controls for the landing. According to De Bruyn, Bertram touched down in a severe nose-down attitude and the aircraft "turned upside down twice and broke into five pieces." Although De Bruyn and two others of the crew survived, five died in this crash.

The crash of P-302 marked the end of the Mariner's Dutch service. The day after the crash, Capt. Adrian J. De Bruijn, commander in chief of the Netherlands Naval Air Service in Netherlands New Guinea, issued a ban on further Mariner operational flying. The Mariners were withdrawn from service. P-300, P301, P-304, P-309, P-310, P-311, P313, P314, and P316 are listed as "Afgevoerd" (withdrawn) from Netherlands service at Biak and P308 in the Netherlands on 15 January 1960. P-315, one of the "spare parts" aircraft, is listed as being scrapped in the Netherlands on 28 June 1958. Four C-47 Dakotas were loaned from the Royal Netherlands Air Force as provisional replacements for the Mariners until modern Lockheed P2V-7B Neptunes arrived in September 1961.

On 1 October 1962 the Netherlands transferred Netherlands New Guinea to the United Nations. On 15 October 1962 the Naval Air Station Biak was closed, ending the activities of the MLD in the Far East.

Mariners in Argentina

In the 1950s the Argentine Naval Air Service, Comando de Aviacion Naval (CAN), purchased a total of nine PBMs. Three were purchased in 1954–55 from Pan Air Corporation, an aircraft broker in the New Orleans area. Flight crews were trained at the U.S. Navy's Advanced Training Unit 700 (ATU-700), Corpus Christi, Texas. The route planned was from New Orleans to Argentina via Key West, Puerto Rico, Trinidad and Belem in Natal, and Rio de Janiero in Brazil.

One of these aircraft, whose U.S. Navy bureau number is not identified, was assigned Argentine permanent serial number (PSN) 0372 and operating code (side number) 2-P-21. It arrived in Argentina on 31 March 1955. During a leg of its delivery flight in February 1955, another Mariner, the former BuNo 84624, carrying operating code 2-P-22, was destroyed by fire at the U.S. Naval Air Station, Trinidad, British West Indies. The aircraft, which had been purchased for $28,000, was never assigned a PSN. BuNo 84624 had been delivered to the U.S. Navy on 5 June 1945. During World War II it had served with VPB-212, a patrol bombing squadron. After the war, it served with patrol squadrons VP-MS-11, VP-MS-2, and VP-MS-6. It received an overhaul in San Diego on 29 April 1949 and later served with VP-661 and ATU-700. It had been stricken from U.S. Navy records on 15 January 1955.

2-P-22 had departed New Orleans on 20 January 1955. Commanded by Comdr. J. Martinez Achaval, the copilot was Lt. G. Sylvester. 2-P-22 suffered left engine problems near Georgetown, British Guiana. It returned to U.S. NAS Trinidad. The engine was changed by Fleet Aircraft Service Squadron 115 (FASRON-115). On 10 February 1955, during the run-up of the new engine, the engine backfired and started a gasoline fire. The fire truck at the scene exhausted its foam extinguisher before the fire could be contained and the aircraft was damaged beyond repair.

George T. Damoff, at the time an aircrewman with Patrol Squadron 34, witnessed the accident. In a letter home he remarked that the accident was doubly unfortunate—the Argentine crew not only lost most of their personal belongings, but many of the gifts they were bringing home to their families.

The third aircraft, identified by an Argentine source as the former BuNo 84649, was assigned PSN 0373 with the same operating code, 2-P-22, as the lost aircraft. It arrived in Argentina on 7 July 1955. Later its operating code was changed to 2-P-201. A former The Flying Lobster of Air Lanes, Inc. (TFLALI) aircraft, it had held the U.S. civil registration NL67904. Some confusion exists because U.S. Civil Aeronautics Administration (CAA) records show NL67904 as having a BuNo of 84659. U.S. records also show NL67904 as being sold to Argentine Purchasing Commission in early 1955, supporting the NL67904/2-P-22 connection. The correct bureau number for 2-P-210 (the second 2-P-22) is probably BuNo 84659.

The Argentine Mariners were based at the Puerto Belgrano Naval Air Station near Bahía Blanca City about seven hundred kilometers south of Buenos Aires. They were assigned to the 2 Escuadrilla Aeronaval de Patrulleros (Number 2 Naval Patrol Squadron), which was under the command of the Escuadra Aeronaval no. 2. Although operations were limited by a lack of spare parts and trained crews, the Mariners flew a total of 439.25 hours during 1956. Most were training flights (293.5 hours) but 77.06 hours supported fleet exercises.

Mariner 2-P-21 was lost on 5 December 1956 on the shores of Rio Gallegos City in southern Argentina. After being torn from its moorings during a violent storm, 2-P-21 was blown on the beach upside down. There were no casualties. 2-P-21 was unique among the Argentine Mariners because it was equipped with three-blade (Hamilton Standard) propellers. All other Argentine Mariners were equipped with four-blade (Curtiss-Electric) propellers.

During the 1957–58 Antarctic exploration campaign, 2-P-22 was used in a single fast naval mail delivery with the Argentine navy oiler *Punta Gorda* standing by for a possible refueling. In early 1959, as a military assistance sale, CAN purchased an additional six surplus PBMs from the U.S. Navy. Saul Alvarez recalled selecting the aircraft from a group in a field at the U.S. Naval Air Station Corpus Christi, Texas, in January 1959. The aircraft were flown to Argentina the following month. The configuration (no bow or dorsal turrets) and the paint scheme of the aircraft indicates that they probably had been used by U.S. Navy's Advanced Training Unit 501 (ATU-501) for flying boat pilot training. The bureau numbers of these aircraft were 59277, 59345, 84746, 84780, 84786, and 85155. They were assigned Argentine PSNs from 0491 through 0496 with operating codes from 5-P-23 through 5-P-28, respectively. Later the operating codes were changed to 2-P-202 through 2-P-207. The delivery flights of these six aircraft were mostly uneventful, although 5-P-25 suffered an engine failure and remained for a month in Guanabara Bay near Rio de Janeiro, Brazil, awaiting repairs. It finally arrived at Puerto Belgrano on 5 March

1959 and was declared out of service the same day because of dangerous wing corrosion. After work at the Taller (Workshops) Aeronaval, Puerto Belgrano, 5-P-25 was released for service on 30 April. It was later recoded as 2-P-204, and remained on active service until 1962.

The U.S. Navy's aircraft history cards detail the assignments of the aircraft before they were transferred to Argentina. BuNo 59277 was delivered 9 March 1945. During World War II it served with VPB-201 and VPB-204. It was placed into storage at Renton, Washington, in June 1947. Brought out of storage for the Korean War, it served in the Pacific with VP-731, VP-892, VP-50, and VP-47. Next, it served with ATU-501, the redesignation of ATU-700, at Corpus Christi. BuNo 59345 was delivered 18 April 1945. After short assignments with VPB-98 and VPB-100, it served with VPB-26 for a year, then with ATU-10, an earlier designation of ATU- 700/ATU-501. Navy records show it was overhauled at Norfolk in December 1949 and then placed in storage. Out of storage, it served with VP-45 in Panama before transfer to Corpus Christi.

BuNo 84746 was delivered 6 June 1945 and significant assignments were to VPB-212 and VP-MS-11. It was overhauled in San Diego in April 1949 and placed in storage. During the Korean War it served with VP-47 and VP-45 and then

ATU-501. BuNo 84780 was delivered after the end of World War II on 28 September 1945. It remained in a "pool" or unassigned status until being placed in storage at Renton, Washington, in 1946. During the Korean War it was assigned to VP-45 and then to ATU-700/ATU-501. BuNo 84786 was delivered on 31 October 1945 and also remained in a pool status until being placed in storage at Renton in 1946. During the Korean War it served in the Far East with VP-892/VP-50 and then ATU-700/ATU-501. BuNo 85155 was accepted on 14 September 1946 and went directly into storage at Renton. During the Korean War it served with VP-40, VP-42, and VP-34. Most of these aircraft completed their U.S. Navy service with the advanced seaplane training unit at Corpus Christi, Texas. Retired in 1958, they were the last operational U.S. Navy Mariners.

After the second group of Mariners was delivered to Argentina, the Mariners were formed into the 2nd Naval Aviation Squadron of Exploration (2 Escuadrilla Aeronaval de Exploracion) in January 1959. This Mariner squadron was integrated into the Flotilla de Exploracion, which operated a total of four squadrons including squadrons of PBY Catalinas and P2V Neptunes. The Mariners operated primarily from Puerto Belgrano, Ushuaia, in Terra del Fuego and from Puerto Deseado in Santa Cruz Province in southern Argentina.

During 1959 there were four Mariners operational and three in "depot" status. Some 620 hours were flown, mainly in the long-range patrol role engaging in both antisubmarine and surface search. Specific missions included participation in Operation Neptuno II, a two week exercise that included U.S. Navy P2V Neptunes operating from Mar del Plata; a search for an unidentified submarine reported in the Golfo San Jorge; and a search for survivors of the merchant ship *Motomar.* Additional missions were flown in support of Argentine Antarctic exploration activities.

During 1960 the Mariners flew some 651.4 hours, of which 166.8 hours were in support of a large-scale antisubmarine operation in the Golfo Nuevo where an unidentified submarine had been observed. To support this effort, the U.S. Navy sent several cargo planes with sonobuoys and depth charges for the Argentine Mariners and Neptunes.

During this period the Argentine Mariners deployed some five times to Laguna del Sauce, Uruguay, for joint exercises with Uruguay's three Mariners. On one occasion, Argentina received five hundred kilograms of spares from Uruguayan stocks and in return performed maintenance on the Uruguayan aircraft at Puerto Belgrano.

The only flying loss of the Argentine Mariners was on 4 January 1961. During a night takeoff from Puerto Belgrano, 2-P-203 hit a buoy and sank. Fortunately, there were no fatalities.

Two of the second-buy Argentine Mariners were withdrawn from service in 1961 along with 2-P-201, the former Flying Lobster Air Lanes aircraft. By 1962 only two Mariners remained airworthy: 2-P-202 and 2-P-204. Consideration was given to transferring these aircraft to Uruguay, but the transfer was never accomplished due to "political circumstances." The political circumstances may well have been a provision in the military assistance sales agreement that prohibited transfer to a third party. 2 Escuadrilla de Exploracion was deactivated during April 1962. The last operational flight of an Argentine Mariner was on 11 May 1962 with a Ushuaia to Puerto Belgrano flight.

Mariners in Uruguay

Through military assistance sales, the Naval Air Service of Uruguay purchased three modified PBM-5S2 Mariners. These aircraft were given the Uruguayan designations A-810, A-811, and A-812. The U.S. Navy bureau number of A-810 was BuNo 84719; A-811 was BuNo 59255, and A-812 was BuNo 59256. Both BuNo 84719 and BuNo 59255 had been delivered to the U.S. Navy late in World War II and had spent many years in storage before being

refurbished for the Korean War. BuNo 84719 served with VP-42, VP-731, and VP-46 and finally with VP-50 during the Korean War. BuNo 59255 was assigned to VP-892, which was later redesignated VP-50. In VP-50, the Mariners operated in the Far East on the Formosa Straits and Korean Patrols, BuNo 59255 as "SE-5" and BuNo 84719 as "SE-12." They had accumulated just under three thousand flying hours each when they were retired from U.S. Navy service in 1956.

In early 1956, with Capitan de Fragata Carlos Mari as chief of mission, flight and maintenance crews flew to the United States. They were given three months of intensive training in the aircraft at the U.S. Navy's advanced flying boat training squadron (ATU-700) at the U.S. Naval Air Station, Corpus Christi, Texas.

The first Uruguayan Mariner, A-810, was flown by its new crew from Corpus Christi to Uruguay via Pensacola, Florida; Guantánamo Bay, Cuba; Trinidad, West Indies; and then through Brazil with stops at Belem, Natal, and Rio de Janiero. These intelligently planned legs permitted daylight landings and takeoffs in unfamiliar seadromes. A-810 arrived in Uruguay on 2 May 1956. Following similar itineraries, A-811 arrived on 21 March 1957 and A-812 on 12 May 1957.

In Uruguay the Mariners operated from the Base Aeronaval No. 2 C/C Carlos A.

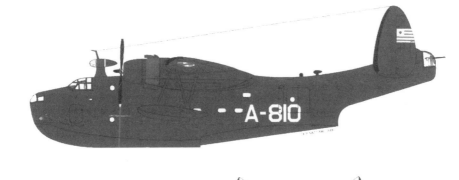

Uruguayan
Mariners (A-810
and A-811),
circa 1957.
P. O. Cerovaz

Curbelo on the Laguna del Sauce near Montevideo. Diverse missions included search and rescue (SAR), long-range surface and antisubmarine search, instrument and navigation training, target towing, and operations with surface ships. The Mariners participated in Operations Unitas I, II, III, and IV, involving coordinated operations with the navies of Brazil and Argentina.

In service from 1956 until 1964, the Uruguayan Mariners flew 449 flights, totaling 1289.2 hours. A-810 remained in service through March 1961 and A-812 through October 1962. In November 1963 A-811, the remaining Mariner, was involved in a spectacular air-sea rescue operation. In honor of Uruguay's Navy Day on 15 November, a ceremony was planned involving an aerial parade of four SNJs, two SNBs, and A-811. During the rendezvous phase of the flyover, at 11:33 AM, SNJ A-254 suddenly entered a steep spiral. Its two pilots bailed out and landed in the waters of the River Plate. The A-811 pilot, Capitan de Fragata (Commander) Luis Rivero, immediately assumed the role of on-scene commander and began rescue operations. He ordered the remaining SNJs to return to base and the two SNBs to orbit the area and keep the survivors in sight. Descending to one hundred feet, he found terrible surface conditions: winds of over thirty knots and nearly ten-foot waves.

With the help of the SNBs, he located one of the survivors from SNJ-254 and dropped a life raft nearby, but the raft was blown away by the violent winds. Rivero then set up for landing and made a superb full-stall open-sea landing at 11:55, stopping within two hundred meters of the survivor. Once on the water, he found the high waves and wind-driven spume limited visibility to only twenty meters. Guided by the SNBs, he was slowly approaching the survivor when an Uruguayan Air Force Bell H-47G helicopter appeared and began a rescue hover. In his fixation with making a rescue, the intrepid helicopter pilot got too low and the tail rotor was struck and destroyed by a wave at 12:05. The two helicopter pilots were thrown into the sea and Rivero immediately turned to save them, but both were lost in the raging waters.

Fortuitously, the crew of A-811 on this day was constituted for SAR and included two qualified frogmen and a medical corpsman. The frogmen used a rubber raft to retrieve the sole survivor of the two crashes, Midshipman Hector Mielniczuk. Mielniczuk, suffering from severe hypothermia, was brought aboard the flying boat at 12:37 PM and treated by the corpsman. He reported that the midshipman required immediate hospital attention.

Because the water was too rough to permit a safe takeoff, Rivero decide to put the aircraft on a nearby beach so the survivor could be taken to the hospital. He informed Curbelo control of his intentions and requested an ambulance meet him on the beach.

With a wonderful display of seamanship, Rivero headed the flying boat into the wind for maximum controllability and let the wind carry him into the shore. When he reached the breaker line, he twisted the aircraft 180 degrees with asymmetric thrust and grounded it bow first on the sandy beach at 1:15 PM. As soon as the survivor was offloaded, Rivero twisted the undamaged aircraft 180 degrees to permit an easy relaunch and set two bow anchors and stern lines.

During the night the wind and sea subsided and by morning the Mariner was high and dry. The retrieval operation consisted of digging a channel to the water and applying strain on a bow line by a tugboat while the aircraft applied full power. Four days after the rescue the Mariner was floated free and flown off.

Remaining in service until 3 February 1964, A-811 was the last operational Mariner in the world. It made its last flight nearly twenty-five years after the first flight of the XPBM-1 in 1939.

CHAPTER EIGHT

COMMERCIAL MARINERS

A few surplus Mariners were used in commercial service in the United States, Colombia, and Portugal. Each employment was interesting and exotic.

Mariners in the Colombian Jungle

The story of the Mariners in the jungle began in early 1946 when Don Carmichael, a former PBM pilot wondering what to do with himself after World War II, accepted a free airplane ride to Bogotá, Colombia. Before leaving New York City, Carmichael was given the address of a mutual acquaintance in Bogotá. Through this source he made friends in Medellin, Colombia's third largest city.

Mariner freighter of Naviera Colombiana, 1946.
Chick Tkachick

While dating the daughters of some of Colombia's leading families, he met officials of Naviera Colombiana, the river steamship line. He learned that in Colombia, the Magdalena River runs southward from Barranquilla on the Caribbean coast to its source in the Andes some five hundred miles away. The river was the country's main artery of surface transportation. For three or four months of the year, however, it dried to depths in some spots of no more than four and one-half feet. During this low water period the steamers could take weeks to travel the route. Many times the paddle-wheel river steamers got stranded and were useless until the water rose. During these stranded periods, high value cargo was vulnerable to pilferage and river piracy.

The Bogotá terminus of the steamers was the river port village of La Dorada. From La Dorada, it was a relatively short truck haul to the city. This situation made Carmichael envision a seaplane freight operation using surplus Martin Mariners to connect the ocean port of Barranquilla with La Dorada. The cost of the air freight in such an operation plus the cost of the short truck haul to Bogotá was thought to be less than the cost of direct air freight by any then-available land plane capable of operating from the 8,660 foot elevation of the Bogotá air field.

The only competition at the time seemed to be Avianca, a Pan American Airways subsidiary. Avianca flew PBY Catalinas with a very limited payload. Transportation needs were heavy and it appeared that there would be business for all.

Carmichael was joined in Medellin by three old friends: Charles "Buddy" Moran, a former U.S. Army Air Force gunnery captain; William Bush, a former U.S. Navy PBM pilot; and Norman Asher, a former U.S. Air Force B-24 pilot. Asher was also a graduate engineer who had spent two years in the aerodynamics group of the Martin Company's engineering division.

The group put together a prospectus for a proposed air freight service and presented it to Naviera Colombiana's board of directors. The board approved the concept and authorized the formation of a new La Division Aerea with Carmichael as manager.

Two PBMs were bought from military surplus in Norfolk, Virginia, in August 1946. After the U.S. Navy removed military electronics, guns, turrets, and armor, Naviera Aerea had the aircraft modified for commercial cargo service. All nonstructural bulkheads were removed. The deck turret opening was reconstructed into a large rectangular overhead hatch through which heavy cargo could easily be loaded by a crane. The bow and tail turret openings were faired over. The aft hull tanks were leveled with the decks and the decking was strengthened to handle heavy loads.

Weight reduction was rigorously pursued by the removal of all unnecessary items such as the cabin heater system, propeller anti-icing system, the sonobuoy air compressor, aft fuel jettison lines, hull tank carbon dioxide (CO_2) purging system, JATO fittings, bombardier and navigator's instruments, and the stove and galley bench. This careful attention to detail reduced the PBM's basic weight by 5,500 pounds, thus providing a very respectable cargo-carrying capacity of 17,500 pounds.

After conversion the two Mariners, Bureau Numbers 85143 and 59160, received the Colombian registration numbers C-56X and C-57X, respectively. They were flown from the United States to their new home: the seaplane base at Barranquilla, Colombia. Barranquilla was one of the world's oldest civil seaplane bases. It had been used by the Sociedad Colombo-Alemana de Transportes Aereos (SCADTA) as early as 1921 for its Junkers floatplane service to La Dorada, and had been a terminus for Pan American Sikorsky S-40s and Consolidated Commodores in the early 1930s. Barranquilla had complete flying boat handling facilities: ramps, aprons, and hangars.

The first Mariner route-survey flight to La Dorada turned out to be an adventure in itself. In Rich Frangella's "Mariners in Civvies," Carmichael recalled:

We had a normal takeoff with appropriate cheers from Barranquilla. Not being familiar with the route, we followed the river as though it were a highway. About an hour out we began noticing mountains and the farther we flew, the higher they seemed and closer and closer to the river.

By the time we sighted La Dorada, we looked around and saw the sheer walls of towering mountains dead ahead. We were in a three-sided pocket of mountains with barely enough room to circle for a landing.

We finally sat down all right and began taxiing toward a buoy the steamship people had placed for us. At that point there was a strong current in one direction and the wind came from the opposite point of the compass. Consequently, we had to make pass after pass at the buoy.

On about the third pass we grounded on a sandbar and did we sweat! Here we were on our first landing and stuck. We shifted ourselves and our cargo fore and aft till we were ready to drop and finally off she came. At last on about the eighth attempt we caught the buoy.

Then the natives piled into dugout canoes and began streaming from the shore. We began wondering whether we were being welcomed or were about to be attacked. Soon, however, most of the dugouts halted and a long 30-footer, power driven with a Ford engine, continued to the PBM. This proved to be the official welcome boat containing the mayor and his entourage, none of whom spoke English. None of the PBM's crew or passengers spoke Spanish. But language was no barrier and with a whoop and holler we were brought aboard.

We found ourselves leading an impromptu parade. Into the town's best cafe we trooped and sat around a rectangular table on a dirt floor. There, under a straw roof and with one side open to gaping onlookers, we drank toast after toast with rum, rum and more rum. And with no chasers!

The next day Carmichael and his crew made depth soundings and planned how to handle their cargo. They developed the technique of beaching the Mariner by running it up upon the soft muddy shore. When the aircraft was beached, a barge would move under the wing and native stevedores would unload the cargo. The barge would then move to a dock where the cargo would be transferred to the trucks for Bogotá.

After obtaining the Colombian CAA permit for commercial operations, La Division Aerea of Naviera Colombiana made its first cargo flight on 21 December 1946. The PBM flew the four hundred mile route from Barranquilla to La Dorada in less than three hours. Although the PBM had been prohibited in its U.S. Navy days from carrying any alcoholic beverages except for medicinal purposes, on this initial trip of its commercial service the ship's cargo was fifteen thousand pounds of French brandy!

From then on the PBM seldom lacked an ounce of capacity loads both ways. Going up, it was often whiskey, brandy, or gin. Returning to Barranquilla it might be potatoes or oil. But cargoes varied and included machinery, medicine, and even cement. Once it included six thousand pounds of uncut picture molding.

Although C-57X was cannibalized for parts, C-56X was carrying capacity loads. This convinced the parent company of the new division's profit possibilities and the directors approved the purchase of additional PBMs. Five additional PBMs were purchased and converted in Norfolk, Virginia, under contract by International Aviation Service of Baltimore. None of the aircraft cost more than five thousand dollars. They were given the Colombian registration numbers C-77X (BuNo 45408), C-78X (BuNo 59034), C-79X (BuNo 59001),

C-81X (BuNo 59013), and C-82X (BuNo 59088). It is possible that C-81X was never flown to Colombia. In correspondence Emil "Chick" Tkachick stated he has a 1948 photo of C-81X in Norfolk.

Tkachick, who had joined Carmichael's operation as a flight engineer, recalled that in May 1948 C-77X and C-78X flew together from Norfolk to Barranquilla via Miami and Kingston, Jamaica. Approaching Kingston the aircraft flew into a squall and were separated. C-77X, piloted by Jim Clews, landed in another harbor to wait out the weather. In Kingston the fuel truck hoses were not long enough to reach the anchored aircraft, so gasoline had to be floated out to the planes in fifty-five gallon drums and hand pumped into the hull tanks.

By the summer of 1948 La Division Aerea of Naviera Colombiana had four flyable PBMs and a fifth for spare parts. All five pilots in the operation were Americans. In addition to Asher, Bush, and Carmichael there were now Howard Hoover and William Fay (both of whom had also flown PBMs in the U.S. Navy). Another crewman was Arturo Polo, a Colombian who was a radio operator. In August Colombian copilots were added to the operation.

In June 1948 a survey was made to examine the possibility of extending the operation to the river port of Puerto

Berrio. Hoover and Tkachick were dropped off at Puerto Berrio by the scheduled Barranquilla–La Dorada flight. The plan was to put the two men and a mooring buoy ashore by an inflatable life raft carried in the aircraft's bomb bay. The plan seemed to be working well until the men got into the raft. The raft would not fit into the bomb bay in a fully inflated condition, so the loading crew had released a lot of the raft's buoyancy air. When Hoover and Tkachick got into the raft, it partially submerged and became uncontrollable. After rescue by a dugout canoe and a diesel tug, they arrived on shore completely soaked. They later planted the buoy, but the current was so swift the buoy would be almost submerged and rapidly clogged with river debris. After a day or so, the buoy was swept away by the current. The plan to add Puerto Berrio to the schedule was subsequently abandoned.

Operations on the Magdalena River were always full of surprises. Early in Carmichael's operation the C-56X Mariner lost a wing tip in a collision with a dock. It was soon returned to service with a replacement wing from the spare parts aircraft.

Tkachick described an event that began on 2 July 1948. It well illustrates some of the unique problems of river flying:

The day we landed, the river was quite low. Our standard operation was to taxi to a sandbar along the riverbanks, using full power with both engines. Utilizing this method enabled us to "drag" the airplane up as far as possible onto the sand to unload our cargo. When we were off-loaded, the airplane was a lot more buoyant so it was quite easy to drag it off the sand with one engine throttled up to allow the PBM to pivot.

While taxiing on the river, we hit a submerged object. I don't know if we struck a rock or one of the huge dead trees that were sometimes carried downstream with the current. The trees were so big and waterlogged that they stayed submerged. We felt an incredible jolt when we hit. I immediately left the flight deck and went below to open an inspection plate located near the main step.

The water was rushing in through the ruptured hull. The crew didn't waste any time in getting the PBM to the nearest sandbar. We used maximum power to bring it up as far as possible but by then the water had already risen to the lower deck and most of the bilge had flooded. After we had off-loaded, it was too late in the day to begin pumping the water out of the hull for our return to Barranquilla.

Imagine our shock the following morning to discover the waterline almost up to the engine nacelles. The river rose several feet overnight. It was unbelievable how the river level changed so quickly

Naviera Colombiana Mariner (C-78X) grounded on sandbank after the river rose, July 1948. *Chick Tkachick*

due to weather patterns high up in the Andes. There was no getting out now. The force and swiftness of the river's current swirling around the hull carried away the sandbar and silt. The airplane settled deeper into the muddy bottom.

I managed to plug the hole from inside the hull. It was quite a challenge, as I had to hold my breath underwater and feel my way through the murky water. Even after we managed to pump most of the water out, the airplane would not float loose. We commandeered a diesel river tug to pull alongside us, using its propeller to force the mud away from the hull. When enough of the mud was removed, there was suddenly a loud suc-

tion sound as the PBM bobbed up as if it was a cork!

Just before floating free, I recall walking about inside the airplane where the water had receded to ankle deep in the waist compartment. All that could be seen out the portholes was water. It was like looking out of a glass bottom boat! We had pumped the water out to several feet below the river level.

We finally towed the Mariner ashore to an abandoned army seaplane base where she was hauled up on the ramp for repairs. The hole was patched with concrete and we manhandled a couple of 55 gallon drums of Aviation Gasoline on board because the hull tanks were contaminated with water. A rotary hand pump was rigged to transfer fuel from the drums during flight to the wing service tanks. Four car batteries were installed to make a 24 volt electrical system as most of the interior below the flight deck was ruined. With the fuel drums secured, and after over three months of salvaging and repair, we took off without any further problems. The return flight to Barranquilla on October 26 was uneventful.

Business was thriving and Carmichael was developing plans to include parachute merchandise deliveries to small towns along the four hundred mile route. However, in October 1948 Naviera's board of directors abruptly decided to end the operation of its Division Aerea. Even though the initial investment had been small, the operating costs of a procedure that required offloading merchandise from aircraft to barges to docks to trucks was high. Competition was appearing in the form of war-surplus C-46s and C-54s that could operate directly to and from the Bogotá airport. By the end of 1948, all of Naviera's Mariners lay abandoned at the Barranquilla seaplane base.

In the 1950s, a U.S. government request for proposal (RFP) was issued for the operation of a seaplane flying service in the Pacific Trust Territories. Carmichael and Tkachick flew to Colombia in July

1951 to inspect the ex-Naviera Mariners for possible use in this service. Alas, the Mariners were no longer fit to fly. They had been stripped of anything useful. They were riddled with bullet holes and corrosion was extensive The story of the jungle Mariners was over.

The Flying Lobster of Air Lanes, Inc.

One of the most unusual chapters in Mariner history is the story of The Flying Lobster of Air Lanes, Inc. (TFLALI).

TFLALI was the brainchild of Harry O. Lee, an imaginative entrepreneur who was also an attorney, actor, and constitutional scholar. During World War II, Lee was a U.S. Marine Corps officer commanding one of the first units to use the Amtrack amphibious landing vehicle. Harry is credited with developing the technique of launching the Amtrack offshore from the ramp of landing ships, a technique widely used in Pacific invasions. After the war Lee "entrepreneured in steel." He joined with a friend in a company called La Rocca Associates and "made a lot of money" brokering steel reinforcing rod, a commodity in high demand in postwar construction.

In 1947 Lee was approached by Carl F. Krogman, a former U.S. Coast Guard pilot, with a proposition to invest in an air cargo business to fly fresh shrimp from Mexico with Martin Mariner flying boats. Mariners were then available from war surplus at a very low price and they seemed to be ideal for such an operation. Lee was interested and advanced the money for the aircraft.

On 6 June 1947 Krogman purchased a Mariner (BuNo 84671) from the War Assets Administration (WAA) for two thousand dollars. The near-new aircraft had most probably been in storage at the Boeing facility in Renton, Washington. Krogman, who was also a TFLALI pilot, obtained the civil registration NL67903 and flew the aircraft to the east coast. During the trip, the Mariner ran into severe icing conditions and was forced to make an emergency stop at Lake Coeur d' Alene, Idaho. On 5 September 1947 Krogman purchased another WAA Mariner (BuNo 84659) on the west coast. It was given the civil registration NL67904. Although Civil Aeronautics Administration (CAA) records of NL67903 were destroyed in 1968, most of the CAA documentation of NL67904 survived. A CAA repair and alteration form indicates NL67904 was on the west coast at least until early November 1947.

On 13 October 1947 Harry O. Lee took title to NL67903 and NL67904. In November he transferred the title to Harmex Company, which he had specifically formed to fly shrimp to the United States from Coxmel, Mexico. At first he planned to operate from the Corpus

Christi Naval Air Station in Texas. After a short stay on the base it became apparent that operating a civilian shrimp-freighting from a naval air station was not practical.

Lee then moved the Harmex shrimp operation to Pan Air Corporation's seaplane base in New Orleans. Lee recalled that two shrimp runs were made, but his primitive refrigeration system was not satisfactory to U.S. Customs and U.S. Department of Agriculture inspectors. He was required to destroy the cargo at considerable expense.

The next transfer of title of the Mariners was in January 1948 from Lee's Harmex to his Caribbean Air Cargo Corporation, formed to fly "fresh meat and produce to armed forces installations in the Caribbean." There is no existing record to indicate whether this activity ever began. In the meantime, Lee had become a partner with Boston financier Frederick C. Adams in a plush Manhattan restaurant called "The Flying Lobster."

Lee came up with the idea of getting his lobsters directly from the fishermen in Newfoundland. He would fly the lobsters to Maine and then truck them down to New York City. Not only was this a cost-effective way to procure lobsters, it made for good publicity! A newspaper article stated that Lee "used hydroplanes to pull lobsters right out of the fisherman's traps and have them back in the water before the mist on their shells dried."

Two Mariners of Flying Lobster of Air Lanes Inc., anchored at Rockland, Maine, 1948. *Glenn L. Martin Museum*

On 17 May 1948 title of the two Mariners was transferred from Caribbean Air Cargo to Air Lanes, Inc., of which Adams was president, and the Flying Lobster operation began. Business headquarters for the Flying Lobster operation was located in Rockland, Maine, but home base for the Mariners was Bar Harbor, which had a nice ramp at the airport bordering on Frenchman Bay.

In a 1994 interview with Rich Frangella for the September 1995 issue of *Mariner/Marlin Association (MMA) Newsletter,* former TFLAFI pilot Tedford M. Blaisdell recalled some of his experiences in the Flying Lobster operation. Blaisdell was a professional airline pilot who had been flying with American Overseas Airlines (AOA). When AOA was bought by Pan American he decided to take a vacation at his Bar Harbor home. During his vacation he flew for the Flying Lobster. Blaisdell recalled going to Norfolk, Virginia, to obtain a second Lobster

Mariner and flying it to Maine, probably in the spring of 1948. Blaisdells's reminiscences provide a wonderful snapshot of TFLALI operations:

I obtained a co-pilot locally, Bob Battie, who was later shot down over North Korea flying a B-29. We made eight trips to Lewisporte, Newfoundland. The crew consisted of pilot, co-pilot, crew chief and a helper. We carried between 12,000 and 20,000 pounds of lobsters per trip which was grossly overloaded. Loading was very carefully carried out and checked by the crew chief and myself to keep the MAC [mean aerodynamic chord] to 16.2%. During our stops we had to tie up to a mooring buoy. The PBM was a BIG machine to grab a buoy and stop, even on a windy day. Sometimes we would make an instrument approach to Gander Airport and hedgehop to Lewisporte sixty miles away. To take-off on calm days I had to go to the whole length of the fjord, about six miles on the step, until we hit some ocean swells to become airborne. Then circle over water until you had 1500 feet altitude and then follow the river at Botwood inland. By the time we were over the interior of Newfoundland, we were up to 5000 feet above several river lanes as emergency landing places.

In Lewisporte we loaded the lob-sters which were packed in cedar crates soaked in brine. Each crate weighed about a hundred pounds making them quite a load. Crates were crammed into all available compartments. The lobsters would make a clicking sound that could be heard over the noise of the R-2800s in flight. Upon our destination at Boothbay Harbor, unloading was accomplished by tossing the crates from the waist hatch into the water to be picked up by a waiting boat.

On return trips to Newfoundland we carried lobster bait in 55 gallon drums, placed far aft for balance. The bait was chopped fishheads and tails or leavings from a sardine factory. It was put in the sun to rot. The riper it became, the more the lobsters liked it. You can't imagine the odor, after a while you didn't notice the smell too much.

The flying was interesting and I really enjoyed the trips. The PBM had a nice big flight deck with a hot plate (galley). We ate lobster on every trip back. The PBM drove like a Cadillac. It was very comfortable.

We flew into Rockland and Boothbay Harbor where it was cheaper to truck lobsters from those locations to New York. My instrument approach was made by using the ADF [automatic direction finding] on a commercial radio tower and picking up the lights on the high-tension electrical lines over a bridge. Night landings were a little tricky. You never were certain that there would be a lobster boat or pleasure craft anchored in the bay with no lights.

TFLALI apparently remained in business until the end of the summer of 1951. David C. Quinn and Rich Frangella's "The Flying Lobster Air Lanes, Inc." quotes a 1995 newspaper biography of Harry O. Lee that recounted that he closed his restaurant and returned to his law practice in Troy, New York.

But the story of the Flying Lobster Mariners was not over. On 5 December 1951 the Lobster Mariners and assorted spares and support equipment were sold by Flying Lobster Air Lanes, Inc., for about ten thousand dollars to Steward-Davis Inc., of Gardena, California. Title was later transferred to Air Power Inc., a corporation owned by Steward-Davis. Apparently most of the sale was reduced to salvage or scrapped, but NL67904 was sold less its engines, instruments, and radio to Bar Harbor Airways on 30 January 1952 for "One Dollar and other considerations." Bar Harbor Airways canceled the registration number on 1 April 1952.

Mariner NL67904, without its engines, was observed on the tarmac of the Bar Harbor airport in 1953 with "Sight Seeing Flights" painted on the side. The aircraft probably was being used as an eye-catching billboard for other airport activities.

On 15 March 1954 Pan Air Corporation of New Orleans stated in a letter to the CAA that it had purchased the aircraft. Pan Air requested that the registration be reinstated for the "ferry flight to New Orleans and for the test flights after overhaul of the aircraft." A photograph of NL67904 dated 23 May 1954 shows it at Bar Harbor with engines installed and presumably ready for flight.

While taxiing in Frenchman Bay preparing for the ferry flight to New Orleans, NL67904 struck a rock. Temporary repairs were made with "concrete and chicken wire." In New Orleans the aircraft was given an extensive overhaul at Pan Air's facilities. It was sold to an Argentine naval commission on 4 January 1955 and arrived in Argentina on 7 July 1955.

In the Argentine naval air service, Comando de Aviacion Naval, the former Flying Lobster NL67904 was assigned the operating code 2-P-22 (later changed to 2-P-201). It served until 1961, one of the last operational Mariners in the world.

Some confusion arises as to the original U.S. Navy bureau number of NL67904/2-P-22/2-P-201. All CAA records indicate BuNo 84659, but an Argentine source states BuNo 84649. The correct bureau number is probably 84659.

The Portuguese Airliner

Although at least forty-nine U.S. Navy and twelve Royal Australian Air Force Mariners had been specially configured and used as cargo/personnel transports, few Mariners were used in postwar civil aviation. Two operated with Flying Lobster of Air Lanes, Inc., during 1947–51, carrying lobsters from Newfoundland to Maine. Seven flew with La Division Aerea de Naviera Colombiana along the Magdalena River in Colombia in 1947–48. No other Mariners are known to have operated in a civil role until 1958.

Since 1949 the British airline Aquila Airways Limited had operated flying boat passenger services linking Southampton, England, with Funchal Bay, Madeira, via Lisbon using Short Hythe (converted Sunderland) and later Short Solent aircraft. The route was subsidized by the Portuguese government through the Portuguese national airline, Transportes Aéreos Portugueses (TAP).

Because of the cost of this subsidy and the unreliable service being provided by Aquila's aging flying boats, in early 1958 the Portuguese government decided to build an airport on Madeira Island. When the airport project was announced, Aquila

chose to request a substantial increase in its subsidy. Until the airport was completed, the Portuguese government had three options: (1) agree to the increase and let Aquila continue with the existing operation, (2) terminate the air service to the islands (not a viable option because of the adverse effect on the Madeira economy) or (3) have TAP assume the route using flying boats.

The Portuguese Government chose the third option. Suffering grave internal problems, Brigadier Freitas, the president of TAP's board of directors, did not feel TAP was capable of undertaking the project. Capt. Durval Mergulhao, TAP's chief pilot, was also a partner in the company Aero Topografica SA (ARTOP) and suggested to Freitas that ARTOP might be interested in the venture.

Freitas gave the go-ahead for ARTOP to explore the concept and the company immediately began a search for an appropriate aircraft. The most direct approach would have been for ARTOP to purchase Aquila's Solents. In fact, Aquila had offered the aircraft and support equipment as a package at a realistic price. Neither TAP nor ARTOP, however, liked the Solent's poor reliability or its lack of rough water capability so the Solent was eliminated from consideration.

At the time the PBY Catalina, the Martin JRM Mars, and the Martin PBM

Mariner were available. These aircraft were analyzed for the route. Considering passenger capacity, capital costs, availability of spares, conversion expense, and time, the choice was narrowed to either the Mars or the Mariner.

On 20 June 1958 ARTOP presented a proposal to the minister of communications for the operation of the Lisbon/Madeira route giving a choice of two aircraft: the four-engined Martin Mars or the two-engined Martin Mariner. Based on a recommendation from TAP, the minister gave approval to the proposed operation using converted Mariners on 25 June 1958.

Having the conversion done in the United States would cause an interruption in the air service to the Madeira Islands. It also would require a significant amount of capital to flow out of the country. Because the conversion did not present any significant technical problems officials decided to have the work done in Portugal. However, first it was necessary to get the necessary approval from Direcção-Geral da Aeronáutica Civil (DGAC), the Portuguese civil aeronautics agency. Negotiations with DGAC established the following ground rules:

The aircraft would fly from the United States to Lisbon with a U.S. ferry permit. The conversion would be done in Lisbon using personnel recruited from the government facility's general workshops of aeronautical material (Oficinas Gerais de Material Aeronautico, OGMA), TAP, or other qualified organizations. ARTOP would be required to choose the most experienced technicians to head all the different technical groups.

DGAC would provide quality control for all phases using its own technicians and inspectors.

DGAC would provide the final certificate of airworthiness.

Contract general conditions were then established with TAP. ARTOP began selection of suitable aircraft to be bought through brokers in the war surplus market. TAP chose the American company Surex Trading of North Bergen, New Jersey, as its agent. Surex was managed by Manuel Garcia, an aeronautical engineer and one of the founders of Aerolineas Argentinas. Surex represented companies such as Lockheed, Curtiss-Wright, Vertol, Convair, etc. It was also charged with the procurement of all the necessary spares and support equipment.

The main focus was to find aircraft with little or no corrosion. Twelve were inspected and two selected, one in Philadelphia and another in San Diego. The aircraft selected were surplus U.S. Navy PBM-5 Mariners (Bureau Numbers

59144 and 45409); they received the Portuguese registrations CS-THA and CS-THB, respectively.

BuNo 59144 (CS-THA) had been delivered to the U.S. Navy in January 1945. It served with Patrol Bombing Squadron 204 (VPB-204) until March 1946. After a reconditioning at Norfolk, Virginia, it was assigned to Patrol Squadrons (Medium Seaplane) 5 (VP-MS-5), then VP-MS-9 and VP-MS-4. It next underwent a second reconditioning at Norfolk during 1948 and was placed in storage. Brought out of storage during the Korean War, it served with the flying boat advanced training unit (ATU) at Corpus Christi, Texas. BuNo 59144 was struck from U.S. Navy inventory and declared surplus in July 1954.

CS-THA was prepared for its Civil Aeronautics Administration (CAA) ferry permit by Atlantic Aviation in Philadelphia. For the flight to Portugal, it was assigned the U.S. civil registration N10162. It arrived in Lisbon on 26 August 1958.

BuNo 45409 (CS-THB) had been delivered to the U.S. Navy in August 1944. It first served with Patrol Bombing Squadron 208 (VPB-208). It was reconditioned at Norfolk in early 1946 and placed in storage in Renton, Washington. After being brought out of storage, it also served with the ATU in Corpus Christi. BuNo 45409 was stricken from U.S. Navy inventory in San Diego and declared surplus in January 1957.

CS-THB was prepared for its CAA ferry permit by Spiders Aircraft Company in San Diego. The permit was granted on 28 August 1958 with U.S. civil registration N7824C. CS-THB departed San Diego on 29 August 1958, arriving at Lisbon on 4 September. It was flown to Portugal by Comdr. Pat Byrnes, a legendary flying boat pilot whose twenty-two thousand plus pilot hours included nearly four thousand in the PBM. Byrnes was also an operational and technical consultant for ARTOP.

After arrival in Portugal, the two aircraft received minor airframe modifications to prepare them for their new civil transport role. The bow and tail gun turrets were removed and the openings were faired over. A nonstructural hull partition was removed. Additional soundproofing and provisions for baggage stowage and passenger seating were added. Eight windows were enlarged and twelve more were converted to be windows that open.

Because the planned route of the Mariners was only three hours and twenty minutes at altitudes below ten thousand feet, some significant modifications to the aircraft systems were also made. The fuel feed system was fixed into a simple cross-feed system. The Mariner was originally designed for flights of up to eighteen hours, which required a complex fuel system utilizing wing service tanks, hull tanks, and bomb-bay tanks controlled by

Interior accommodations of Portuguese Aero Topografica SA (ARTOP) Mariner after conversion, 1958. *Jose Mergulhao*

a flight engineer. The engine compressors were fixed in the "low blower" position. This was justified by the planned low altitude operation. Electrical and radio installations were modified. Dual automatic direction finding (ADF) equipment was installed. Although a later accident investigation report stated that "reverse" propeller control was eliminated, this modification probably was not necessary. The only Mariners known to be equipped with reversing propellers were the PBM-5Gs used by the U.S. Coast Guard and the PBM-5A amphibian. If reverse thrust

had been installed in CS-THA and CS-THB, it should have been retained. Reverse thrust propellers allow precise maneuvering on the water, and eliminate the need for crew members to handle clumsy canvas "sea anchors" for slowing and turning. Inasmuch as these system modifications seemed to eliminate the need for a flight engineer, the minimum flight crew complement for the civil Mariners was established at pilot, copilot, and radio operator.

Except for some passenger accommodations, CS-THA completed conversion on

26 September 1958. ARTOP decided to use CS-THA for test flying while CS-THB was being completely finished. CS-THA did several flights on 27 September under a DGAC special flight test permit. The flights were successful and the aircraft was issued a certificate of airworthiness to start air service on 1 October 1958.

On 29 September 1958 Aquila flew its last flight on this route. The next day it ceased operations altogether. Because of "bureaucratic delays," the certificate of airworthiness was not activated as scheduled, so CS-THA continued test flights with a temporary certificate. During October it accumulated nearly 140 hours.

CS-THB completed its complete conversion on 2 November 1958. A test flight revealed only two minor problems that were immediately corrected. After generator balancing on 8 November a certificate of airworthiness was requested and granted. CS-THB was scheduled for a revenue flight to Madeira on 9 November.

On 9 November 1958 CS-THB, which had been christened "Porto Santo," was scheduled to depart Lisbon for Madeira at 0700. Because of weather conditions at Madeira, the flight was delayed twice, finally lifting off at 1223. On board was a crew of six and thirty passengers.

The pilot in command was Harry Broadbent, an experienced flying boat captain who had flown Solents with Aquila and with Trans Oceanic Airways in Australia. Broadbent had nearly ten thousand pilot hours and had been checked out in the ARTOP Mariners by Commander Byrnes. Copilot Thomas Rowell was another experienced ex-Aquila pilot with nearly four thousand pilot hours. Radio operators were two very qualified Portuguese: Joaquim Pereira Bairrao Ruivo and Joaquim Luis. The cabin crew consisted of Fernando Pereira Rego, flight steward, and Maria Vilao Antunes, the onboard assistant.

At 1230 CS-THB established voice contact with the center of regional air traffic control of the continent. At 1240 the pilot requested a change in assigned altitude from eight to six thousand feet. The request was granted.

Enroute communications by Morse code were established at 1247, estimating passage of the thirteenth meridian at 1407. Normally the next message from CS-THB would be to provide the exact time of passage. However, at 1321 the center of regional air traffic control received the Morse international "Q" signal "QUG" followed by the plain language word "EMERGENCIA." The "QUG" signal means, "I am forced to land immediately."

No further transmissions from the aircraft were received, and the aircraft did not respond to queries from air traffic control.

The American embassy in Lisbon was requested to ask the U.S. Air Force base at Sidi-Silmane, Morocco, if any transmissions from CS-THB had been received. Sidi-Silmane replied in the negative.

Search and rescue (SAR) procedures were activated. A massive search by civil and military aircraft and merchant and naval ships began, centered about an estimated position of 37°12' N, 11°16' W. The SAR effort was truly international, including British Shackletons from Gibraltar; U.S. Navy P2V Neptunes and a UF-1 Albatross from Port Lyautey, Morocco, and Rota, Spain; Portuguese Neptunes and PV-2 Harpoons; and a number of U.S. Air Force SA-16 Albatrosses of the 56th Air Rescue Squadron from Sidi-Silmane. The search was also joined by CS-THB's sister ship, Mariner CS-THA. The search continued night and day until 14 November, but not the slightest trace of CS-THB was ever found.

On 10 November 1958, the day after the accident, the director general of civil aeronautics (DGAC) of Portugal appointed a commission of inquiry headed by Lt. Col. Carlos Esteves Beja, director of the Lisbon Airport, to investigate the accident. There were no witnesses or survivors. No wreckage was ever recovered. Inasmuch as there was nothing beyond the single radio message, the commission's investigation was limited to an examination of equipment and crew records and a physical examination of CS-THA, the lost plane's sister ship.

Equipment records for CS-THB showed that although it had been delivered to the U.S. Navy in 1944, it had spent many years in U.S. Navy preserved storage. Upon its arrival in Portugal the airframe had accumulated only 2,240 flight hours. Engine logs showed both engines were low time engines with less than four hundred hours since overhaul. The engines apparently performed flawlessly on the 43.8 hour ferry flight from San Diego, California, to Lisbon. Propeller records indicated both propellers were given a complete inspection in Portugal at the general workshops of aeronautical material in October 1958. CS-THB's flight logs showed one hour and thirty-four minutes flight time between its arrival in Portugal and the fatal flight. This was the test flight after completion of modifications. The flight crew's licenses were all current and in order. The flight crew appeared to be exceptionally well qualified.

Inasmuch as CS-THB and its sister ship CS-THA were of the same model and general history and had undergone identical modifications for ARTOP passenger service, CS-THA was physically examined by the commission. The airframe was found to be in excellent condition and the modifications made to convert it to civilian use did not appear to weaken the structure in any way. Modifications to aircraft systems appeared to be correct. The modifications had been tested in a month's flight service of CS-THA and no problems were reported.

The examination of CS-THB's crew and aircraft records and the physical examination of CS-THA yielded no clues as to the cause of the accident. The commission then considered the following possibilities:

Failure of one of the engines. This possibility was eliminated because according to the flight handbook, at the licensed maximum weight of forty-eight thousand pounds, CS-THB should have been able to maintain flight at an altitude of 710 m (over 2,000 ft). The radio operator would have had ample time to communicate details of any problem.

Simultaneous failure of both engines. In this situation, again according to flight handbook data, the aircraft should have taken about four minutes to descend from flight altitude to sea level. This should have given ample time to communicate with air traffic control, assuming electrical power was available to the radio. Even if electrical power was not available, the pilots were extremely experienced in flying boats. With the estimated sea conditions of six to eight feet, they should have been able to make a controlled sea landing.

However, in this situation, flaps would probably not be available. Any open-sea landing is hazardous, so the aircraft may have broken up during an attempted landing.

An explosion in flight. This seemed to be a reasonable possibility, but the commission concluded that this situation should have resulted in some wreckage being recovered. Although no wreckage was ever found, an explosion may have occurred. Many U.S. Navy Mariner crews were uneasy about the reliability and safety of the gasoline-fueled cabin heater and refused to use it even in the coldest weather. The crew of CS-THB may have turned on the cabin heater for the comfort of the passengers, resulting in an in-flight fire and explosion.

With no concrete evidence, however, the commission was unable to determine the exact cause of the accident. The commission believed the simultaneous loss of both engines was the possible cause, as it concluded in its final report on 18 February 1959.

Another possible cause of the crash could have been a propeller malfunction. On 20 August 1958 Netherlands Navy PBM-5A P-303 crashed in Abadan, Iran. Just after take-off P-303 developed an engine problem. The pilot was returning to the airport when the aircraft made a violent turn to the right and crashed. The Dutch crash investigating commission concluded the starboard propeller had gone into reverse pitch. Because it is known that CS-THB had some sort of modification to the propeller control system, that system is suspect. A possibility could be that trouble developed in one of the engines and the pilot attempted to feather the propeller. If the propeller went into reverse instead of feather, the aircraft would have entered a violent spin and crashed vertically into the sea.

As soon as CS-THA was released by the accident commission, Captain Mergulhao had it broken up for scrap. His son says

this action was an expression of remorse over the loss of CS-THB. Despite financial difficulties resulting from the Mariner venture, ARTOP paid all of its debts and remained in business.

Two former Aquila Solents—Awatere-G-ANYI and Aotearoa II- G-AOBL—had been flown to Lisbon on 20 December 1958 in anticipation of their use. Shortly after the loss of CS-THB, a group headed by "a financier from the Azores" requested a Portuguese government permit to operate the two Solents on the Lisbon-Madeira route, but the permit was not granted. The Solents remained derelict in Lisbon until they were scrapped in 1971.

CHAPTER NINE

THE MARINER'S SEAPLANE TENDERS

The Mariner was part of an integrated naval weapon: the flying boat/tender system. The seaplane tender concept was pioneered by Great Britain. In World War I the British tender-based seaplanes were used at the battle of Jutland and in the Dardanelles campaign.

With the post–World War I integration of the long-range Curtiss F5L flying boats into the fleet, the U.S. Navy used the large minelayers *Shawmut* and *Aroostook* and the small minelayer *Sandpiper* as seaplane tenders without official designation as such. Additional large ships were converted from other classes and formally designated as seaplane tenders (AVs). These were transport *Wright* (AV-1), colliers *Jason* (AV-2)

Large seaplane
tender
Chandeleur
(AV-10), 1943.
*U.S. Naval
Institute Photo
Archive*

and *Langley* (AV-3), and oiler *Patoka* (AV-6). None of these ships is known to have operated with the Mariner.

Bird-class minelayers and four-stack destroyers were converted and designated as small seaplane tenders (AVPs or AVDs). Many of these ships operated with Mariners throughout World War II.

Large Seaplane Tender (AV)

With the introduction of the PBY and the PB2Y into the fleet, there was an obvious need for improved seaplane tenders. Authorized in 1937, two modern purpose-built seaplane tenders were launched and commissioned in 1940: *Curtiss* (AV-4) and *Albemarle* (AV-5). These were large ships, 527 feet long with a limiting displacement of 13,777 tons. They were equipped with cranes capable of lifting a PBM and had deck room for one PBM. Another PBM with wings removed could be stored in the hangar. Each seaplane tender carried 270,000 gallons of aviation fuel. Each ship was intended to support two VP squadrons.

Four improved *Curtiss*-class ships were ordered in 1940: *Currituck* (AV-7), *Norton Sound* (AV-11), *Pine Island* (AV-12), and *Salisbury Sound* (AV-13). Slightly larger than the *Curtiss,* the *Currituck*s were 540 feet long with a limiting displacement of 15,092 tons. The *Currituck*s had deck space for two PBMs as well as hangar space for one PBM with its wings removed. *Currituck* was commissioned in 1944; the others in the same class were commissioned in 1945. All serviced the Mariner in World War II and beyond.

To augment the purpose-built tenders, seven Maritime Commission C-3 merchant ships were converted to AVs: *Tangier* (AV-8), *Pocomoke* (AV-9), *Chandeleur* (AV-10), *Kenneth Whiting* (AV-14), *Hamlin* (AV-15), *St. George* (AV-16), and *Cumberland Sound* (AV-17). All were 492 feet long with a limiting displacement of 14,200 tons. Although none had a hangar, each had a crane capable of lifting a PBM and had deck space for one aircraft. Each converted merchant ship could carry over 300,000 gallons of aviation gasoline. *Tangier* and *Pocomoke* were commissioned in 1941, *Chandeleur* in 1942, and the others in 1944. All played an important part in Mariner history.

Albemarle commenced its long involvement with Mariners in 1941. Starting in April it operated with planes of VP-55 and VP-56 in Narragansett Bay, Newfoundland, and Iceland. During 1942 *Albemarle* acted as fast transport for personnel and material to the new naval air bases in the Caribbean and the Pacific

coast of South America. In 1943 it expanded these transport runs to Trinidad and Brazil and in 1944 to North Africa. In 1945 the ship resumed seaplane tending, servicing Mariners of VPB-201 and VPB-210 at Guantánamo Bay and VPB-213 at Trinidad. In February and March it tended VPB-214 at Almirante Bay, Panama, and VPB-74 and VPB-209 in the Galápagos.

Curtiss was damaged at Pearl Harbor on 7 December 1941. Although active throughout the Pacific War, it apparently never operated with PBMs. *Currituck* tended VPB-25 during the Leyte operations. *Norton Sound* supported VPB-26 at Okinawa, where *Pine Island* supported Dumbo aircraft. *Tangier* was also at Pearl Harbor. It tended VPB-20 and VPB-28 during the Philippine campaign.

Pocomoke's initial assignment was in the Atlantic, but she was transferred to the Pacific Fleet in late 1942. In June 1944, *Pocomoke* tended VPB-16 during the Saipan and Palau invasions. Its next deployment was during the Philippine campaign, tending VPB-17 and VPB-20 at Palawan and Tawi Tawi Islands.

Chandeleur tended VPB-18 and VPB-216 at Saipan and Palau and VPB-21 at Saipan and Okinawa. *St. George* tended VPB-19 at Iwo Jima and VPB-18 at Saipan and Okinawa. *Hamlin* tended VPB-17 at Saipan and also participated in the Iwo

Jima and Okinawa invasions. The same squadron was tended by *Kenneth Whiting* at Palau. *Cumberland Sound* supported VPB-22 at Ulithi and Eniwetok.

After the war all the converted AVs were decommissioned. In 1946 *Norton Sound* tended the PBMs of Operation Nanook in Greenland. In 1948 it was converted to a mobile missile-launching platform. *Pine Island* and *Currituck* served the PBMs of Operation Highjump in the Antarctic in 1947. *Currituck* was placed out of commission in reserve in August 1947. *Pine Island* was placed out of commission in May 1950, *Albemarle* in August 1950. *Salisbury Sound* remained active as a seaplane tender in the postwar era, servicing Mariners throughout the Far East.

Shortly after the outbreak of the Korean War, *Curtiss* joined the Seventh Fleet and supported Mariners and British Sunderlands at Iwakuni and Kure, Japan. After this deployment, *Curtiss* ceased acting as a seaplane tender. It began to serve as a scientific command ship.

Pine Island was put back in commission in 1950, and *Currituck* and *Kenneth Whiting* in 1951. *Pine Island, Salisbury Sound,* and *Kenneth Whiting* rotated serving Mariners and later Marlins at Okinawa, Japan, and the Pescadores. *Kenneth Whiting* was decommissioned in 1958, but *Pine Island* and *Salisbury Sound* remained active

until the phase-out of the Marlin in 1967.

Currituck was the only Atlantic Fleet AV during the era. It tended Mariners in the Caribbean and participated in the 1952 Operation Mainbrace in Northern Europe. After retirement of the Mariner, *Currituck* continued to service the Marlin.

The Small Seaplane Tender (AVP and AVD)

The Bird-*Class Minelayer Conversion*

The first series of standardized small seaplane tenders were conversions of the *Bird*-class minelayers of 1917–18. These were sturdy and versatile ships, steel hulled, and 188 feet long. Limiting displacement was 1,350 tons. They had been designed and built for World War I's North Sea mine barrage. After the Armistice, they served as fleet jack-of-all-trades: minesweeping, tending seaplanes, towing targets, performing patrols, and engaging in tactical maneuvers.

In 1936 nine of these ships—*Lapwing, Heron, Thrush, Avocet, Teal, Pelican, Swan, Gannet,* and *Sandpiper*—were reclassified as small seaplane tenders (AVP) and assigned the class numbers 1 through 9, respectively. Each ship carried thirty thousand gallons of aviation gasoline and was equipped to support six patrol planes.

At the outbreak of World War II *Lapwing, Thrush, Gannet,* and *Sandpiper*

Small seaplane
tender *Lapwing*
(AVP-1), 1941.
*U.S. Naval
Institute Photo
Archive*

were part of the Atlantic Fleet. *Pelican* joined the Atlantic Fleet in 1943.

Lapwing tended Mariners at Recife, Brazil, from May to August 1944. *Thrush* serviced VP-212 and VP-213 in Brazil, Puerto Rico, and the British West Indies. In 1942 *Gannet* serviced VP-74 in Bermuda. On 7 June 1942, while engaged in a search for survivors of a torpedoed merchantman, *Gannet* was torpedoed and sunk. Twenty-two survivors were rescued by two PBM-1s of VP-74, which had made hazardous landings in heavy seas. Forty others were saved by *Hamilton* (DMS-18), which had been guided to the area by one of the PBM-1s. From September 1943

until June 1944 *Sandpiper* supported Fleet Air Wing 16's Mariners in Brazil.

Pelican was transferred from the Pacific to the Atlantic Fleet in May 1943. It alternated duties between tending seaplanes and serving as a convoy escort. *Pelican* supported VP-212 Mariners at Essequibo, British Guyana, and Paramaribo in May 1944. No records have been found to indicate whether any *Bird*-class AVPs serviced Mariners in the Pacific during World War II.

The "Four-Piper" Destroyer Conversion

In 1938–39, seven four-piper destroyers of World War I vintage—*Childs, Williamson,*

George E. Badger, Clemson, Goldsborough, Hulbert, and *William B. Preston* were reclassified as small seaplane tenders (AVP) and assigned the class numbers AVP-14 to AVP-20, respectively. Seven other old destroyers were programmed for seaplane tending duties: *Belknap, Osmond Ingram, Ballard, Thorton, Gillis, Greene,* and *McFarland.* In August 1940 all fourteen were redesignated "seaplane tender, destroyer" (AVD) with the class numbers AVD-1 through AVD-14, respectively. The designators AVP-14 through AVP-20 were retired.

The conversion from destroyer (DD) to seaplane tender, destroyer (AVD) involved removing all torpedo equipment, two 4-inch guns, one 3-inch gun, the depth charge racks, and the forward two boilers. Additional deckhouse space was added forward. Internal arrangements were made to accommodate aircraft personnel and for the storage of aviation gasoline. A boat derrick was added to handle a pair of thirty-foot motor launches for tending aircraft. Four .50-caliber machine guns were added for antiaircraft protection.

The AVDs were trim vessels, 318 feet long, with a limiting displacement of 1,900 tons. Even with their two remaining boilers they were capable of twenty-five knots. They were equipped to service twelve patrol planes.

Although most Mariner AVP support was from the newer *Barnegat* class, the AVDs played a significant role in Mariner operations. *Goldsborough, Belknap,* and *George E. Badger* supported PBMs in Newfoundland and Iceland, *Osmond Ingram* in Ecuador and the Galápagos, *Ballard* at Saipan and Palau, *Williamson* at Palau, and *Gillis* and *Williamson* at Okinawa. As the *Barnegat*s joined the fleet, many of the AVDs were assigned new duties. One AVD was redesignated a destroyer (DD) and one an AVD (escort) in 1943; five AVDs were designated as assault transports (APD) in 1944. All the ships that had been designated AVD were scrapped after the war.

The Barnegat/Humboldt Class

Authorized in 1938, six vessels of a new class designed from the keel up as small seaplane tenders were launched in 1941. *Barnegat* (AVP-10), *Biscayne* (AVP-11), *Casco* (AVP-12), and *Mackinac* (AVP-13) were built at the Puget Sound Navy Yard. *Humboldt* (AVP-21) and *Matagorda* (AVP-22) were built at the Boston Navy Yard.

The *Barnegat* class was destroyer sized, 311 feet in length with a 41-foot beam. Capable of eighteen knots, each ship had a limiting displacement of twenty-eight hundred tons. They were well equipped with antiaircraft protection. In order to maximize the space for aircraft support, the main propulsion plant of each *Barnegat*

Small seaplane tender *Matagorda* (AVP-22), 1942. *U.S. Naval Institute Photo Archive*

was diesel. Diesel drive was more compact than a boiler/steam engine plant and required less fuel.

The *Barnegat*s were designed to support up to a full squadron of flying boats. They could lay sea lane and mooring buoys, had extensive aircraft repair and supply facilities, and provided messing and rest facilities for aircrews. Although they could not hoist a flying boat on board, each ship was equipped with a suite of refueling, rearming, and personnel boats. Each *Barnegat* carried eighty-five thousand gallons of aviation gasoline.

The *Barnegat* class was such a successful design that series production of an additional forty-five ships was planned with building to be done at two shipyards near Seattle: the Lake Washington Shipyard and Associated Shipbuilders. Although sixteen ships of this program would later be canceled, twenty-nine were delivered: twenty-five as AVPs and four as motor torpedo boat tenders (AGPs). *Absecon* (AVP-23) never tended flying boats. Fitted with a catapult, it was used for the training of scout/observation (VO/VS) pilots. *Timbalier* (AVP-54) and *Valcour* (AVP-55) were completed by the Puget Sound Navy Yard and commissioned in 1946. Most of the thirty-one *Barnegat*-class AVPs serviced Mariners, both in World War II and in the Korean War.

During World War II in the Atlantic, *Barnegat, Humboldt, Matagorda, Rehoboth* (AVP-50), *Unimak* (AVP-31), and *Rockaway* (AVP-29) serviced Mariners in the Canal Zone, the Galápagos, Cuba, Jamaica, Ecuador, Nicaragua, and in many Brazilian ports. *Barnegat*s became active with Mariners in the Pacific by 1943. *Mackinac, Chincoteague* (AVP-24), *Casco,* and *Onslow* (AVP-48) operated under CFAW-2 in the Marshalls. *San Pablo* (AVP-30), *Half Moon* (AVP-26), *Orca* (AVP-49), *San Carlos* (AVP-51), and *Barataria* (AVP-33) operated under CFAW-10 in the New Guinea–Philippine Theater. Under CFAW-1, *Barnegat*s also participated in Pacific invasions: *Chincoteague* at Iwo Jima; *Mackinac, Casco,* and *Onslow* at Palau; and *Coos Bay* (AVP-25), *Yakatat* (AVP-32), *Shelikof* (AVP-52), *Suisun* (AVP-53), *Castlerock* (AVP-35), *Bering Strait* (AVP-34), and *Corson* (AVP-37) at Saipan. *Mackinac, Chincoteague, Cosco, Yakutat, Shelikof, Onslow, Suisun, Bering Strait, Gardiners Bay* (AVP-39), and *Duxbury Bay* (AVP-38) supported Mariners during the Okinawa invasion.

With the end of World War II, most *Barnegat*s were mothballed or assigned to other duties. Eighteen were transferred to the U.S. Coast Guard for service as weather ships, four were converted to hydrographic survey ships, and others were transferred to foreign governments. *Corson* was placed in

reserve in 1946. After supporting the Mariners of VPB-32 and VH-4 during the Bikini A-bomb tests, *Orca* was placed in reserve in 1947. Seven remained as seaplane tenders: *Gardiners Bay, Floyds Bay,* and *Suisun* in the Pacific and *Greenwich Bay, Timbalier, Valcour,* and *Duxbury Bay* in the Atlantic.

At the beginning of the Korean War in 1950, *Gardiners Bay* established a seadrome for Mariners at Iwakuni, Japan. In September it established an advanced base at Inchon, Korea, for Mariners engaged in mine reconnaissance and destruction. The advanced base was moved to Chinhae, Korea, in October. *Gardiners Bay* continued to support Mariners throughout the Korean War, rotating with *Floyds Bay, Suisun,* and the recommissioned *Corson* and *Orca.* Beginning in 1951 the AVPs primarily supported the Formosa Straits Patrol, establishing seadromes as necessary in Okinawa and the Pescadores Islands. The Pacific AVPs began to be retired as the Mariner was phased out. *Orca* and *Floyds Bay,* however, remained in commission until 1960.

In the Atlantic Fleet during this era, three of the four AVPs were employed in roles other than tending seaplanes. From 1950 through 1960, *Duxbury Bay, Greenwich Bay,* and *Valcour* rotated duty as the flagship for the commander of the Middle East Force. *Timbalier* was the only

Atlantic Fleet AVP employed as a traditional seaplane tender. *Timbalier* supported Mariners in the Caribbean and in Iceland during Operation Mainbrace.

Seaplane Tenders at War

The Pacific campaigns of World War II fully justified the investment in the seaplane/tender team. Seaplane tender operations reached a height that was never seen again. A March 1948 *Naval Aviation News* article, quoted in Capt. Albert Raithel et al.'s *Mariner/Marlin,* wonderfully summarizes the contribution of the seaplane tenders to the campaigns.

> In June 1944, one of the largest fleets ever assembled was lying off Saipan in the Marianas. It was of paramount importance that the fleet not be subjected to surprise attack. To prevent this, long range patrol planes had to establish a wide search perimeter through which no enemy unit could penetrate undetected.
>
> The nearest airfield to Saipan that could base heavy patrol planes was Eniwetok. This was too far away for planes based there to conduct the protective screen needed. The answer, of course, was the Navy's PBM Mariner seaplanes, which needed no hard paved airfield.
>
> On D-day, the mechanical mamas of the seaplane outfits, the seaplane ten-

> ders, took up position several miles offshore and quietly set about preparing a seadrome area for the flying boats. Shortly the big awkward Mariners landed on the open sea and taxied up to the buoys. Fuel and food were brought aboard, sectors were assigned and the first patrols took off from Saipan. It was a familiar pattern, from Tarawa to Okinawa, seaplanes filled the space between invasion and the opening of landfields on the islands that had been secured. The seaplanes operated out of reef-filled lagoons or open sea areas. Home base was where a tender dropped her hook.
>
> Every need of the plane and crew were taken care of by the tender. The PATSU [patrol aircraft service unit] crew based on the tender maintained and repaired the plane: the ship furnished the crew haircuts and beds. She carried bombs and gas, cigarettes, food and limited recreational facilities.
>
> The big AV class tenders, like the *Curtiss* and *Hamlin,* had limited overhaul and repair facilities aboard and they could pick up and handle three PBM type aircraft on their fantails at the same time. The smaller AVP class were equipped with adequate spare parts and could do emergency repair work. They were equipped with machine shops and carried a PATSU detachment. They could

not pick up a PBM with their small cranes. The small tenders gassed planes over the stern and occasionally by bowser [refueling boats]. Bombs and ammo were loaded by rearming boat.

The apogee of tender operations was at Okinawa. Based in Kerama Retto, fourteen seaplane tenders serviced nearly one hundred flying boats during and after the invasion. Even after landplane facilities were secured, the tender-based flying boats continued aggressive operations, attacking Japanese convoys and land facilities in Japan itself. The seaplane tenders provided the vital support that permitted the Mariner to be a fighting flying boat.

CHAPTER TEN

FLOTSAM AND JETSAM

In the long history of the Mariner there have been some very unique and interesting operational configurations and dispositions. In 1943 one Mariner received a civil registration to support war-essential nickel mining in Cuba. In 1944 a Mariner made an emergency landing on a dry lake bed in Arizona. It was repaired on site and flown off as a landplane. One aircraft was used in 1945 as a testbed for an unusual radar by the Naval Electronics Laboratory. The last production Mariner flying boat was extensively rebuilt by the Martin Company for aerodynamic and hydrodynamic experiments in 1948–52, leading to the design of the P5M Marlin and P6M Seamaster. A Mariner was used at the Naval Air Test Center during 1960–61 for hydroski experiments and became the last Mariner in U.S. Navy service. The hulk of a former U.S. Coast Guard Mariner was used by the General Dynamics Company in 1960–61 for nonflying spar buoy experiments to investigate techniques of reducing seaplane motion on the water.

Although no Mariners were preserved by the U.S. Navy, an aircraft sunk in the fresh water of Lake Washington near Seattle in 1949 became the subject of a complex (and unsuccessful) salvage operation in 1996. Another Mariner, sunk in Kwajalein Lagoon, was surveyed for possible recovery in 1998 but logistics considerations precluded salvage.

The last Mariner is a PBM-5A amphibian that is currently on display at the Pima Air and Space Museum in Tucson, Arizona. After being in a derelict state for thirty years, it was restored by the Mariner/Marlin Association in 2001 as a living memorial to the "fighting flying boat" and its crews.

A Civilian Mariner in World War II

During World War II a single PBM-3R Mariner (BuNo 6469) was registered as a civilian aircraft and assigned the civil registration number NX28995. The U.S. Navy's aircraft history card for the aircraft indicates that it was delivered on 14 August 1942 and assigned that same day to "TTS LANT," the Transitional Training Squadron Atlantic. There is no other entry on the card until over a year later on 15 November 1943, when assignment to a transport squadron is indicated. The navy record of the aircraft is blank between August 1942 and November 1943.

However, a summary Federal Aeronautics Administration (FAA) Aircraft Registration Record accounts for the period. BuNo 6469 was described on an application for a civil airworthiness certificate as a Glenn L. Martin Co. PBM-3 (transport version) to be registered for "[c]onfidential purposes in international operation." It was described as having five crew and twenty removable seats for passengers.

On an Application for Foreign Flight Authorization (Civil Aeronautics Administration Form ACA 776) dated 31 August 1942, the purpose of the foreign flight was given as "unlimited flights to Jamaica and Cuba at various times in connection with design and construction of facilities for recovery of nickel in Cuba." The sponsor of these flights was the Defense Plant Corp. The agent was listed as the Nicaro Nickel Co. The aircraft was assigned the radio call sign "khize."

On 1 November 1942 NX28995 was involved in an accident at Miami, Florida (Biscayne Bay), while under the command of Charles S. Collar, its civilian captain.

The aircraft was beached in six and one-half feet of water to prevent sinking after the tunnel gun hatch cover worked loose while taxiing out for takeoff. An "[e]xcited passenger damaged watertight door to forward hull contributing to damage."

The aircraft was salvaged and probably continued in its civilian role until October 1943. Bookkeeping entries in the FAA record show the aircraft was returned to U.S. Navy control on 18 October 1943. The navy's aircraft history card shows assignment on 15 November 1943 to Air Transport Squadron 6 (VR-6).

The Civil Aeronautics Administration (CAA) canceled the civil registration at the navy's request on 11 April 1944. BuNo 6469 was stricken from navy inventory on 31 August 1945.

The Desert Mariner: The Mirage of Willcox Dry Lake

One of the most publicized incidents in Mariner history was an emergency landing on a dry lake bed near Willcox, Arizona. In Capt. Albert Raithel et al.'s *Mariner/Marlin,* Lt. Scott Fitzgerald, the pilot, recalled:

> On March 28, 1944, three PBM aircraft left Eagle Mountain Lake, Texas for San Diego, California. The mission for this flight was to transport machine guns, a large quantity of ammunition and the valuable Norden Bomb Sight which we had been told to protect at all cost.
>
> Of the three aircraft, I, as a NATS [Naval Air Transport Service] ferry pilot, was piloting PBM-3D, side number 5-228. I took off and climbed to an altitude of 10,000 feet using solid instruments. This means I was unable to see outside the aircraft because of fog and I depended entirely on instrument readings. Approximately three hours into the flight, our aircraft broke into clear skies. I remember seeing El Paso, Texas through the clouds. It was a short time later when the flight engineer advised me of port engine problems. Glancing out my window, I could see a large quantity of oil streaming from the wing. We let the engine run until the oil pressure started to drop. At that point we feathered the prop on the port engine and set up for a single engine operation for the duration of the flight.
>
> Weather was clear, but there was extreme air turbulence. Since we were now flying with a single engine, we had lost a couple hundred feet of altitude and would not be able to reach that altitude again. In order to maintain our present altitude, we had to jettison all cargo except for the Norden Bomb Sight.
>
> In the constant confusion of stabilizing our altitude, I knew there was no

PBM-3D (#5-228) after landing at Willcox Dry Lake, Arizona, 28 March 1944. *U.S. Navy via Capt. Al Raithel*

way we were going to make it to our destination. With this thought plaguing my mind, I was trying to locate the closest body of water. Our navigator advised me that there were two possible locations, San Carlos Reservoir or Hoover Dam. With these two locations in mind, I began comparing the two. If we went to either, we would have to fly up a canyon to one of the lakes. If we reached this point, we were not sure we would have enough altitude to get over the dam, then we would need to turn the aircraft around and there might not be room to do this.

With neither of these locations seeming promising, the navigator advised me of a dry lake bed 70 miles east of Tucson, Arizona. After studying the map,

I decided this was the best alternative. I knew that this was dangerous, but chances of landing the huge craft here were better. Knowing the danger of this landing, I gave the crew the option of either parachuting or riding the craft onto the dry lake bed. All the crew chose the latter.

We were soon approaching the dry lake bed. We had been gradually descending and we were now level with the mountain tops. We eased her down to about ten feet off the deck. At this point, I raised the nose slightly so that it would not dig into the ground too hard. As the aircraft touched down ever-so-gently, it felt as if you were drawing your fingers through the sand. We maintained a straight course for approximately 177

PBM-3D (#5-228) being repaired on Willcox Dry Lake, Arizona, April 1944. *U.S. Navy via Capt. R. C. Knott*

yards. At this point aileron control was lost. The starboard wing dropped down knocking the float off which tumbled backwards and did slight damage to the flap. All seven crew members were safe and uninjured.

The aircraft was guarded by U.S. Army Air Corps personnel while Lt. (j.g.) E. C. Miller, San Diego's naval air station crash and salvage officer, and Martin service representative Paul Mitendorff prepared a salvage plan. Their plan called for the damage to be repaired in place and the aircraft to be flown off the lake bed using modified beaching gear for wheels. Glenn L. Martin was consulted and he personally endorsed the plan.

San Diego's assembly and repair facility modified a set of standard beaching gear by removing the flotation tanks and inserting locking bolts to prevent the wheels from swiveling during the takeoff. Provisions were made to permit the gear to be jettisoned in flight. A special tail skid was added to provide an optimum aircraft angle of attack for the takeoff. Turrets and all combat equipment were removed to lighten the plane as much as possible. Ramped pits were dug alongside the aircraft to allow the gear to be attached. After gear attachment, the aircraft was pulled forward onto the level surface of the lake bed.

On 22 May 1944 the desert Mariner was ready to fly. The pilot selected for the mission was Lt. (j.g.) Flynn. He was a veteran

pilot with a total of 2,650 hours in flying boats, of which 650 hours were in PBMs. When the wind was right, just after noon, Flynn made a smooth takeoff, circled back to jettison the gear, and flew on to an uneventful water landing in San Diego Bay.

The Three-Domed Mariner

A very hazy, undated Naval Electronics Laboratory photo exists that depicts a one-of-a-kind Mariner. It was configured with three radomes. The Mariner had one radome in place of the bow turret and two side-by-side radomes on top of the hull just aft of the cockpit in place of the usual APS-15 doghouse radome. The caption to the illustration indicated a "triple radome installation by NAF" for meteorological research in the Far East. "NAF" probably stands for Naval Aircraft Factory. Nothing more is known of this aircraft.

The XP5M-1 and M-270

The last production PBM-5 flying boat,

PBM-5 (BuNo 98616) reconstructed as Martin Model M-270 for P6M seamaster hull testing, 1951. *Glenn L. Martin Museum*

BuNo 98616, was reconstructed in 1947 as the prototype for the new Marlin. It received the designation XP5M-1. First flying on 20 May 1948, it was used in rough water, open-ocean tests of the Marlin's new hull design until the summer of 1950.

In May 1951 the XP5M-1 was returned to the Martin Company for conversion to a test vehicle for the 15:1 length-to-beam ratio hull being considered for the jet-powered P6M Seamaster. The reconstruction was designated Martin model M-270. All M-270 test goals were met and the data proved invaluable in reaching the final Seamaster hull design.

Hydroski Experiments

After World War II a great deal of work was done to improve the rough water capabilities of the seaplane. Basic hull design was refined from a length-to-beam ratio of about 6:1 to 15:1. Aerodynamic improvements were made to reduce lift-off and touch-down speeds. Hydrofoils and hydroskis were investigated to discover their ability to reduce impact forces on landing and takeoff.

The hydroski was a promising approach. It was mechanically simple. It could be configured to offer minimum

PBM-5 (BuNo 84764) during hydrofoil landing tests at the Naval Air Test Center, Patuxent River, Maryland, 1961.
Glenn L. Martin Museum

aerodynamic drag and it could be located on the aircraft so as to minimize adverse pitching movements. The idea behind the hydroski-equipped flying boat was to take advantage of the hydrodynamic lift generated by the hydroski. During the takeoff run the hydroski lift would assist in raising the hull out of the water, thereby reducing overall drag, improving acceleration, and reducing the impact of wave and swell. During landing the lift and distance of the ski from the hull would allow deceleration of the aircraft so that the hull contacted the water at a slower-than-normal speed. Because impact forces are proportional to the square of the speed, hydroskis might prove beneficial.

While the concept of the hydroski was simple, determination of the optimum ski configuration (area, length-to-beam ratio, deadrise angle, and strut length) required full-scale experimentation. PBM-5 BuNo 84764 was assigned to the Naval Air Test Center (NATC) Patuxent River, Maryland, for hydroski experiments and tests.

BuNo 84764 was the last Mariner in U.S. Navy service. Testing continued until 1961 when the aircraft was destroyed in a freak hangar fire. Navy seaplane hydrofoil experiments then continued into the 1960s using a single-engined Lake amphibian. Although the Lake amphibian tests were quite satisfactory, all seaplane hydroski experiments were terminated when the navy decided to end the use of seaplanes.

Project Stilt: Spar Buoy Experiments

With the emergence of the Soviet submarine threat after World War II, antisubmarine

warfare (ASW) became the U.S. Navy's top priority. Every conceivable physical phenomena that might be useful in the detection, tracking, and destruction of submarines was explored. Despite extensive research and experimentation of the promise shown by infrared detectors, exhaust emission detectors, plankton detectors, the Japanese "C" radio system, and blue-green lasers, sonics remained as the only practical detection system.

As part of a broad sonics development program that eventually led to the successful Jezebel system, the concept of a truly open-ocean capable seaplane as a platform for a large active/passive sonar was born. A competition for the open-ocean seaplane

was held and won by Convair with its P6Y design. The navy simultaneously awarded a contract to the Martin Company to install a prototype seaplane sonar in two P5M-2 Marlins in order to conduct a practical examination of the concept before committing to series production of the P6Y. This examination was done by Air Development Squadron 1 (VX-1) in 1958–59.

Although the sonar eventually performed well, serious operational problems with the seaplane sonar concept were shown by the VX-1 trials. One of the most serious was that the crew suffered from seasickness when the aircraft sat on the ocean with the sonar deployed.

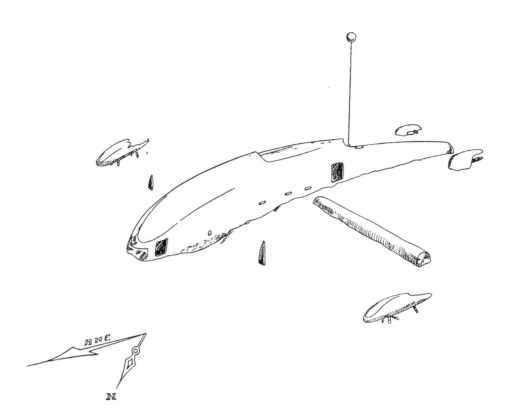

Illustration of
BuNo 59172
resting on the
bottom of Lake
Washington,
1994.
U.S. Navy

Convair conceived an inflatable spar buoy configuration to reduce this motion and constructed a steel spar buoy rig for test. The hulk of the last U.S. Coast Guard Mariner, a PBM-5 (BuNo 59148), was mounted on the test rig and tested in the open sea off of San Diego. While the spar buoy arrangement reduced aircraft motion, the cancellation of the P6Y program ended interest.

The Lake Washington Mariner

PBM-5 (BuNo 59172) sank on 6 May 1949 while being ferried from Sand Point Naval Air Station in Seattle to the Boeing Company seaplane ramp at Renton, Washington, for storage. After landing at Renton and during taxi to the Boeing ramp, rapidly changing wind conditions caused the aircraft to hit a piling. One of the stabilizing floats was damaged. This caused the aircraft to capsize and sink upside down. The crew escaped unharmed.

Through the years, BuNo 59172 has been the subject of a number of salvage attempts. During a 1980–81 effort, over one hundred artifacts were removed from the aircraft and put into the custody of the National Museum of Naval Aviation at Pensacola, Florida. Another salvage attempt took place in 1990 with assistance provided by the navy supervisor of salvage and by Naval Reserve Mobile Diving Salvage Unit 1's Detachment 522 (NRMDSU-1 Det 522). The project was discontinued following the unfortunate work-related death of a detachment 522 diver due to a preexisting heart condition.

Personnel from NRMDSU-1 returned to the wreck site in March 1994 to assess the feasibility of another salvage attempt. Their survey showed the wreck of BuNo 59172 resting on its back in seventy-one and a half feet of water. It was embedded in a dense silt bottom, with between five and nine feet of overburden deposited over the wreck. The hull projected approximately twelve feet above the bottom at its highest elevation.

NRMDSU-1 personnel concluded that a recovery of the aircraft was feasible. Recovery would not only place the aircraft in the collection of the National Museum of Naval Aviation but would also provide a valuable and challenging training exercise for a number of the U.S. Naval Reserve's mobile diving and salvage unit detachments.

In 1995 the Mariner/Marlin Association made a formal request to the chief of naval operations and the Naval Historical Center

to recover BuNo 59172. In 1996 NRMDSU-1 was tasked to undertake this activity. Some logistical support was provided by NRMDSU-1 Det 522, the Naval Historical Center, and the Mariner/Marlin Association. Other agencies that became involved in supporting this cooperative effort included the Washington State Office of Archaeology and Historic Preservation; the U.S. Army Corps of Engineers, Seattle District; and the Advisory Council on Historic Preservation, Western Review Office. The Boeing Corporation provided a substantial amount of additional cooperation and logistical support during the course of the project.

The project to recover BuNo 59172 took place from 19 August through 23 October 1996. The basic objectives of the exercise were to recover the aircraft and to provide a marine salvage training evolution for mobile diving and salvage unit detachments. Over five hundred dives were conducted. They provided an exceptional level of realistic training in difficult conditions and used a variety of different tools and techniques.

While the training objective of this mission was achieved, the goal of recovering the aircraft intact was not. After over a month and a half of laborious overburden removal efforts, and several unsuccessful attempts to free the upside-down aircraft from bottom suction, the final introduc-

Portions of PBM-5 (BuNo 59172) recovered from Lake Washington, 1996.
Dr. Grabe Harman

tion of strain caused the rear of the aircraft to separate from the rest of the fuselage.

Decisions were made to (1) recover the tail section, document it, and turn it over to the National Museum of Naval Aviation; (2) suspend salvage operations; (3) remove all potentially hazardous features on the site; and (4) seal off all accessible penetration points in order to make the site safe for sport divers. The tail section was later transported to the Pima Air and Space Museum in Tucson, Arizona, to be part of an exhibit featuring the last surviving intact PBM.

The Kwajalein Mariner

Aircraft salvor Gary Larkin made dives on a sunken Mariner in Kwajalein Lagoon off Ebeye Island in 1998. Videotapes show a complete Mariner airframe sitting upright on a sandy bottom in about 120 feet of water. Although there was no visible damage to the airframe, the aircraft had no engines, turrets, or radome. It is believed that the aircraft had been stripped of useful parts and then scuttled during or immediately after World War II.

Larkin desired to raise and salvage the

aircraft. Although the raising appeared simple and straightforward, logistic considerations prevented the execution of his plan.

Kwajalein is a U.S. Army ballistic missile test site located about twenty-one hundred miles east of Hawaii. All surface and air transportation is in support of the site mission. Furthermore, fresh water was in short supply and copious amount of water would have been necessary to conserve the airframe if it were brought to the surface. The Kwajalein Mariner remains on the bottom of the lagoon.

The Mariner Legacy

BuNo 122071, a PBM-5A amphibian, was accepted by the U.S. Navy on 6 May 1948. In July it was assigned to Patrol Squadron Medium Amphibian 3 (VP-MA-3) based in Norfolk, Virginia. VP-MA-3 was redesignated VP-33 on 1 September 1948.

After an extensive operational evaluation, the U.S. Navy concluded that the PBM-5A amphibian did not have the operational usefulness of the PBM-5 flying boat so VP-33 was disestablished on 15 December 1949. With its armament removed, BuNo 122071 was then transferred to the air facility of the U.S. Naval Academy for use in the midshipman aviation indoctrination program. In September 1953 the aircraft was sent to

the naval air facility at Litchfield Park, Arizona, for storage. It was stricken from navy service on 17 December 1956.

On 11 July 1958 the aircraft was sold as scrap for $2,251.02 to Frontier Flying Service of Visalia, California. On 10 March 1959 it was sold to Clayton Curtis and Ralph Ponte for "$1 and other considerations." The pair reportedly had plans to convert the Mariner into a fire bomber. The aircraft was made flyable, assigned the civil registration N3190G, and flown to Porterville, California. Nothing appears to have been done to the aircraft at Porterville. It was sold on 15 July 1960 to the Bacon Aircraft Company of Thermal, California, for "$10 and other considerations." The Mariner was flown from Porterville to Thermal in December 1961 by John B. Muoio, a pilot for Cal Air Motive who had flown Mariners in World War II. While serving with VPB-20 in November 1944, Muoio had attacked and badly damaged the Japanese submarine Yu-2. The submarine was later sunk by a follow-up destroyer attack.

During its decade at Thermal, the Mariner was stripped of its original navy paint. Its engines and control surfaces were stored in an old hangar. And it went through six ownership changes and a lien sale!

In 1972 the Mariner was acquired by Bob Gallaher of Allied Aircraft Sales in

Tucson, Arizona. Gallaher reasoned that a museum would either buy this now very unique aircraft or trade other aircraft for it. Gallaher had the aircraft made flyable and had it flown to Tucson.

Gallaher's speculation paid off. On 8 August 1972 the National Air and Space Museum (NASM) traded him three Grumman SA-16 Albatrosses, a Boeing F4B-4, and a Lockheed R5O Lodestar for his Mariner. NASM placed the Mariner on temporary loan to the Pima Air and Space Museum while developing plans for display at its projected Dulles, Virginia, facility. Discussions were held with International Aviation of Tucson on the work required to make the aircraft flyable for a ferry flight from Tucson to Dulles. Replacement engines were identified and reserved at the Davis-Monthan Air Force Base in Tucson.

After the failure to salvage the Lake Washington Mariner in 1998, the Mariner/Marlin Association requested per-mission from NASM to move the former BuNo 122071 Mariner from Pima Air and Space Museum to the National Museum of Naval Aviation in Pensacola. Although NASM indicated that it had no current plans to move the aircraft to Dulles, it denied the request because of a lack of display space inside the Pensacola museum.

The Mariner/Marlin Association then requested permission to refurbish the exterior of the Mariner. NASM agreed and placed the aircraft on a long-term loan to Pima Air and Space Museum. The exterior restoration was completed in 2001. At NASM direction, the aircraft was painted in the Korean War colors and displays the insignia of Air Transport Squadron 21.

BuNo 122071 is currently on display at Pima Air and Space Museum in Tucson, Arizona. It is the only known surviving intact example of the U.S. Navy's twentieth-century "fighting flying boat."

APPENDIX: CASUALTIES IN THE MARINER, 1941–1959

In the long service of the Mariner, there were over one hundred incidents that resulted in the loss of life. The details of these incidents in themselves present a chronology of the Mariner's worldwide operations. This chronology also serves as an honor roll of the names of those who gave their lives flying the Mariner.

During World War II crewmen were killed and Mariners were shot down in battles with German U-boats and with Japanese aircraft and surface ships. In the Korean War era, five Mariners were attacked by Red Chinese MiG-15 jet fighters. Although no Mariners were shot down, three suffered hits from MiG cannon fire and two crewmen were killed and two were wounded.

Many Mariner losses were due to weather, navigational error, and mechanical problems. Weather forecasting was primitive and electronic navigation aids were almost nonexistent. With some assistance from radar, navigation was by drift measurement, dead reckoning, and celestial observation. Changing weather conditions coupled with primitive navigation capability caused a number of losses.

The R-2600 engines in the PBM-3 series were quite unreliable, and engine failures resulted in many crashes and casualties. After the introduction of the more reliable R-2800 engine in the PBM-5 series, engine failures were fewer. Yet, the poor single engine performance of the Mariner caused unfortunate losses.

Most of the information for the years 1941–52 is from microfilmed U.S. Navy aircraft accident reports (AARs), obtained from the Naval Historical Center in Washington, D.C. The AARs list every crewman lost in a specific accident. Except for some World War II combat losses, all PBM losses until 1952 are contained on one microfilm roll and are listed chronologically. World War II combat losses, however, were not always reflected in the AARs. Details of those combat losses were obtained from an examination of microfilmed copies of squadron war diaries, also obtained from the Naval Historical Center. In a few cases names are barely readable.

The notation "(n)" denotes no middle initial. Records of the World War II era contain many typographical errors and in some cases these errors cause some confusion about the proper enlisted rating. The identification for most enlisted rating abbreviations was found in Charles A. Malin's 1970 book, *Abbreviations Used for Navy Enlisted Ratings.* When identifying a few obscure abbreviations, however, the rating given represents a best informed guess. Despite the utmost care trying to ensure that each and every casualty name is correctly listed herein, the listing may contain inadvertent errors or omissions. The author takes full responsibility for any such errors or omissions.

After 1952 a different AAR system was used. It was necessary to know the date of the accident to obtain data. The dates of post-1952 PBM accidents were obtained by cross-referencing Capt. Michael Roberts's second volume of *Dictionary of American Naval Aircraft Squadrons,* the *New York Times* index, and Nevis Frankel's "VPNAVY Website." With a date established, the Aviation History Branch of the Naval Historical Center was able to locate the appropriate AAR.

Names of the U.S. Coast Guard casualties were obtained from the U.S. Coast Guard Historian's Office in Washington, D.C. The name of the Royal Air Force casualty was provided by Colin A.

Pomeroy. Names of the Netherlands Navy casualties were provided by VP International's "Book of Remembrance." The names of the crew lost in the ARTOP commercial Mariner crash were obtained from the official Portuguese accident report.

Special thanks are due to Nevis Frankel's "VPNAVY Website," Historian Terry Geary, Norm Donovan of VP International's "Book of Remembrance," Roy Grossnick and Mark Evans of the Aviation History Branch at the Naval Historical Center, Capt. Dave Carruth, Capt. Al Raithel, Matt Rodina, Frank Hannig, Bill Pierce, Bill Kushman, Joe St. Louis, Graybill Harman, Bruce Handler, and the many Mariner/Marlin Association (MMA) members who contributed information to make this listing as complete and accurate as possible.

U.S. Navy Casualties

2 November 1941
BuNo 1248: PBM-1, VP-74. BuNo 1248 was returning to its base at Krisuvik, Iceland, in bad weather after patrol. No instrument approach was available in the 1940s. After circling the base while awaiting improvement in visibility, the pilot was forced to make a visual approach when fuel ran low. The PBM crashed into a mountain at eight hundred feet.

Ens. C. M. Thornquist
Ens. Carl Bialek
Second Lt. William P. Robinson, U.S. Army
Aviation Machinist's Mate 1st Class Vern H. Anderson
Aviation Machinist's Mate 1st Class Walter V. Garrison
Radioman 1st Class Oran G. Knehr
Seaman 2nd Class M. Ground
Seaman 2nd Class E. L. Cooper
Aviation Machinist's Mate 1st Class (Naval Aviation Pilot) Coy M. Weems
Radioman 2nd Class Joseph S. Wanek
Aviation Machinist's Mate 3rd Class Andrew R. Brazille
Aviation Ordnanceman 3rd Class W. Gordon Payne

3 June 1942
BuNo 1250: PBM-1, VP-74. BuNo 1250 was listed as missing in action on strike mission. The aircraft was believed to have been caught in a downdraft at approximately 37° N, 66° W while circling at low altitude.

Ens. John H. Cushman
Ens. William B. Trapp
Ens. Alton W. Davies

Warrant Machinist Anthony
   Javonovich
Aviation Machinist's Mate 1st Class
   Harvey Peterson
Electrician's Mate 1st Class Edward W.
   Leidy
Aviation Machinist's Mate 2nd Class
   George W. Eddy
Radioman 2nd Class David G. Stone
Radioman 3rd Class Hugh M.
   Brantham
Aviation Ordnanceman 3rd Class
   Thomas E. McMillian
Aviation Machinist's Mate 3rd Class
   William F. Marshall
Aviation Machinist's Mate 3rd Class
   Richard L. Amburn
Aviation Machinist's Mate 3rd Class
   Walter L. Kuhlman

11 November 1942
BuNo 1256: PBM-1, TTS-ATL. Fire in the
air resulted in a crash landing and explosion of BuNo 1256 at NAS Banana River
in Melbourne Beach, Florida.

Lt. (j.g.) Glen David Schroeder
Ens. James H. Littlehales
Ens. C. W. Hanna
Ens. Howard Sage
Aviation Machinist's Mate 3rd Class
   J. M. Wages
Aviation Machinist's Mate 3rd Class
   F. W. Cole

Radioman 3rd Class Walter H. Smith
Seaman 2nd Class L. A. Rivard
Apprentice Seaman G. R. Wheeler

31 December 1942
BuNo 6527: PBM-3C, VP-203. BuNo
6527 crashed on takeoff at San Juan
Harbor, Puerto Rico.

Lt. (j.g.) Edward M. Vogel
Aviation Ordnanceman 3rd Class Izzie
   Goldberg
Aviation Machinist's Mate 3rd Class
   Edwin James Sipowsky

17 February 1943
BuNo 6482: PBM-3R, VP-209. BuNo
6482 stalled on takeoff and crashed at NAS
Norfolk, Virginia.

Ens. James H. Van Leer
Aviation Machinist's Mate 2nd Class
   H. R. Best
Chief Radioman Francis X. Wentworth
Aviation Ordnanceman 3rd Class
   Joseph N. Clark
Radioman 3rd Class John C. Kestyal
Quartermaster 3rd Class Kenneth K.
   Smart
Aviation Metalsmith 1st Class John B.
   Lynch

10 June 1943
BuNo 6534: PBM-3C, VP-205. BuNo

6534 disappeared during a submarine search mission in the Trinidad sector. Crew was listed as missing in action.

Lt. (j.g.) O. W. Haenel
Lt. (j.g.) L. H. Neu
Aviation Pilot 1st Class A. E. Temple
Aviation Machinist's Mate 2nd Class R. O. Marshall
Aviation Radioman 2nd Class W. R. Smith
Aviation Machinist's Mate 3rd Class W. R. Forsyth
Aviation Ordnanceman 3rd Class E. P. Anderson
Aviation Radioman 3rd Class J. O. Hove
Aviation Machinist's Mate 3rd Class L. J. Chouinard
Seaman 2nd Class J. F. O'Barr
Seaman 2nd Class U. E. Kitchens

3 July 1943
BuNo 6571: PBM-3C, VP-74. While on a night ASW patrol, the aircraft crashed forty-seven miles south of the entrance to Rio de Janiero, Brazil. Probable cause of the loss was enemy action. The aircraft was believed to have been shot down by U-199. The crew was listed as killed in action.

Lt. (j.g.) Harold C. Carey
Lt. (j.g.) John A. Helms
Ens. Robert G. Smith
Aviation Chief Machinist's Mate James

L. Mason
Aviation Machinist's Mate 2nd Class Joseph J. Kofka
Aircrewman William E. Magie Jr.
Aviation Radioman 2nd Class Robert R. Hundt
Aviation Machinist's Mate 2nd Class Norman A. Miller
Seaman 2nd Class James E. Burke
Aviation Ordnanceman 2nd Class George W. Persinger

30 July 1943
BuNo 6718: PBM-3S, VP-204. During night patrol on an antisubmarine search mission BuNo 6718 was located at 07°58' N, 54°58' W. The seaplane was hit by 30-caliber machine-gun fire from a U-boat believed to have been U-572. One PBM crewman was killed

Lt. (j.g.) R. K. Hersey

3 August 1943
BuNo 6722: PBM-3S, VP-205. After contact with an enemy submarine that resulted in the sinking of German submarine U-572 (Oberleutnant Heinz Kummetat commanding), BuNo 6722 disappeared in the Trinidad sector. Its crew was listed as missing in action.

Lt. (j.g.) C. C. Cox
Lt. (j.g.) O. K. Lacraft

Lt. (j.g.) W. H. Schwant

Lt. (j.g.) E. G. Wood

Aviation Machinist's Mate 2nd Class
W. J. Dier

Aviation Machinist's Mate 2nd Class
Robert S. Courtney

Aviation Radioman 3rd Class Ralph A.
Guthrie

Aviation Radioman 3rd Class Keith G.
Anderson

Aviation Ordnanceman 2nd Class
Clifford R. Campbell

Seaman 2nd Class W. L. Bickman

Aviation Ordnanceman 3rd Class John
B. Martin

Seaman 2nd Class Samuel C. Boggs

6 August 1943

BuNo 6713: PBM-3C, VP-205. The PBM
engaged German submarine U-615 during
a submarine search in the Trinidad sector.
U-615 was heavily damaged and later sunk
by other aircraft. BuNo 6713 disappeared
and its crew was listed as missing in action.

Lt. A. R. Matuski

Lt. (j.g.) J. L. Milmoe

Lt. (j.g.) C. B. Donahue

Aviation Machinist's Mate 2nd Class
R. M. Gilrist

Aviation Radioman 2nd Class S. L.
Egnew

Aviation Radioman 2nd Class G. T.
Worrell

Aviation Radioman 3rd Class M. G.
Rankin

Aviation Ordnanceman 3rd Class C. R.
Steele

Aviation Machinist's Mate 2nd Class
R. B. Fisher

Aviation Ordnanceman 1st Class H. E.
Fredrickson

Seaman 2nd Class E. W. Moore

6 August 1943

BuNo 6735: PBM-3C, VP-204. During
an antisubmarine search mission BuNo
6735 attacked U-615 at 12°40' S,
64°50' W. Hit by gunfire, the plane suffered minor damage, but the pilot was
killed.

Lt. (j.g.) John W. Dresbach

18 August 1943

BuNo 6716: PBM-3S, VP-210. Twelve
miles south of Montauk Point, Long
Island Sound, New York, the PBM
crashed during an attack on a simulated
submarine target.

Lt. (j.g.) Joseph Prentice Willetts

Lt. (j.g.) William S. Anderson

Lt. (j.g.) John R. Wensel

Aviation Machinist's Mate 1st Class
William G. O'Brien

Aviation Radioman 1st Class Frank E.
Verran

Aviation Ordnanceman 2nd Class
  Arthur Eager
Aviation Machinist's Mate 3rd Class
  Jack Burnett Bubb
Radioman 3rd Class Thomas Joseph
  Marshall
Radioman 3rd Class Irwin Leroy
  Davies
Seaman 2nd Class Dale H. Pitser
Seaman 2nd Class Bruce Franklin
  Shankle
Aviation Machinist's Mate 3rd Class
  Richard John Willnauer

24 September 1943
BuNo 01668: PBM-3S, VP-212. During
night landing training on Perquiman River,
Brazil, BuNo 01668 nosed in and crashed.

Lt. William Jefferson Walker, pilot
Aviation Ordnanceman 3rd Class
  William F. Piety
Aviation Machinist's Mate 3rd Class
  George Anderson Schofield
Aviation Radioman 3rd Class
  Alexander V. Dardynski
Aviation Ordnanceman 3rd Class
  Robert Knute Johnson Jr.
Seaman 2nd Class Thomas Rodney Averitt

13 December 1943
BuNo 48126: PBM-3S, VP-213. BuNo
48126 disappeared during a routine patrol
at 36° N, 75° W.

Lt. (j.g.) George Lincoln Nordby
Chief Aviation Pilot Charles Hardy
Ens. Charles Ireson Briggs
Ens. Sylvester Mazur
Ens. Warren O. Gruber
Aviation Ordnanceman 3rd Class
  Jospeh Barriuso
Aviation Machinist's Mate 3rd Class
  Henry Lloyd Campbell
Aviation Machinist's Mate 3rd Class
  James Warren Claytor
Aviation Machinist's Mate 3rd Class
  Paul Stewart Gahres
Radioman 3rd Class Charles Herbert
  Hayden
Aviation Radioman 3rd Class Vivian
  Chase Kellogg
Seaman 2nd Class Joseph Phillip Kelly
Seaman 2nd Class Walter Andrew
  Kozma
Radioman 3rd Class Harold Max
  Levine
Aviation Ordnanceman 3rd Class
  Warren Frederick Lucas
Aviation Machinist's Mate 2nd Class
  Frederick Walter Mitterwald
Aviation Radioman 2nd Class John
  Henry Ross
Aviation Machinist's Mate 2nd Class
  Michael Francis Michalski Jr.

21 January 1944
BuNo 6644: PBM-3, VP-211. Flying out
of NAF Aratu, Brazil, on an ASW training

mission, BuNo 6644 was hit by its own bomb blast. The aircraft crashed and exploded.

Ens. Thomas C. Donahue
Ens. F. A. Rowe III
Aviation Ordnanceman 2nd Class
    William John McGrath
Aviation Ordnanceman 3rd Class
    Stephen Eli Odydine
Aviation Radioman 3rd Class
    Constantine Livanis

22 January 1944
BuNo 48141: PBM-3S, VP-214. While on an ASW bombing practice mission at 24°31' N, 82°10' W, BuNo 48141 was hit by its own bomb blast which ripped off the aircraft's tail, causing it to crash.

Ens. Charles Thomas Worley
Ens. John Jackson Carmack
Seaman 2nd Class William Edgar Canoe
Photographer's Mate 2nd Class Lloyd
    David Dahl

26 January 1944
BuNo 48134: PBM-3S, VP-213. During a night landing at NAS Key West, Florida, the aircraft hit an ammunition magazine mound and crashed.

Chief Aviation Pilot Donald Ray Meyer
Ens. George Henry Pigion

Ens. William E. Hudson
Aviation Machinist's Mate 2nd Class
    William John Achenbach Jr.
Radioman 3rd Class Marvin
    Christopherson
Seaman 2nd Class Delbert S. Harris
Aviation Ordnanceman 3rd Class
    Edwin Douglas Isbell
Seaman 2nd Class Albert Martines
    Moran Jr.
Seaman 2nd Class Joseph Milton
    Pilachonski
Aviation Machinist's Mate 2nd Class
    Walter Frank Pgoroszewski
Aviation Machinist's Mate 3rd Class
    James Phillip Smith

16 February 1944
BuNo 48182: PBM-3D, VP-202. Returning from a search mission, the aircraft made a hard night landing at Kwajalein Atoll. It caught fire and sank.

Lt. (j.g.) Welburn Ennis Piercy
Ens. Alexander King Wiggins
Aviation Radioman 1st Class William
    Shifler
Aviation Radioman 2nd Class Romers
    Rene Munn
Seaman 1st Class David William Smith

11 April 1944
BuNo 48222: PBM-3D, VP-16. During an extended flight, the aircraft suffered an

engine failure and crashed fifteen miles east of Columbus, New Mexico.

Lt. R. K. John Jr.
Lt. W. F. McIndoo
Ens. N. R. Boyce
Ens. L. R. Bradshaw
Aviation Machinist's Mate 2nd Class Donald M. Wilmot
Aviation Machinist's Mate 3rd Class C. C. Kisielewski
Aviation Machinist's Mate 2nd Class William F. Jacobs
Seaman 1st Class George O. Rizzolo
Aviation Machinist's Mate 2nd Class Francis S. Waldron

31 May 1944
BuNo 45263: PBM-3D, VP-21. During bombing practice, the aircraft experienced a high-altitude stall and crashed at Harvey Point, North Carolina.

Lt. (j.g.) Farquhar Macrae Jr.
Lt. (j.g.) Sidney C. Poage
Ens. James David Dea
Aviation Machinist's Mate 2nd Class Anthony Nykyforczyn
Aviation Radioman 2nd Class William Joseph Westhoven
Aviation Radioman 2nd Class Arthur Henry Leclare
Aviation Machinist's Mate 2nd Class Joseph Tobi Jr.

Seaman 2nd Class James Craig Sloan
Seaman 1st Class John Frederick Schrade

16 June 1944
BuNo 6497: PBM-3R, VR-2. Shortly after takeoff on a training flight, BuNo 6497 exploded and crashed into the San Francisco Bay. The cause was not determined.

Lt. William Frank Hess Jr.
Lt. (j.g.) John Lewis Roberts
Lt. (j.g.) Elbridge Keuley McWha
Aviation Machinist's Mate 1st Class Robert Edward Booker
Aviation Machinist's Mate (Flight Engineer) 3rd Class Rolland Merle Blanchard
Aviation Machinist's Mate (Propeller) 1st Class George Frank Rehrer
Aviation Machinist's Mate (Flight Engineer) 1st Class Paul William Poticha
Aviation Radioman 3rd Class John Sterling Rhodes Jr.
Aviation Ordnanceman 2nd Class Alma Dale Clark

19 June 1944
BuNo unknown (plane 16-P-1, Pilot Lt. Blocker), PBM-3D, VP-16. During the Marianas campaign, the aircraft was attacked by U.S. Grumman Hellcat fighters and one crewman was killed.

Apparently the PBM's IFF equipment was inoperative.

Aviation Machinist's Mate 2nd Class
Gilbert R. Person

21 June 1944
BuNo 45216: PBM-3D, VP-16. During the Marianas campaign, BuNo 45216 was reported missing on patrol and it was believed to have been shot down by U.S. destroyers of Task Force 58. Apparently the aircraft's IFF equipment was inoperative.

Lt. Cmdr. Harry R. Flachsbarth
Ens. Larson G. Ruth
Ens. Lyman E. Benson
Aviation Machinist's Mate 1st Class
Robert E. Wise
Radioman 3rd Class Cecil H. Wiggs
Radioman 3rd Class James T.
Greenfield
Aviation Ordnanceman 3rd Class
Wallace B. Grant
Aviation Machinist's Mate 3rd Class
Austin E. Hoskins
Aviation Machinist's Mate 3rd Class
Alexander Hilton Jr.
Aviation Machinist's Mate 3rd Class
George Plant
Aviation Machinist's Mate 3rd Class
Ray Moorman
Seaman 1st Class Lee R. Douglas

1 July 1944
BuNo 01697: PBM-3S, VP-210. During takeoff from NAF Great Exuma, British West Indies, for a convoy coverage mission, the aircraft water looped to avoid another aircraft. The aircraft hit a buoy, exploded, and sank.

Lt. (j.g.) Herschel B. Douglas
Ens. Edwin H. Booth
Aviation Machinist's Mate 1st Class
Lloyd T. Jones
Aviation Machinist's Mate 2nd Class
Miles H. Jenson
Aviation Ordnanceman 2nd Class John
E. Dzendran
Aviation Ordnanceman 3rd Class
Luther D. Stanford

12 July 1944
BuNo 45244: PBM-3D, VP-20. On a training mission fifty miles west of Monterey, California, the deck turret accidentally fired into the tail, killing the tail gunner.
Aviation Machinist's Mate 2nd Class
Edwin Tugwell Tucker

15 July 1944
BuNo 01726: PBM-3S, VP-204. On a low altitude antisubmarine sweep mission about 140 miles west of Trinidad, British West Indies, one engine failed and the aircraft flew into the sea.

Lt. (j.g.) John Vincent Bruno

Ens. Everett Paul Simonson

Ens. David Sherman

Aviation Radioman 1st Class Larry
Thomas Bostic

Aviation Radioman 1st Class Richard
Stanley Atkinson

Aviation Ordnanceman 2nd Class
Robert Lee Elders

Aviation Machinist's Mate 2nd Class
James Theodore Hall

Radioman 2nd Class Arthur C. Howland

Aviation Ordnanceman 3rd Class John
Joseph Klist

16 July 1944
BuNo 6600: PBM-3C, VP-209. While on
an antisubmarine patrol mission, the aircraft crashed at the approximate position
10°22' N, 79°02' W. It was making a
searchlight run on the U.S. merchant ship
SS *O. M. Bernuth.*

Lt. Robert Donald Spammuth

Ens. Lawrence Dixon Kiker

Ens. Sidney Faim

Aviation Machinist's Mate 2nd Class
Anthony John Block

Aviation Machinist's Mate 3rd Class
George Carl Kurz

Aviation Machinist's Mate 1st Class Bill
Hudspeth

Aviation Radioman 2nd Class Calvin
Ernest Furlong

Aviation Radioman 3rd Class Wallace
Joseph Gillow

Radioman 2nd Class Paul Raymond
Lanigan

Aviation Ordnanceman 2nd Class
Daniel Joseph Welch Jr.

Aviation Chief Machinist's Mate
Bernard Robert Lisle

Seaman 2nd Class Matthew
Sierakowski

Seaman 2nd Class Joseph Frank
Serranti

Seaman 2nd Class Walter Morgan

20 July 1944
BuNo 6679: PBM-3C, VP-203. While on
an antisubmarine patrol near Rio de
Janerio, the aircraft crashed during an
investigation of a suspected target about
two miles from the merchant ship SS *John
Marshall.*

Lt. Livio DeBonis

Ens. Paul Bishop Blair

Ens. Robert James Moots

Aviation Radioman 2nd Class John
Charles Bacon

Aviation Radioman 3rd Class Martin
Stanislaus Beamko

Aviation Machinist's Mate 2nd Class
Dominic John Campagna

Aviation Machinist's Mate 2nd Class
Granvelle Sanford Holt

Aviation Ordnanceman 2nd Class

Wilmer John Kamp
Aviation Machinist's Mate 1st Class
James Worth Reece
Seaman 1st Class Willie Joe Cameron

20 August 1944
BuNo 6717: PBM-3C, VP-207. On a
training flight, BuNo 6717 crashed and
exploded at a position about twenty miles
north of Bermuda. The cause of the accident was unknown.

Lt. (j.g.) Stanley Charles Smith
Ens. Joe Billy Langhorne
Aviation Machinist's Mate 2nd Class
Marion Daniel Colvard
Aviation Machinist's Mate 3rd Class
Fleming Whitley
Seaman 1st Class Will Mitchel Haire
Aviation Ordnanceman 1st Class
Joseph Ellswort Cook
Aviation Ordnanceman 2nd Class
James Lloyd Noel
Aviation Radioman 2nd Class Robert
Chester Taylor

5 September 1944
BuNo 45226: PBM-3D, squadron
unknown. VP-200 was erroneously list on
the accident report; however, there was no
VP-200. The aircraft was on a ferry flight
when an engine failed. BuNo 45226
crashed and sank after an emergency landing at 06°22' N, 176°25' W.

Aviation Ordnanceman 3rd Class John
Francis Kerwin
Seaman 1st Class John Howan Peters
Aviation Machinist's Mate 1st Class
John Joseph Pedgorski
Aviation Ordnanceman 3rd Class
Charles Joseph Fox

29 September 1944
BuNo 48165: PBM-3D, VP-16. BuNo
48165 was on a patrol southeast of Palau
Island when the engines failed. The aircraft
crashed at sea.

Lt. Daniel U. Thomas
Ens. Wilburn R. Caudle
Ens. Lourde L. Costello
Aviation Machinist's Mate 1st Class
Evan E. Frost
Aviation Radioman 3rd Class Edward
B. Reavis
Aviation Ordnanceman 2nd Class
William P. Mulcahy
Aviation Machinist's Mate 3rd Class
Robert J. Gonzales
Aviation Machinist's Mate 3rd Class
Harold G. Green
Seaman 1st Class Morris O. Hamilton
Aviation Machinist's Mate 3rd Class
Willis W. Harris

6 October 1944
BuNo 48189: PBM-3D, VP-216. While
on a combat patrol, BuNo 48189 experi-

enced engine problems and was forced to make a night open-sea landing at 08°15' N, 136°10' E near Noulu Atoll. During the landing, the aircraft broke up and sank.

Ens. Harry F. Mulkey
Aviation Chief Radioman (Air Crew) Harry E. Schopf
Aviation Radioman 3rd Class Arthur E. Artley

18 October 1944
BuNo 45279: PBM-3D, VP-216. BuNo 45279 was on a local test flight in Kossol Passage. It stalled on landing and crashed.

Aviation Radioman 1st Class Arthur W. Boydston
Aviation Machinist's Mate 2nd Class Robert Dietrich

22 October 1944
BuNo 45287: PBM-3D, VPB-19. While on patrol, BuNo 45287 suffered an engine failure and made a forced landing at sea at 21°57' N, 158°09' W. The aircraft broke in two and sank.

Lt. Grady Lamar Mullins
Lt. (j.g.) Norman Archer Taylor
Aviation Ordnanceman 1st Class Arthur Carlos Foust
Aviation Radioman 1st Class William Walter Herlihey

Aviation Machinist's Mate 3rd Class Rudolph John Rozman
Aviation Machinist's Mate 1st Class Odie Esther Williams Jr.
Aviation Machinist's Mate 3rd Class Clarence Roger Garwood
Aviation Machinist's Mate 1st Class John Floyd Wall
Aviation Radioman 3rd Class Clifford S. Sonon

27 October 1944
BuNo 45304: PBM-3D, VPB-21. On a search and rescue (SAR) mission, BuNo 45304 landed to pick up survivors from USS *Hancock* about six hundred miles from Kossol Passage. The aircraft hit a submerged object on landing, but attempted to take off with survivors. It crashed on takeoff.

Aerographer's Mate 3rd Class Samuel Payan (buried at sea)

7 November 1944
BuNo 45307: PBM-3D, VPB-21. BuNo 45307 was moored at the buoy riding out a typhoon at Palau Island. It was torn from the buoy by the typhoon and sank.

Lt. Phillip G. Umhook

16 November 1944
BuNo 01676: PBM-3S, Hedron 12. While engaged in low-altitude bombing practice,

the wing tip of BuNo 01676 hit the water. The aircraft cartwheeled, crashed, and sank.

Ens. Harold Colin Smith
Ens. John Edward Winkler
Aviation Machinist's Mate 3rd Class
   J. A. Beaver
Aviation Machinist's Mate 3rd Class
   James Earl Roper
Aviation Machinist's Mate 3rd Class
   Earl George Spaulding
Aviation Machinist's Mate 3rd Class
   Edward Joseph Hill
Aviation Radioman 3rd Class Charles
   Patrick Kelly
Aviation Ordnanceman 3rd Class
   Raymond Franklin Lyerly
Aviation Ordnanceman 3rd Class
   Walter Ray Hermanson

21 November 1944
BuNo 01669: PBM-3S, VPB-211. On a night training flight to Aratu, Bahia, Brazil, BuNo 01669 crashed at sea, due to unknown causes. Its estimated position was near 12°48' S, 38°08' W.

Lt. Robert H. Lind
Lt. (j.g.) John A. Carroll
Ens. Edmund F. Burke
Aviation Radioman 2nd Class Edward
   A. Crawford
Aviation Machinist's Mate 3rd Class
   Henry D. Duncan Jr.
Aviation Ordnanceman 1st Class

Thomas E. Poquette
Aviation Machinist's Mate 1st Class
   George R. Ruth
Aviation Radioman 3rd Class Samuel
   B. Tipton

22 November 1944
BuNo 45422: PBM-5, VPB-208. Landing at NAS Alameda, California, BuNo 45422 caught fire in the air while on base leg. It subsequently crashed and sank in San Francisco Bay.

Ens. Walter F. Demsey
Ens. James R. Suggs
Aviation Machinist's Mate 2nd Class
   C. T. Brawner

30 November 1944
BuNo 45415: PBM-5, VPB-208. After taking off in the overcast from NAS Alameda, California, on a transpacific flight, the aircraft hit Mt. Tamalpais in Marin County, California, at two thousand feet. All hands were lost.

Lt. J. L. Resley
Lt. (j.g.) Thomas B. Miller
Lt. (j.g.) Thomas W. Oliver
Aviation Chief Machinist's Mate Harry
   L. Holland
Aviation Machinist's Mate 2nd Class
   Thomas J. Joyce
Aviation Machinist's Mate 2nd Class
   Rodney Jeffers
Aviation Radioman 2nd Class John R.
   Kelly

Aviation Ordnanceman 2nd Class
Wayne D. Paxson

12 December 1944
BuNo 48194: PBM-3D, squadron unknown. While being serviced by a boat from USS *Currituck,* a bomb dropped into the water and exploded. BuNo 48194 sank at its mooring.

Aviation Radioman 2nd Class Daniel Joseph Casias
Aviation Radio Technician 2nd Class Robert Adie Hoehme

12 December 1944
BuNo 45382: PBM-3D, VPB-28. During a patrol mission, the aircraft became lost and was forced to ditch at 21°13' N, 151°35' W after running out of fuel. Three survivors were picked up by the merchant ship SS *Cape Lopez* on 16 December.

Lt. C. T. M. Goertz
Ens. C. H. Harrison
Ens. J. B. Higgins
Aviation Machinist's Mate 2nd Class F. X. O'Connell
Aviation Machinist's Mate 3rd Class J. W. Chandler
Aviation Radioman 2nd Class P. V. Mackey
Aviation Radioman 3rd Class A. J. Myers

25 December 1944
BuNo 59017: PBM-5, VPB-27. During a landing in the Kaneohe, Hawaii, seadrome, the aircraft bounced, stalled, and crashed into the water nose first.

Ens. C. B. R. Fennock
Aviation Ordnanceman 3rd Class D. E. Blatt
Aviation Machinist's Mate 2nd Class D. T. Hughes Jr.
Aviation Radioman 3rd Class R. J. McCain
Aviation Ordnanceman 3rd Class D. W. Parmeeter
Aviation Machinist's Mate 3rd Class A. E. Smith

26–27 December 1944
Bureau Numbers unknown: two PBM-3Ds, VPB-28. On 26–27 December a four-plane attack was made on a Japanese task force that was bombarding the beachhead in Mangarin Bay, Mindoro, Philippines. The Japanese force consisted of a heavy cruiser, a light cruiser, and six destroyers. Two aircraft were shot down. A third ran out of fuel and was refueled in enemy waters by a crash boat with a PT escort. Lt. Warren M. Cox's aircraft was hit by intense antiaircraft fire so he ditched it in the bay. All twelve crewmen were rescued by a PBY from VPB-54. Lt. James V. Fallon's Mariner was riddled by fire from a Japanese destroyer and ditched a half mile away from the scene of the battle.

Fallon and his crew reached Canipo Island two days later. They received aid from guerrillas. They were evacuated by a VPB-54 PBY three weeks later, but one man died after rescue.

Aviation Machinist D. W. Schnur

14 January 1945
BuNo 45266: PBM-3D, VPB-28. On taking off from Mangarin Bay, Mindoro, Philippines, on a patrol, BuNo 45266 experienced an engine fire during the take-off run. It hit Cajui Reef and burst into flames. Whaleboats from USS *Half Moon Bay* and USS *San Pablo* went to the crash site and rescued numerous survivors, but the aircraft was a complete wreck.

Lt. (j.g.) Donald A. Riedl
Aviation Machinist's Mate 3rd Class
    Henry R. Shaffer

23 January 1945
BuNo 59015: PBM-5, VPB-27. While on an ASW training exercise about two miles northwest of Kaneohe, Hawaii, BuNo 59015 experienced an engine failure. During the resulting emergency landing attempt, the aircraft stalled and crashed into the sea.

Ens. H. M. Anderton
Aviation Ordnanceman 3rd Class H. L.
    Gheesling Jr.

Aviation Machinist's Mate 3rd Class
    K. E. Brenneman
Aviation Machinist's Mate 3rd Class
    O. McCoy
Aviation Radioman 3rd Class G. W.
    Dickens
Aviation Machinist's Mate 1st Class
    D. B. Barnum
Aviation Machinist's Mate 1st Class
    J. C. Smith
Aviation Machinist's Mate 2nd Class
    G. T. Shaw

29 January 1945
BuNo 45309: PBM-3D, VPB-25. While on a search mission, BuNo 45309 was damaged by antiaircraft fire from a Japanese ship. It was forced to land near Tam Quan, Indochina. All crewmen reached shore and where aided by French resistance. Aviation Radioman 2nd Class Charles L. Hamilton was rescued by an Australian submarine. Aviation Radioman 3rd Class Vincent M. Grady and Ens. William Arthur Quinn were captured by the Japanese, but survived. The rest of the crew were killed or executed by Japanese forces.

Lt. J. L. Stevenson
Ens. Dwaine Meridith Peterson
Aviation Machinist's Mate 3rd Class
    Warren H. Daley
Aviation Machinist's Mate 3rd Class
    Thomas J. McGowan

Aviation Machinist's Mate 3rd Class
Donald H. Douglas

Aviation Machinist's Mate 2nd Class
Frederick C. Barnes

Aviation Ordnanceman 3rd Class
Gordon Hugh Yates

Seaman 1st Class Joseph N. Venditti

8 March 1945

BuNo unknown: PBM-3D, VPB-28.
Piloted by Lt. W. E. Hermanson on a night
low-level bombing mission on a Japanese
ship, the aircraft was hit by ship gunfire.
The bow gunner was killed.

Aviation Ordnanceman 3rd Class
Charles N. Boyle

22 March 1945

BuNo 59077: PBM-5, VPB-100. While
on a training mission, BuNo 59077
experienced an engine failure. The aircraft crashed at sea at position 21°50' N,
157°50' W.

Lt. (j.g.) Walter Lee Hanson

Ens. Alfred Meredith Cole

Ens. Thomas Micklin Whitaker Jr.

Aviation Ordnanceman 3rd Class John
Dale Blair

Aviation Ordnanceman 3rd Class Costa
Harismides

Aviation Ordnanceman 3rd Class
Emmett Robert Dorton Jr.

Aviation Ordnanceman 3rd Class
Bernard Wesley Martens

Aviation Machinist's Mate 3rd Class
Amos Barton Polen

Aviation Machinist's Mate 2nd Class
James Winton Repass Jr.

Aviation Radioman 3rd Class Ernest
Anthony Spagnola

Aviation Radioman 3rd Class Morton
Abraham Wirtner

29–30 March 1945

BuNo 59117: PBM-5, VPB-20. The aircraft was shot down during a night formation attack on a Japanese convoy.

Lt. (j.g.) Wesley O. Glaze, Plane
Commander

Lt. George K. Larson

Lt. (j.g.) Mervin S. Hammond

Ens. Leland J. McDonald

Seaman 1st Class Frank A. Blengino

Aviation Radioman 3rd Class Marvin
L. Boock

Aviation Machinist's Mate 1st Class
Wiley H. Edison

Aviation Radioman 3rd Class Roger L. Foss

Aviation Machinist's Mate 3rd Class
Steve Kowak

Aviation Ordnanceman 2nd Class
Gayle J. Moe

Seaman 1st Class Bernard F. Nelson

Aviation Machinist's Mate 3rd Class
John A. Walling

6 April 1945
BuNo 59082: PBM-5, VPB-98. After take-off on a transpacific flight, the aircraft lost altitude when the flaps were raised. BuNo 59082 bounced and stalled, crashing nose down. It sank in forty-five feet of water.

Lt. James P. O. Lyle
Aviation Ordnanceman 3rd Class
    Robert L. Miller
Aviation Ordnanceman 3rd Class
    Dayton E. Friend
Aviation Machinist's Mate 3rd Class
    Alfred Burton
Aviation Ordnanceman 3rd Class
    Harold G. Kunz
Aviation Radioman 3rd Class Donald
    G. Biggs
Aviation Ordnanceman 3rd Class
    Harold H. Seward
Aviation Radioman 3rd Class Martin
    N. Capral

10 May 1945
BuNo 59204: PBM-5, VPB-100. BuNo 59204 was forced to ditch at sea after a fire began inside the wing between the fuselage and the engine. Nine crewmen were killed in the crash. Three survivors were rescued the next day.

Ens. E. B. Roux
Seaman 1st Class R. C. Brill
Aviation Machinist's Mate 3rd Class
    H. E. Chancellor

Aviation Radioman 3rd Class W. G.
    Crumpler
Aviation Ordnanceman 3rd Class D. A.
    DelMato
Seaman 1st Class E. T. Epps
Aviation Ordnanceman 3rd Class G. R.
    Geuther
Seaman 1st Class W. R. Hanson
Seaman 1st Class J. C. Lawton Jr.

11 May 1945
BuNo 59134: PBM-5, VPB-2. While taking off from NAS Banana River, Florida, on a night radar bombing flight, BuNo 59134 lost power and crashed.

Ens. William R. McLure
Aviation Machinist's Mate 2nd Class
    Robert P. Williams

15 May 1945
Bureau Numbers unknown (believed to be 59038 and 59107): PBM-5, VPB-18. VPB-18 lost two aircraft to Japanese fighters in the Tsushima Straits with a total loss of fifteen crewmen. Records do not separate the casualties by specific aircraft. Lt. (j.g.) Irving E. Marr and his entire crew were lost when shot down by Japanese fighters at about 33°12' N, 128°46' E. Three crewmen were lost when Lt. Marvin E. Hart's aircraft was forced to ditch after being damaged by Japanese fighters at about the same posi-

tion. The rest of crew was rescued by U.S. submarine.

Lt. (j.g.) Irving E. Marr

Ens. Rollo Hecht

Ens. Harold N. Robuck

Ens. Kenneth W. Wagner

Aviation Radioman 3rd Class Clyde L. Varney

Aviation Radioman 3rd Class Howard C. Barnes

Aviation Ordnanceman 3rd Class Jack Carroll

Aviation Machinist's Mate (Flight Engineer) 3rd Class Edmund L. Day Jr.

Aviation Machinist's Mate 3rd Class Richard L. Esler

Aviation Ordnanceman 2nd Class Richard F. Morey

Aviation Machinist's Mate 3rd Class Alfred F. Priest

Aviation Machinist's Mate 3rd Class Carl W. Taylor

Aviation Machinist's Mate 3rd Class Jack Davis Wahl

Aviation Machinist's Mate 3rd Class Leroy Waite

25 May 1945

BuNo 59126: PBM-5, VPB-17. While making a night masthead bombing attack on a Japanese destroyer in the China Sea, BuNo 59126 crashed as a result of damage that was caused by enemy fire.

Ens. A. Ligrani

Aviation Machinist's Mate 1st Class Chester M. Shoemaker

Aviation Machinist's Mate 2nd Class Oliver M. Plumb

Aviation Radioman 3rd Class Marion L. Nutter Jr.

Aviation Radioman 3rd Class Robert D. White

Aviation Ordnanceman 3rd Class William S. Cass

Aircrewman Ralph G. Halstead

Aviation Ordnanceman 3rd Class G. R. Suck

Aviation Ordnanceman 3rd Class D. E. Marks

Seaman 2nd Class Paul E. Oberdorfer

4 June 1945

BuNo 59062: PBM-5, VPB-20. Lt. Deland J. Croze attacked two Japanese transports and an escort vessel in the Makassar Straits, sinking the transports, but his aircraft received damage from the antiaircraft fire of the escort. Croze made a forced landing on the beach at Lingayen Island near the northwestern tip of Celebes. One crewman died of wounds. Three were later rescued by a squadron PBM: Dale Hunt (arm taken by shark), Dalton C. Stephenson, Brodus Lyle Bumpas. Four were captured and beheaded by the Japanese. The Japanese officer responsible was hung after a war crimes trial. No evidence of the exact fate of six crewmen is known.

Lt. Deland J. Croze

Ens. Marshall H. Hicks Jr.

Aviation Radioman 3rd Class Edward A. Calhoun

Aviation Ordnanceman 3rd Class Kenneth J. Crow

Aviation Machinist's Mate 2nd Class Robert B. Jezewski (USS *Pocomoke*)

Aviation Ordnanceman 3rd Class Joe H. Garcia

Aviation Radioman 2nd Class Owen D. Huls

Aviation Machinist's Mate 1st Class John P. Igoe

Aviation Ordnanceman 3rd Class Charles W. Moorfield

Aerographer's Mate 2nd Class Donald M. Pell (USS *Pocomoke*)

15 June 1945

BuNo 01728: PBM-3S, VPB-2. While landing at NAS Corpus Christi, Texas, BuNo 01728 hit a channel marker and crashed.

Lt. R. D. Hotchkiss

Lt. A. J. Englander

Aviation Machinist's Mate 3rd Class J. J. Frey

Aviation Machinist's Mate 3rd Class G. R. Olsen

Seaman 1st Class H. J. O'Hare

Seaman 2nd Class J. J. Ventura

Aviation Chief Machinist's Mate M. D. Dye

18 June 1945

BuNo 59068: PBM-5, VPB-21. While on a Yellow Sea patrol, BuNo 59068 experienced an engine failure. During a forced landing at sea, it crashed and sank at 35° N, 123°36' E.

Aviation Ordnanceman 3rd Class Jackie Neil Camden

Aviation Ordnanceman 3rd Class Peter Anthony Colby

Aviation Machinist's Mate 3rd Class Robert George Fertig

Aviation Ordnanceman 1st Class Donald Laughran

Aviation Radioman 3rd Class Donald Elliott Parkinson

28 June 1945

BuNo unkown: probably a PBM-3D, VPB-18. The aircraft disappeared on a combat search mission in the Western Pacific.

Lt. (j.g.) Edward Podlogar

Aviation Machinist's Mate 2nd Class Eugene R. Foster

Aviation Radioman 1st Class Thomas A. Parsons

Aviation Ordnanceman 3rd Class Dane
Roland Moreland

Aviation Ordnanceman 3rd Class
William Roscoe Autrey

30 June 1945

BuNo 59200: PBM-5, VPB-17. BuNo
59200 was on a search mission in the
Philippines. Because of water contamination
in the fuel, it experienced a double engine
failure. The aircraft crashed and burned.

Ens. Edgar H. Stadler

Aviation Machinist's Mate 3rd Class
Douglas Spencer John Jr.

Aviation Machinist's Mate 3rd Class
Stanley Bruce Ekar

Aviation Machinist's Mate 3rd Class
Richard Duane Bentz

Aviation Radioman 3rd Class Walter S.
Dalyie

Aviation Radioman 3rd Class Walter
Fairfield Flynn

Aviation Machinist's Mate 3rd Class
Kenneth Kerr

Seaman 1st Class Richard Kirash

10 July 1945

BuNo 6510: PBM-3C, VPB-2. BuNo
6510 disappeared on a radar patrol out of
NAS Banana River, Florida. Last reported
position was 25°22' N, 77°34' W.

Lt. (j.g.) J. B. White

Ens. Wendall Eugene Lavoy

Ens. Wesley Elliot Lewis

Aviation Machinist's Mate 3rd Class
James E. Eisley

Aviation Machinist's Mate 3rd Class
Thomas A. Garner

Seaman 1st Class John E. Hurt

Seaman 1st Class Edward J. Wayatt

Aviation Ordnanceman 3rd Class
Thomas C. Oliver

Seaman 1st Class Gene S. Boyer

Seaman 1st Class Bernard M. Zlotwick

Seaman 1st Class Stephen Wororeck

Seaman 1st Class Glen L. Winder

28 July 1945

BuNo 59071: PBM-5, VPB-208. BuNo
59071 bounced during takeoff from the
Chimu Wan Seadrome in Okinawa. The
aircraft nosed in, broke in two, and sank.

Lt. Charles A. Turner, pilot

Lt. (j.g.) W. Garber

Aviation Machinist's Mate 3rd Class E.
E. Casper

Seaman 1st Class G. H. Bullock Jr.

Aviation Radioman 1st Class E. H.
Kunzler

Aviation Radioman 2nd Class M. M.
Zetrouer

Aviation Ordnanceman 2nd Class
W. C. Massey Jr.

Aviation Ordnanceman 3rd Class C. L.
Byrne

Aviation Radioman 2nd Class R. M.
Schilz

7–8 August 1945
BuNo 59145: PBM-5, VPB-27. BuNo
59145 disappeared on a night shipping
strike off Formosa. It was believed to have
been caused by enemy action.

Lt. (j.g.) Bernard Austin Gallagher
Ens. Albert Preston Breeden Jr.
Ens. Ralph Elmer Wolfe
Aviation Machinist's Mate 3rd Class
John Lucian Gregory
Aviation Machinist's Mate 3rd Class
Lamar Eldory Howsare
Aviation Radioman 3rd Class Joseph
Augustin Boarman
Aviation Radioman 3rd Class Hollis
"B" Looney
Seaman 1st Class James Edwin Wood
Aviation Ordnanceman 3rd Class
Harley William Blake
Seaman 1st Class Paul Golnik
Seaman 1st Class Francis Curry Goodian
Seaman 1st Class Paul Richard Kelly

7–8 August 1945
BuNo 59023: PBM-5, VPB-27. BuNo
59023 disappeared on a night shipping
strike off Formosa. Its loss was believed to
have been caused by enemy action.

Lt. (j.g.) Otho Leonard Edwards
Lt. (j.g.) James Leslie Bistodeau

Ens. William McMaster Holligan
Aviation Machinist's Mate (Flight
Engineer) 1st Class Carl Paul Bach
Aviation Ordnanceman 3rd Class
George Patrick Neary
Aviation Machinist's Mate (Flight
Engineer) 3rd Class John Daniel
Heath
Aviation Machinist's Mate (Flight
Engineer) 2nd Class James Clifford
Stewart
Aviation Radioman 1st Class Jack
Lee
Aviation Ordnanceman 2nd Class
Robert Wheeler Shaw
Aviation Ordnanceman 3rd Class
Micheal Martyak
Aviation Radioman 2nd Class Fred
Micheal Korzin
Aviation Radio Technician 2nd Class
Wallace Carey Sumner

5 September 1945
BuNo 59185: PBM-5, VPB-98. BuNo
59185 was conducting night searchlight
practice off San Diego, California. The aircraft crashed at sea. It was surmised that
the pilot suffered vertigo.

Lt. (j.g.) Howard A. Harvey
Lt. (j.g.) Joseph L. Fitzpatrick
Aviation Ordnanceman 3rd Class
George W. Baylor
Aviation Ordnanceman 3rd Class
Robert N. Brown

Aviation Ordnanceman 3rd Class
 Kenneth C. Davis
Aviation Ordnanceman 3rd Class
 Richard A. Frandsen
Aviation Radioman 3rd Class Richard
 P. Kennelly
Aviation Radioman 2nd Class Antonio
 B. Risi
Aviation Radioman 2nd Class Galvin
 Ryder
Aviation Radioman 3rd Class Louis M.
 Hansen
Aviation Machinist's Mate 3rd Class
 Edward W. Albright
Aviation Radioman 2nd Class Lawry B.
 McDaniel

12 September 1945
BuNo 84617: PBM-5, VH-1. While taking
off from Chimu Wan, Okinawa, BuNo
84617 collided with a Grumman J2F. The
collision sheared off the tail of the PBM,
causing it to crash.

Lt. (j.g.) Herman G. Sale
Aviation Machinist's Mate (Flight
 Engineer) 2nd Class Charles B. Kendall
Aviation Machinist's Mate 2nd Class
 George A. Bolex
Aviation Ordnanceman 3rd Class
 Donald B. McGarvah
Aviation Machinist's Mate 1st Class
 Kenneth Defenderffer
Aviation Machinist's Mate 2nd Class
 Joseph B. Ferguson

Aviation Machinist's Mate 3rd Class
 Russell L. Hamilton
Aviation Machinist's Mate 2nd Class
 Henry H. Lafreniere
Aviation Machinist's Mate 2nd Class
 James T. Riller
Aviation Machinist's Mate 3rd Class
 Harry C. Nelson
Aviation Machinist's Mate 3rd Class
 Charles H. Rienhart
Aviation Machinist's Mate 3rd Class
 Robert E. Towns

18 September 1945
BuNo 59716: PBM-5, VPB-27. During a
typhoon, BuNo 59716 was broken loose
from its mooring. It was blown ashore and
destroyed.

Seaman 1st Class Robert C. Wensling

2 October 1945
BuNo 59336: PBM-5, VPB-205. BuNo
59336 disappeared on a patrol. It was
found on 19 November 1948 about five
miles northeast of Wada-Nagano, Honshu,
Japan.

Lt. Gilbert D. Lizer
Ens. Kazimer Oelnski
Aviation Machinist's Mate 2nd Class
 Frank Frederick Kissinger
Aviation Machinist's Mate (Flight
 Engineer) 3rd Class Jack Conrad
 Mallory

Aviation Radioman 2nd Class Herbert
Andrew Kilgour Jr.

Aviation Radioman 3rd Class Donald
Henry Hawthorne

Aviation Ordnanceman 3rd Class
Luther Earl Shaw Jr.

Aviation Machinist's Mate (Flight
Engineer) 3rd Class Albert J.
Schale Jr.

Seaman 1st Class Robert Herbert Johnson

Rear Adm. W. D. Sample

Capt. Charles C. McDonald

18 October 1945
BuNo 59113 and BuNo 01710: PBM-5
and PBM-3S, VPB-2. These two aircraft
collided and exploded about two and half
miles north of NAS Corpus Christi, Texas.

Crew of BuNo 01710:

Lt. (j.g.) J. W. Rosson

Lt. (j.g.) L. F. Cox

Lt. Cmdr. P. Moore

Ens. W. O. Nowlin

Aviation Radioman 3rd Class W. O.
Nowkin

Aviation Machinist's Mate 3rd Class S.
D. Cole

Aviation Ordnanceman 3rd Class J. J.
Fitzsimmons

Aviation Machinist's Mate 3rd Class
H. A. Stern

Aviation Ordnanceman 3rd Class E. A.
Knie

Aviation Radioman 3rd Class H. K.
Breckenridge

Crew of BuNo 59113:

Lt. (j.g.) D. W. Wright

Ens. W. B. Rickard

Ens. D. P. Kelly

Aviation Machinist's Mate 1st Class
T. W. Drake

Aviation Machinist's Mate 3rd Class
J. E. Smith

Aviation Radioman 2nd Class W. F.
Howard

Seaman 1st Class C. W. Cavallaro

Seaman 1st Class W. J. Danezich

Seaman 1st Class R. H. Barberio

Seaman 1st Class W. T. Hopkins

Seaman 1st Class H. A. Thompson

5 December 1945
BuNo 59225: PBM-5, VPB-2. BuNo
59225 was on a night emergency search
and rescue mission from NAS Banana
River, Florida. The aircraft exploded at sea
from an unknown cause at approximate
position 28°59' N, 80°25' W.

Lt. (j.g.) Walter C. Jeffrey

Lt. (j.g.) Harry Grimes Cone

Ens. Charles R. Arceneaux

Ens. Roger Murry Allen

Ens. Lloyd A. Eliason

Aviation Ordnanceman 1st Class Alfred
Joseph Zywicki

Aviation Ordnanceman 3rd Class James

Fredrick Osterheid

Aviation Ordnanceman John Thomas
Menendez

Aviation Radioman 1st Class Phillip B.
Neenan

Aviation Radioman 3rd Class James
Frederick Jordan

Aviation Radioman 3rd Class Robert
C. Cameron

Aviation Machinist's Mate 1st Class
Wiley David Cargill

Aviation Machinist's Mate 1st Class
Donald Edward Peterson

28 July 1946
BuNo 84734: PBM-5, VP-26. Flying out
of NAB Sangley Point, Philippine Islands,
BuNo 84734 was reported missing while
on a search for a missing C-47. The PBM
crashed on a ridge on Mindoro Island at an
approximate position of 13°11' N, 120°56'
E. The crash was attributed to bad weather.
It was found on 6 August 1946.

Lt. Claude W. Adams

Lt. Lionel G. Tetley

Ens. Garland S. Morrison

Aviation Ordnanceman Roger T. Mills

Machinist's Mate 1st Class Walter
Olinkiewiz

Air Controlman 2nd Class Joseph
Adamusko

Aviation Machinist's Mate 2nd Class
Donald R. Manis

Aviation Ordnanceman 3rd Class
Marion K. Norland

Aviation Machinist's Mate 2nd Class
Doyle E. Brownlee

Aviation Ordnanceman 2nd Class
Calvin M. Wilson

Yeoman 3rd Class John F. Ferreira

30 September 1946
BuNo 85145: PBM-5, VRF-1. BuNo 85145
was being ferried to Seattle for storage. It
crashed after takeoff from NAS Corpus Christi,
Texas. Cause of the accident was unknown.

Aviation Communications Technician
M. Ross

Aviation Chief Machinist's Mate G. E.
Gurney

Aviation Machinist's Mate 1st Class
R. M. Allen

Radioman R. J. Woody

Chief Storekeeper J. G. Hay USCG

10 November 1946
BuNo 59343: PBM-5, Hedron 2, FAW-2.
On a test flight from NAS Kaneohe,
Hawaii, BuNo 59343 had to make a forced
landing because of engine failure.

Aviation Machinist's Mate 1st Class
Horst Weigand

30 December 1946
BuNo 59098: PBM-5, VJ-Unit from USS

Pine Island (AV-12). On a photographic reconnaissance mission over the Antarctic continent in the vicinity of Cape Dart, BuNo 59098 flew into the ground during a snow squall. The aircraft then exploded. Survivors were rescued thirteen days later.

Ens. Maxwell A. Lopez, pilot/navigator
Aviation Radioman 1st Class Wendell
  K. Hendersin
Aviation Machinist's Mate 1st Class
  Frederick W. Williams

10 January 1948
BuNo 84606: PBM-5, VH-2. While BuNo 84606 was taking off from the bay in Tsingtao, China, one of the JATO units exploded, resulting in a fire. The aircraft was destroyed.

Air Crew Ordnanceman Maston E.
  Rifenberg

10 February 1948
BuNo 84772: PBM-5, ATU-10. BuNo 84772 was on a navigation training flight from NAS Jacksonville, Florida. The aircraft flew into trees on the west shore of the St. Johns River, about three miles south of Doctors Inlet.

Lt. Morris V. Cromer
Lt. (j.g.) Harry W. Pressell

8 July 1949
BuNo 84655: PBM-5. BuNo 84655 was being overhauled and repaired at NAS Coco Solo, Canal Zone. On a test flight it experienced an engine fire. It crashed and sank at position 09°34' N, 79°58' W.

Cmdr. Edward D. Killian
Lt. Kermit F. Johnson
Chief Aviation Machinist's Mate
  William C. Evans Jr.
Aviation Machinist's Mate 1st Class
  Raymond K. Wardel
Chief Aviation Electronics Technician
  Martin F. Fite
Air Controlman 1st Class Coleman W.
  Henshaw
Aviation Electronics Technician 3rd
  Class Robert T. Willett
Chief Aviation Structural Mechanic
  Mate Arthur J. Melanson
Parachute Rigger 2nd Class Arthur E.
  Bourassa

31 August 1949
BuNo 84770: PBM-5S, VP-46. BuNo 84770 crashed shortly after takeoff from the seadrome at NAS San Diego, California.

Lt. H. T. Kollmorgan
Lt. (j.g.) James W. Wettengel
Ens. Walter L. Brown

Ens. M. J. Barry
Chief Aviation Machinist's Mate
    George Olliver
Aviation Machinist's Mate 3rd Class
    Harry W. Sweezey
Aviation Ordnanceman 1st Class
    Donald A. Sletten
Aviation Electronics Man 3rd Class Ray
    W. Lavender
Airman (Aviation Electronics
    Technician) Dwayne D. Hull
Airman (Aviation Machinist's Mate)
    Johnnie J. Boyd

10 February 1950
BuNo 84704: PBM-5, ATU-10. BuNo
84704 was on a navigation training flight
from NAS Corpus Christi, Texas. There
was no contact with the aircraft after a
routine position report at 28°22' N,
95°26' W. Debris from the aircraft was
later found on a beach southwest of
Galveston, Texas.

Lt. (j.g.) Alfred F. Lemmel
Midn. Thomas M. Baxter Jr.
Midn. Nelson R. Nitz
Midn. William Boyse
Midn. Harry W. Brown
Aviation Machinist's Mate 1st Class
    William R. Wallace
Aviation Machinist's Mate 2nd Class
    Kenneth G. Light

Aviation Electronics Man 3rd Class
    Wayne T. Tate
Aviation Machinist's Mate 2nd Class
    John A. Biggs

5 November 1950
BuNo 84769: PBM-5, VP-46. BuNo
84769 was on a combat patrol over the
China Sea, flying from Sangley Point in
the Philippines to Buckner Bay,
Okinawa. The aircraft disappeared after
a last reported position of 22°20' N,
117°25' E.

Lt. (j.g.) Lester Louis Mische
Lt. (j.g.) Cassiur Allen Williams
Ens. Joseph W. Gardiner
Aviation Electronics Man 1st Class
    James Bryan Burt Jr.
Chief Air Controlman Warren Henry
    Faubel
Parachute Rigger (Naval Aviation Pilot)
    John R. Franchino
Airman Lawrence Oliver Larsen
Seaman Clifford Henderson
Aviation Electronics Man 1st Class
    Raymond Paul Schwerer
Chief Aviation Machinist's Mate Carl
    Cecil Stevenson
Aviation Machinist's Mate 3rd Class
    Donald Wilkes
Chief Aviation Machinist's Mate Nick
    Milus

11 January 1951
BuNo 84662: PBM-5S, VP-46. BuNo 84662 sank after water looping on a landing at Amani O Shima.

    Lt. Col. Maurice H. Rahe, U.S. Army
    Lt. Col. William J. Leight, U.S. Army
    Maj. King C. Hayes, U.S. Army
    Aviation Ordnanceman 1st Class P. W. Blackstock
    Aviation Electronics Man 1st Class Eugene Howard Swanson
    Aviation Machinist's Mate 2nd Class Robert E. Schaefer
    Patrick J. Ginley, civilian

22 April 1951
BuNo 84663: PBM-5, VP-892. While on a combat weather reconnaissance mission out of Iwakuni, Japan, BuNo 84663 experienced an engine failure. Forced to make a single-engine emergency night landing, it crashed at sea at position 34°58' N, 132°15-58' E.

    Lt. George L. Hardgrave
    Aviation Structural Mechanic 3rd Class Wilbur T. Callis
    Aviation Electronics Technician 3rd Class Robert E. Kibler
    Airman Rodrick D. Layton
    Aviation Ordnanceman (Utility) 3rd Class Wendell L. Johnson

14 June 1951
BuNo 85148: PBM-5, VP-731. BuNo 85148 made a hard landing in Manila Bay and sank.

    Aviation Photographer's Mate 1st Class R. P. Wallace
    Seaman C. W. Lantz
    Airman V. Latorre

19 June 1951
BuNo 84691: PBM-5, VP-40. After taking off from Iwakuni, Japan, on a defensive antisubmarine task force escort mission, BuNo 84691 hit a mountain during the climb-out near Okurokami Shima at 34°09-10' N, 132°24-27' E.

    Lt. V. L. Flint
    Lt. B. P. Kritzmacher
    Lt. (j.g.) George C. Ryan
    Aviation Machinist's Mate (Engine Mechanic) 1st Class Dwight E . Asby
    Aviation Structural Mechanic (Air Crew) William B. Braaten
    Aviation Ordnanceman 1st Class Wilbur Gray
    Chief Aviation Machinist's Mate Frederick L. Owens
    Chief Aviation Electronicsman W. H. Torum
    Aviation Electronics Man 3rd Class R. K. Reinke
    Airman R. L. Edgerton

Airman (Aviation Electronics
Technician) R. L. Jones
Airman I. T. Martinez

29 June 1951
BuNo 98610: PBM-5, VX-1. BuNo 98610
experienced engine failure during takeoff
from NAS Key West, Florida, and crashed.

Lt. Comdr. J. J. Ebnet
Lt. Comdr. O. W. Myers
Lt. P. N. Fenton
Chief Aviation Machinist's Mate R.
Edwards
Aviation Electronics Technician 1st
Class O. L. Edwards
Aviation Electronics Man 2nd Class
M. R. Flood
Aviation Machinist's Mate 2nd Class
J. T. Taylor
Aviation Machinist's Mate 2nd Class
C. J. Tufarella

25 November 1951
BuNo 84622: PBM-5, VP-46.
Returning to Iwakuni, Japan, after an
antisubmarine patrol, BuNo 84622
bounced on landing because of high
winds and crashed.

Chief Aviation Electronicsman John M.
Lindsay Jr.
Airman (Aviation Ordnanceman)
Franklin D. Gaut

Airman (Aviation Electronics
Technician) Dale H. Poole
Aviation Machinist's Mate 3rd Class
William M. Beckett

27 November 1951
BuNo 59223: PBM-5, VP-731. During stall
practice at NAS San Diego, California, BuNo
59223 spun in from eight thousand feet.

Lt. Comdr. Harold S. Wilson
Lt. R. C. James
Lt. Ralph C. Kitchen
Aviation Machinist's Mate 1st Class
Harold E. Huffman
Aviation Electronics Man 2nd Class L.
C. Johnson
Aviation Ordnanceman (Utility) 3rd
Class Bruce H. Thompson
Airman (Aviation Electronics
Technician) Roy W. Sheppard Jr.
Airman Apprentice Eugene H.
Radtke
Airman Warren V. South
Airman Apprentice Larry C. Jones
Airman Apprentice Julian R. Morris

31 December 1951
BuNo 84682: PBM-5, VP-47. While tak-
ing off from Kowloon Bay, Hong Kong,
BuNo 84682 stalled and crashed.

Aviation Machinist's Mate 1st Class
J. W. Britton

Aviation Machinist's Mate 3rd Class
    A. E. Baxter
Airman J. F. Finau
Airman S. V. Neville

31 July 1952
BuNo 59277: PBM-5, VP-731. While on a
routine reconnaissance patrol over the
Yellow Sea, BuNo 59277 was attacked by
Chinese MiG-15 fighters. The MiG can-
non fire caused the deaths of two crewmen.

Aviation Machinist's Mate 3rd Class
    Harlan Goodroad
Airman Apprentice Claude Playforth

7 August 1952
BuNo 84774: PBM-5, VP-892. BuNo
84774 took off from Sangley Point,
Philippines, in bad weather. The aircraft
experienced an engine failure and hit a
mountain while returning to base in instrument conditions.

Lt. T. L. Rhodes
Lt. (j.g.) R. F. Bahlman
Ens. L. M. Moore
Aviation Machinist's Mate 1st Class C.
    Chauncey
Airman E. J. Gimburek
Aviation Machinist's Mate 3rd Class
    William E. Bailey
Aviation Electronics Man 1st Class
    John S. Pedmon

Aviation Electronics Man 3rd Class
    James A. Smith Jr.
Aviation Electronics Technician 3rd
    Class William F. O'Hare
Aviation Electronics Technician 3rd
    Class Forrest B. Nance
Aviation Ordnanceman 2nd Class
    Tommy T. Simmons
Airman Sidney P. Krashesny
Aviation Photographer's Mate 2nd
    Class Donald R. Spence

8 August 1952
BuNo 84782: PBM-5,VP-892. BuNo
84782 took off at night from Iwakuni,
Japan, to participate in a fleet exercise. The
aircraft crashed into a mountain during
climb-out.

Lt. Howard L. "Sam" Cornish, Patrol
    Plane Commander (PPC)
Lt. Ebbie D. Wells, Squadron
    Maintenance Officer
Lt. (j.g.) Donald E. Richardson
Lt. (j.g.) S. A. Dobbins
Ens. Wayne P. Grogan
Chief Aviation Machinist's Mate Travis
    Lee Ladd
Aviation Machinist's Mate 2nd Class
    George J. Brambrinck
Aviation Machinist's Mate 3rd Class
    John Edward Meriwether
Aviation Electronics Man 2nd Class
    William Morrison Grayson

Aviation Electronics Man 3rd Class
    Joseph Arnold Hall Jr.

Aviation Ordnanceman 3rd Class
    Truman Doyle Mauney

Airman Roy Roscoe Benge

Airman (Aviation Electronics Man)
    Jimmie L. Lovell

Airman (Aviation Electronics Man)
    George A. Murray Jr.

26 December 1952

BuNo 84787: PBM-5, VP-47. On patrol off the coast of Korea, BuNo 84787 experienced an engine failure. The aircraft ditched and exploded at position 39°30' N, 129°15' E.

Lt. D. W. Anderson

Lt. W. E. Bancroft

Aviation Machinist's Mate 1st Class G.
    E. Haigh

Aviation Electronics Man 2nd Class
    J. A. James

Aerographer's Mate 2nd Class R. L.
    Mounce

Aviation Electronics Man 3rd Class
    R. L. Newman

Aviation Structural Mechanic 3rd Class
    W. D. Wynn

Airman E. N. Franklin

Airman (Aviation Ordnanceman) F. C.
    Lynch

Airman (Aviation Ordnanceman) C. B.
    Macklin

22 March 1953

BuNo 85151: PBM-5, VP-34. BuNo 85151 was tender based on *Currituck* (AV-7) at San Juan, Puerto Rico, for Exercise PHIBEX II-53. The aircraft disappeared during a night exercise patrol. Its last position report was from 23°37' N, 70°07' W.

Lt. Emil Radovich

Lt. Mark R. Armour

Lt. (j.g.) John D. Wick

Aviation Machinist's Mate 1st Class
    Wallace J. Livingston

Aviation Machinist's Mate 3rd Class
    Daniel J. Eames

Aviation Machinist's Mate 3rd Class
    Robert L. Harrington

Aviation Electronics Man 2nd Class
    Daniel G. McLaughlin

Aviation Electronics Technician 3rd
    Class Leonard J. Piersante

Airman (Aviation Electronics
    Technician) Howard E. Appelt

Aviation Ordnanceman 1st Class
    Clarence E. Holder

Airman (Aviation Ordnanceman)
    Charles R. West

2 July 1953

BuNo 85158: PBM-5, VP-42. Flying out of Adak, Alaska, BuNo 85158 experienced a fire in flight. The aircraft attempted an emergency landing at sea in heavy fog. Unsuccessful, the aircraft crashed with the loss of the entire crew.

Lt. Comdr. D. W. McMeekin

Lt. J. L. Burchfield

Lt. J. B. Cornwell

Aviation Machinist's Mate 1st Class
J. E. Griffin

Aviation Electronics Man 1st Class
L. W. Mueller

Aviation Ordnanceman 1st Class R. E.
Ware

Aviation Machinist's Mate 3rd Class
R. T. Graham

Aviation Photographer's Mate 3rd Class
C. D. Macpherson

Aviation Electronics Technician 3rd
Class J. T. McDow

Aviation Electronics Man 3rd Class
W. H. Reagen

Airman (Aviation Machinist's Mate)
L. L. Christense

Airman (Aviation Ordnanceman) G. E.
Walker

30 July 1953

BuNo 84760: PBM-5S2, VP-48. BuNo 84760 was flying a Charlie Patrol out of NAS Sangley Point, Philippines. After a fire in the port engine, the aircraft was ditched at 18°00' N, 119°30' E. Five crewmen were rescued by a U.S. Coast Guard PBM.

Lt. Comdr. Orzond S. Fowler

Lt. Walter H. Meier Jr.

Lt. Daniel A. McManus

Aviation Ordnanceman 3rd Class
Stanley R. Zuba Jr.

Airman Richard E. Ospiert

Aviation Machinist's Mate 1st Class
Charles C. Stewart

Aviation Structural Mechanic 3rd Class
John H. Kugler

Aviation Ordnanceman 2nd Class Steve
A. Walbec

Aviation Electronics Technician 3rd
Class Ronald J. Whitaker

Aviation Electronics Man 1st Class
John L. Hall

10 November 1953

BuNo 85152: PBM-5S2, VP-50. Flying from Iwakuni, Japan, BuNo 85152 was en route to a Yellow Sea patrol when the merchant vessel SS *Swordknot,* sailing near Cheju Island, Korea, reported seeing "dense fire and smoke" about five miles away. *Swordknot* proceeded to the area of the smoke and recovered two wing floats and other debris. No cause for the accident could be determined.

Lt. Paul Elvin Nielsen

Lt. (j.g.) Laurence John Dacasto

Lt. (j.g.) John Crawford Dudley

Ens. James Francis Johnston

Aviation Machinist's Mate 1st Class
Orvis Roger Mee

Photographer's Mate 1st Class Gerald
Robert Hendrick

Aviation Machinist's Mate 2nd Class
　Alvin Clair Haney
Aviation Electronics Technician 3rd
　Class Teddy Arthur Dobrenz
Aviation Electronics Man 3rd Class
　Gilbert Fletcher Gauldin
Aviation Ordnanceman 3rd Class Larry
　Eugene Norton
Airman (Aviation Machinist's Mate)
　Elton Raymond Davis
Airman (Aviation Electronics
　Technician) Kenneth Wilbur Goff
Airman Harlan Paige Cobb
Airman James Mitchell Hill

5 May 1954
BuNo 59143: PBM-5, ATU-700. BuNo
59143 was on a navigation training flight
from NAS Corpus Christi, Texas, when it
disappeared. Wreckage was found later
about ninety miles south-southwest of
Brownsville, Texas.

Lt. Harold Jennings
Lt. Jim W. Martin
Lt. (j.g.) Benjamin D. Guttenian
Lt. (j.g.) William E. McCall
Lt. (j.g.) P. G. Tiefer, USCG
Aviation Machinist's Mate 3rd Class
　Wendell W. MacIntosh
Aviation Machinist's Mate 3rd Class
　Loyd F. Barela
Aviation Electronics Man 3rd Class
　Quentin R. Killon

Airman (Aviation Machinist's Mate)
　Roy Lee Walker
Airman (Aviation Electronics Man)
　Ronald H. Vincent

9 June 1954
BuNo 84779: PBM-5S2, VP-47. BuNo
84779 was en route to Hong Kong from
Iwakuni, Japan, when it hit the top of a mountain on Yaku Shima Island, south of Kyushu.

Lt. Wallace R. Carter
Lt. (j.g.) Cecil F. Hackeny Jr.
Lt. (j.g.) William Bull Hedrick
Lt. (j.g.) Wallace H. Wertz
Ens. John D. McCathy
Ens. Homer F. Trotter Jr.
Ens. Berje Weramian
Electronics Technician 2nd Class
　Douglas C. Campbell
Electronics Technician 3rd Class Ira E.
　Crider
Aviation Electronics Technician 3rd
　Class Jerrold D. Edwards
Aviation Structural Mechanic 2nd
　Class Ronald D. Graham
Photographer's Mate 3rd Class Donald
　D. Landon
Aviation Ordnanceman 2nd Class
　James E. Landon
Aviation Electronics Technician 1st
　Class Laurence E. Stone
Aviation Machinist's Mate Walter R.
　Raab

Maj. James R. O'Moore, U.S. Marine
    Corps
Capt. Theodore R. Moore, U.S.
    Marine Corps

31 October 1955
BuNo 59232: PBM-5S2, VP-34. BuNo
59232 was taking off from Coco Solo,
Canal Zone, when the starboard engine
failed. On a single engine the aircraft hit a
rock seawall, caught fire, and exploded.
Nine crewmen were killed. The one survivor was Airman Apprentice (Aviation
Machinist's Mate) Charles Airhart.

Lt. (j.g.) David J. Ryan, pilot
Ens. Wallace H. Sperlich
Aviation Machinist's Mate 1st Class
    McClellan L. Chidress
Aviation Electronics Technician 3rd
    Class Carroll W. Church Jr.
Airman William N. Hopking
Aviation Ordnanceman William A.
    Ward Jr.
Chief Photographer's Mate George E.
    Etheridge
Photographer's Mate 1st Class John R.
    Myers

U.S. Coast Guard Casualties
22 February 1947
BuNo 45435: PBM-5, USCGAS San
Diego. BuNo 45435 was returning to San
Diego after a fourteen hundred mile mercy

flight into Mexico when the aircraft struck
the hills near Tijuana, Mexico, in adverse
weather.

Lt. (j.g.) E. W. Miles
Aviation Pilot 1st Class F. J. Kestell
Aviation Machinist's Mate 2nd Class
    E. A. Widener
Aviation Radioman 1st Class W. C.
    Williams
Aviation Ordnanceman 3rd Class Q. V.
    Buchanan
Aviation Radioman 1st Class M. J.
    Murphy
Aviation Ordnanceman 2nd Class J. G.
    Steuer
Aviation Machinist's Mate 1st Class G.
    Tracy
Aerographer's Mate 1st Class R. G. Peshek
G. C. Leavitt, civilian

31 March 1947
BuNo 59002: PBM-5G, USCGAS St.
Petersburg, Florida. Aircraft water looped
and exploded with resultant fire while
landing at Tampa, Florida.

Aviation Machinist's Mate 3rd Class
    D. L. Vigrelli

27 May 1952
BuNo 84740: PBM-5G, USCGAS Port
Angeles, Washington. BuNo 84740 was
departing Port Angeles for the scene of

an air force crash near Prince Rupert, British Columbia, when it crashed on takeoff.

> Lt. (j.g.) R. J. Tomozer
> Aviation Electronics Man 1st Class B. Moore
> Aviation Electronics Man 2nd Class B. E. Woodward
> Technical Sergeant H. P. Colbeck, U.S. Air Force

18 January 1953

BuNo 84738: PBM-5G, U.S. Coast Guard Air Detachment, U.S. Naval Station Sangley Point, Philippine Islands. The aircraft was on mission to rescue crewmen of a navy P2V that had been shot down by Chinese fire. Lt. Comdr. John Vukic landed safely and took P2V crewmen on board. However, on takeoff, one engine failed and the aircraft crashed. Four navy men and five coast guardsmen were lost.

> Lt. (j.g.) G. W. Stuart
> Chief Aviation Electronicsman W. J. Hammond
> Aviation Electronics Man 1st Class C. R. Tornell
> Aviation Ordnanceman 1st Class J. R. Bridge
> Aviation Machinist's Mate 3rd Class T. W. Miller

Royal Air Force Casualty

19 July 1943

JX101 (ex–BuNo 6686): PBM-3C, RAF Ferry Command. JX101 was taxiing for take-off for a flight from Bermuda to Canada when the aircraft sank because of an unsecured tunnel hatch. One passenger drowned; the rest of the crew and passengers were uninjured.

> Leading Aircraftsman (LAC) L. L. Scott

Royal Netherlands Navy Casualties

12 August 1957

MLD No. 16-312 (ex–BuNo 122470): PBM-5A, 321 Squadron. On takeoff from the Merauke airstrip in New Guinea, the aircraft failed to clear some trees. It crashed and burned.

> Luitenant-ter-zee der tweede klasse oudste categorie (Lieutenant) W. H. Asselbergs
> Luitenant-ter-zee der tweede klasse oudste categorie G. Smelik
> Majoor vliegtuigtelegrafist (Chief Petty Officer First Class; telegrafist = wireless operator) H. C. van Winderden
> Sergeant Vliegtuigmaker (Chief Petty Officer; vliegtuigmaker = airman) A. Moens
> Sergeant Vlieger (Chief Petty Officer; vlieger = pilot) G. J. van Donkelaar
> Korporaal Vliegtuigmaker (Petty Officer) A. A. de Bruin

Vliegtuigmaker konstabel (Airman;
konstabel = ordnance) J. de Ruiter
Two Papuan policemen

20 August 1958
MLD No. 16-303 (ex–BuNo 122608):
PBM-5A, 321 Squadron. After engine
replacement in Abadan, Iran, the aircraft
took off for Holland, but a severe oil leak
developed in the port engine. The pilot
requested an emergency landing. About one
hundred meters before reaching the runway,
the aircraft made a violent turn to the right
and crashed in flames. The crash investigation commission concluded that the cause
of the crash was that the starboard propeller
had gone into reverse pitch.

Luitenant-ter-zee vlieger der eerste
klasse (Lieutenant Commander;
plane captain) Th. M. A. Hoebink
Luitenant-ter-zee der tweede klasse
oudste categorie J. Andreas
Luitenant-ter-zee der tweede klasse
technische dienst (Sub-lieutenant;
technical officer) J. A. Wurtz
Sergeant Vliegtuigmaker G. de Charon
Saint Germain
Sergeant Vliegtuigmaker H. Q.
Spiessens
Sergeant Vlieger P. J. M.
Paardenkooper
Korporaal Vliegtuigmaker J. Bosma
Korporaal Vliegtuigmaker A. Rompies

Korporaal Vliegtuigmaker K. W. Smits
Korporaal Vliegtuigtelegrafist J. J. F.
Schrijver

10 June 1959
MLD No. 16-306 (ex–BuNo 122084):
PBM-5A, 321 Squadron. En route from
New Guinea to Holland for overhaul, an
engine failed on the leg between Nagumbo,
Ceylon, and Karachi, Pakistan. The pilot
requested an emergency landing at
Portuguese Goa. The aircraft hit a low wall
just short of the runway at Goa and
burned.

Luitenant-ter-zee der tweede klasse
oudste categorie P. A. M. Landsdall
Luitenant-ter-zee der tweede klasse
oudste categorie J. Quispel
Luitenant-ter-zee waarnemer der
tweede klass (Sub-lieutenant; waarne-
mer = navigator) M. J. A. Baarspul
Sergeant Vliegtuigmaker A. Dijkema
Sergeant Vliegtuigmaker C. Koster
Sergeant Vlieger S. Bruin
Sergeant Vliegtuigtelegrafist C. N.
Gabeler
Korporaal Vliegtuigmaker L. H. Bemer

17 December 1959
MLD No. 16-302 (ex–BuNo 122085):
PBM-5A, 321 Squadron. Landing at Fak
Fak in the Patipi Bay, New Guinea, the
copilot touched down in a nose-down atti-

tude. The aircraft "turned upside down and broke into five pieces." Two of the crew survived, but five died.

> Luitenant-ter-zee vlieger der eerste
> klasse J. Adriaanse
> Luitenant-ter-zee der tweede klasse
> H. K. Bertram
> Sergeant Vliegtuigmaker A. J. Wams
> Korporaal Vliegtuigmaker A. F. G. van
> Baalen
> Vliegtuigmaker Konstabel der eerste
> klasse (Airman First Class; konstabel
> = ordnance) A. W. van Loon

Portuguese Airline Aero Topografica SA (ARTOP) Casualty
9 November 1958
Portuguese Registry CS-THB (ex–BuNo 45409): PBM-5. Just after noon CS-THB departed Lisbon, Portugal, on its maiden revenue flight to Madiera Island. About one hour later the aircraft made an emergency signal, then disappeared. No trace of CS-THB was ever found.

> Pilot Harry Broadbent
> Copilot Thomas Rowell
> Radio Operator Joaquim Bairrao Ruivo
> Radio Operator Joaquim Luis
> Flight Steward Fernando Pereira Rego
> On Board Assistant Maria Vilao
> Antunes
> Thirty passengers

BIBLIOGRAPHY

Books

Blair, Clay. *Hitler's U-Boat War: The Hunted, 1942–1945.* New York: Random House, 1998.

Breihan, John R., Stan Piet, and Roger S. Mason. *Martin Aircraft 1909–1960.* Santa Ana, Calif.: Narkiewicz/Thompson, 1995.

Cagle, Malcolm W., and Frank A. Manson. *The Sea War in Korea.* Annapolis, Md.: Naval Institute Press, 1957.

Dunning, Eugene J. *Voices of my Peers: Clipper Memories.* Nevada City, Nev.: Clipper Press, 1996.

Freeman, Brett. *Lake Boga at War.* Swan Hill, Australia: Catalina Press 1995.

Hendrie, Andrew. *Flying Cats: The Catalina Aircraft in World War II.* Shrewsbury, U.K.: Airlife Press, 1999.

———. *Short Sunderland in World War II.* Shrewsbury, U.K.: Airlife Press, 1998.

Jablonski, Edward. *Seawings.* Garden City, N.Y.: Doubleday and Company, 1972.

Kammen, Michael G. *Operational History of the Flying Boat: Open-Sea and Seadrome Aspects.* Washington, D.C.: Bureau of Aeronautics, Navy Department, 1959.

Knott, Richard C. *The American Flying Boat.* Annapolis, Md.: Naval Institute Press, 1979.

Lee, James. *Operation Lifeline.* Chicago: Ziff-Davis Publishing Company, 1947.

Lewis, Comdr. Charles F. Lewis. *Flying Seaplanes for the Navy during World War II.* Bryan, Texas: private printing, 1997.

Malin, Charles A. *Abbreviations Used for Navy Enlisted Ratings.* Washington, D.C.: Bureau of Naval Personnel, 1970.

Meekcoms, Ken. *The British Air Commission and Lend-Lease.* Woodbridge, U.K.: Air Britain, 1999.

Mooney, James L., ed. *Dictionary of American Naval Fighting Ships.* Washington, D.C.: Government Printing Office, 1979.

Morison, Samuel Eliot. *History of United States Naval Operations in World War Two.* Edison, N.J.: Castle Books, 2001. Originally published by Little, Brown and Company in 1947.

Oliver, David. *Flying Boats and Amphibians since 1945.* Annapolis, Md.: Naval Institute Press, 1987.

Pearcy, Arthur. *U.S. Coast Guard Aircraft since 1916.* Annapolis, Md.: Naval Institute Press, 1991.

Pomeroy, Colin A. *The Flying Boats of Bermuda.* Hamilton, Bermuda: Printlink Ltd., 2000.

Raithel, Capt. Albert L., Jr., USN (Ret.), Lt. Comdr. David Rinehart, USCGR (Ret.), and Robert M. Smith. *Mariner/Marlin: "Anywhere, Any Time."* Paducah, Ky.: Turner Publishing Company, 1993.

Roberts, Capt. Michael. *Dictionary of American Naval Aircraft Squadrons,* Volume 2. Washington, D.C.: Naval Historical Center, undated. Available on CD-ROM from Superintendent of Documents, Pittsburgh, Pa., S/N 008-046-00195-2.

Sakaida, Henry. *Aces of the Rising Sun.* Botley, U.K.: Osprey Publications Ltd., 2002.

Sherman, Adm. Frederick C. *Combat Command: The American Aircraft Carriers in the Pacific War.* New York: E. P. Dutton and Company, 1950.

Smith, Bob. *PBM Mariner in Action.* Carrollton, Tex.: Squadron Signal Publications, 1986.

Smith, Comdr. D. F. *Fleet Air Wings in WW2.* Washington, D.C.: Chief of Naval Operations, 1951.

Sweet, Donald H. *The Sailor Aviators.* Burnsville, N.C.: Celo Valley Books, 1996.

———. *Seaplanes at War.* Burnsville, N.C.: Celo Valley Books, 1999.

Sweet, Donald H., Lee Roy Way, and William Bonvillian. *The Forgotten Heroes: The Story of Rescue Squadron VH-3 in World War II.* Ridgewood, N.J.: Pronto Printing, 2000.

Waters, Capt. John M., Jr. *Rescue at Sea.* Princeton, N.J.: D. Van Nostrand Company, 1966.

Wegg, John. *General Dynamics Aircraft and their Predecessors.* Annapolis, Md.: Naval Institute Press, 1990.

Wills, Richard. *The Wreck of the U.S. Navy PBM-5 Mariner BuNo 59172: History and Archaelogical Assessment.* Washington, D.C.: Naval Historical Center, Underwater Archaeology Branch, 1997.

Articles and Papers

Banfield, Greg. "Philip Mathiesen: Flying Boat Experiences." *Man and Aerial Machines* (Australia), March–April 1996.

Berry, Peter. "Transatlantic Flight 1938–1945." *Journal, American Aviation Historical Society,* Fall 1995.

Byrd, Richard E. "Our Navy Explores Antarctica." *National Geographic Magazine,* October 1947.

Erb, Richard I. "Attack by Chinese MiG-15." *Mariner/Marlin Association (MMA) Newsletter,* December 2001.

Frangella, Rich. "Fate of the Flying Lobster." *Mariner/Marlin Association (MMA) Newsletter,* February 1994.

———. "The Flying Lobster Experience." *Mariner/Marlin Association (MMA) Newsletter,* September 1995.

———. "Mariners in Civvies." *Mariner/Marlin Association (MMA) Newsletter,* September 1999.

———. "The Rio Magdalena Incident." *Mariner/Marlin Association (MMA) Newsletter,* December 1998.

Friederichsen, Roland C., and Bill Lower. "Recollections of Crossroads." *Mariner/Marlin Association (MMA) Newsletter,* September 2001.

Grant, James Ritchie. "From Three to Two." *Air Enthusiast,* July/August 1996.

"History of PBM-5A BuNo 122071." Paper. Pima, Ariz.: Pima Air and Space Museum, 2001.

Hoffman, Richard A. "The Worst Mariner Disaster." *Propliner* 85 (winter 2000).

Kelly, Graham. "VR-2 Wartime Operations." Letter. *Mariner/Marlin Association (MMA) Newsletter,* June 1997.

McCarty, Owen. "Dead Men's Diary." *Saturday Evening Post Magazine,* 17 May 1947.

Nelson, Frank. "VP-42 MiG Attack, 11 May 1952." *Mariner/Marlin Association (MMA) Newsletter,* March 2003.

Palmer, Dick. "Reminisces." *Mariner/Marlin Association (MMA) Newsletter,* February 2002.

Palmer, Richard W. "That Maverick 'Mariner': Saga of a Few PBM-5As." *Mariner/Marlin Association (MMA) Newsletter,* February 2001.

Peltzer, Milo. "Mystery of the Desert Mariner." *Warbirds International,* September 2000.

Quinn, David C., and Rich Frangella. "The Flying Lobster Air Lanes, Inc." *Mariner/Marlin Association (MMA) Newsletter,* February 1998.

Raithel, Capt. Albert A., Jr. "Patrol Aviation in the Atlantic in World War II." *Naval Aviation News,* November/December 1994.

———. "Patrol Aviation in the Pacific in World War II." *Naval Aviation News,* September/October 1992.

Rankin, Lt. Col. Robert, USMC, and Norman Rubin. "The Story of Coast Guard Aviation." *Naval Institute Proceedings,* June 1959.

Robbins, Jim. "Operation Nanook: A Personal Account." *Mariner/Marlin Association (MMA) Newsletter,* September 1998.

Schipporeit, Al. "PBM Ditching." *Mariner/Marlin Association (MMA) Newsletter,* December 2002.

Schultz, Capt. Melvin Ray. "Crew Eight." *Wings of Gold,* February 1998.

Untitled. *Mariner/Marlin Association (MMA) Newsletter,* December 1993. This untitled article includes copies of two *Chicago Tribune* clippings: "Is for Sale, 18 Others, Too" (7 June 1959) and "Battered Seaplane Sinks" (August 1959).

Way, Lee Roy. "First PBM Rescue in Pacific?" *Mariner/Marlin Association (MMA) Newsletter,* September 2002.

Weber, Comdr. John A., USCG (Ret.). "Rescue, Reunion, Recognition." *Capital Weekly* (Augusta, Maine), 19 October 2000. Reprinted in *Mariner/Marlin Association (MMA) Newsletter,* June 2001.

Wilson, David. "The Martin PBM Mariner." *Wings* (Royal Australian Air Force magazine), winter 1987.

Web Sites

Frankel, Nevis. "VPNAVY Website." http://www.vpnavy.com/SEARCH.HTM.

Graham, Wynnum. "ADF Serials." http://www.adf-serials.com. This site provides the correlation of RAAF serial numbers to U.S. Navy bureau numbers.

Lee, AOC [Chief Aviation Ordnanceman] J. R., USCG (Ret.), and Lt. Col. Ted A. Morris, USAF (Ret.). "You Have to Go Out, You Don't Have to Come Back." http://www.jacksjoint.com.

Mason, Capt. Jerry Mason, USN. "U-Boat Archive." http://www.uboatarchive.net.

Oliver, Capt. David, USCG (Ret.). "My Life in the Coast Guard." http://www.uscg.mil/hg/g-cp/history/OLIVER.

VP International. "Book of Remembrance." http://www.vpinternational.ca/BOOK/BORM mainpage.htm.

Personal Communication

Alvarez, Saul. Correspondence with the author, 1999. Alvarez, of Buenos Aires, had flown Argentine Mariners. He provided valuable data on Argentine operations.

Damoff, George T. Correspondence with the author, 1999. Damoff, an MMA member, provided an eyewitness account and color photos of the 2-P-22 fire in Trinidad.

da Silva, Luis Lima. Correspondence with the author, 2000. Director of the accident investigation bureau of the Portuguese Instituto Nacional de Aviacao Civil (INAC), da Silva provided the author with a copy of the complete 18 February 1959 accident report on CS-THB and other official records on both CS-THA and CS-THB.

Davis, John M. Correspondence with the author, 2002. Davis, of Wichita, Kansas, provided the U.S. Navy bureau numbers of the Naviera Colombiana aircraft.

Day, Graham. Correspondence with Paul Warrener, 2001. Day, of the Air Historical Branch, Ministry of Defence, London, provided access to RAF Form 78s and No. 524 Squadron's Form 540s.

Dingemans, Theo. Correspondence with the author, 1999. Dingemans, of the Netherlands, had been a PBM flight engineer in No. 321 Squadron. He provided valuable background and crash details of the Dutch Mariners.

Durbin, Jack. Conversations with the author, La Jolla, California, May 2001. Durbin was a passenger on Royal Air Force (RAF) Mariner JX101 when it sank.

Frangella, Rich. Correspondence with the author, 1999–2002. The author is indebted to Frangella, an MMA member. The Flying Lobster Mariner story would not have been possible without the patient research of historian Rich Frangella. Over many years Frangella collected documents, photographs, articles, and reminiscences pertaining to the Lobster. He graciously contributed his entire collection to the Mariner/Marlin Association archives.

Guerreiro, Carlos, Mario Canongia Lopes, and Lt. Duarte Monteiro, Portuguese Air Force magazine *Mais Alto*. Correspondence with the author, 1999. Lopes provided an excellent background summary of the ARTOP story and a photograph of one of the ARTOP Mariners. Monteiro pointed out that records might be available from the files of the Portuguese Instituto Nacional de Aviacao Civil (INAC) because the 9 November 1958 incident was a civil accident.

Hagedorn, Dan. Correspondence with the author, 1999. Hagedorn, of the National Air and Space Museum (NASM), is perhaps the most knowledgeable person in the United States on the history of South American aviation. He graciously shared his files and rare photographs on the South American PBMs.

Larkin, Gary. Correspondence with the author 2001. Larkin, a salvor of historic aircraft, provided information concerning the Kwajalein Mariner.

Lee, Harry O. Conversations with the author, Camp Pendleton, California, 11 January 2002. Perhaps the most enjoyable part of researching this episode was the opportunity to meet with Harry O. Lee at the Amtrac Museum, U.S. Marine Corps Base, Camp Pendleton, California. Lee not only provided the true story of the genesis of TFLALI but some wonderful history on World War II Pacific island campaigns.

Lopes, Commandant. Correspondence with the author, 2000. The director of the Portuguese Instituto Nacional de Aviacao Civil (INAC), Lopes arranged for the author to be provided with a copy of the complete 18 February 1959 accident report on CS-THB as well as other official records on both CS-THA and CS-THB.

Luzardo, Sr. Eduardo. Correspondence with the author, 1999. Luzardo, an Uruguayan aviation historian, provided many wonderful photos and articles describing the delivery flights and the A-811 rescue mission. He also forwarded the beautiful artwork of Pedro Otto Cerovaz and a copy of the Mariner section of a comprehensive history of Uruguayan Naval Aviation being written by Nelson P. Acosta and Alberto Del Pino.

Mergulhao, Jose. Correspondence with the author, 2001. Mergulhao, the son of Aero Topografica SA (ARTOP) founder Capt. Durval Mergulhao, contributed previously unavailable information, personal reminisces, and marvelous photographs of ARTOP's operation.

Nunez Padin, Jorge. Correspondence with the author, 1999. Nunez Padin, of Argentina, provided complete and accurate information on the procurement, operation, and losses of the Argentine Mariners.

O'Rourke, Mike. Correspondence with the author, 2002. O'Rourke, of the Ancient Order of the Pterodactyls, provided details of the U.S. Coast Guard's PBM inventory.

Pomeroy, Colin A. Correspondence with the author, 2001. Pomeroy is the author of *The Flying Boats of Bermuda.*

Raithell, Capt. Al, USN (Ret.). Correspondence with the author, 2001. Raithel provided a copy of the 1943 U.S. Navy Bureau of Aeronautics document that discussed the Lend-Lease allocation and a copy of Comdr. D. F. Smith's *Fleet Air Wings in WW2.*

Sinclair, Capt. Andrew, USN (Ret.). Correspondence with the author, February 2003. Sinclair provided details concerning Operation Nanook.

Tibbetts, Comdr. David K.,USN, Office of Defense Cooperation Montevideo. Correspondence with the author, 1999. Tibbetts acted as liaison with Capitan de Navio Federico Strasser, commandant of Uruguayan Naval Aviation in obtaining usage data on the Uruguayan aircraft.

Tkachick, Emil "Chick." Correspondence with the author, 2002. Tkachick shared his memories and wonderful photographs.

Tornjii, Gerben. Correspondence with the author,

1998. Tornjii, of the Netherlands, supplied a copy of James Ritchie Grant's *Air Enthusiast* magazine article that described Australia's use of both the Dornier DO-24 and the Mariner. Tornjii also provided a partial English translation of an article about the Dutch PBMs from the Netherlands Ministry of Defence magazine *Alle Hens.*

van der Feltz, Dr. C. A. C. W. Correspondence with the author, 1999. Van der Feltz is a historian with the Netherlands Institute for Maritime in The Hague, Netherlands. The institute provided data on the procurement, sparing, training, and deployment of the Dutch aircraft and the wonderful photographs, and also corrected the author's many misinterpretations of Dutch/English translations.

van Royen, Dr. P. C., Correspondence with the author, 1999. Van Royen is the Director of the Netherlands Institute for Maritime History in The Hague, Netherlands. Van Royen arranged for Ing. Nico Geldhof, an aviation historian, and Dr. C. A. C. W. van der Feltz of the institute to provide information and photographs of the Dutch Mariners.

Warrener, Warrant Officer Paul, RAF (Ret.). Correspondence with the author, 2002–3. An essential member of the author's research team, Warrener tracked down RAF and Air Britain information and obtained photos of the Mariners in RAF livery.

Wilkins, Paula, Assistant to the Curator, RAAFA Aviation Heritage Museum of Western Australia. Correspondence with the author, 2001. Located in Bull Creek, Western Australia, the museum provided excellent photos of Mariner operations.

Wilson, David. Correspondence with the author, 1996–97. Wilson, of the Royal Australian Air Force (RAAF) Archives and History Branch in Canberra, Australia, provided copies of the RAAF Mariners' aircraft record cards, the monthly reports of the commanding officer of No. 41 Squadron, and other valuable historic papers.

Wilton, Dave. Correspondence with the author, 2001. Wilton added notes extracted from the official history of the USAF 56th Air Rescue Squadron that provided a wonderful overview of the massive search and rescue effort for the ARTOP Mariner.

INDEX

ABOUT THE AUTHOR

Capt. Richard A. Hoffman, U.S. Navy (Retired), graduated from the U.S. Naval Academy. He holds a bachelor's degree in aeronautical engineering from the U.S. Naval Postgraduate School and a master's degree in seaplane hydrodynamics from the Stevens Institute of Technology. He is a former pilot of Martin PBM Mariners as well as other flying boats and amphibians. As a member of Patrol Squadron 892/50, he flew PBMs during the Korean War. As a test pilot he worked on the P-3 Orion trials and later commanded an operational P-3 squadron. After retirement from the navy, Hoffman worked for Martin Marietta Aerospace, Lockheed Aircraft, and McDonnell Douglas Astronautics. He has published articles in *Proceedings, Approach,* and other aviation journals and magazines. Hoffman currently resides in La Jolla, California.